Bits *of the* Bible *We* Barely Believe

Bits *of the* Bible *We* Barely Believe

Blind Spots of Today's Church in the West

MARK SIMPSON

RESOURCE *Publications* • Eugene, Oregon

BITS OF THE BIBLE WE BARELY BELIEVE
Blind Spots of Today's Church in the West

Resource Publications
An Imprint of Wipf and Stock Publishers
199 W. 8th Ave., Suite 3
Eugene, OR 97401

www.wipfandstock.com

PAPERBACK ISBN: 979-8-3852-4947-3
HARDCOVER ISBN: 979-8-3852-4948-0
EBOOK ISBN: 979-8-3852-4949-7

VERSION NUMBER 021826

Contents

Acknowledgments

I NEVER INTENDED TO write a book. I didn't think I was the type. As you work your way through these pages, you may find yourself agreeing.

On the other hand, it wasn't exactly my idea. (Big decisions rarely seem to be.) While teaching the ministry training course of my regional gospel partnership, a few students suggested that I put something in writing, relating largely to some asides to the actual teaching matter. (How often asides turn out to be the most interesting parts when it comes to teaching. But here I go making asides again.) Eventually I thought it might make a good article for a magazine or something. But as I began to put words on paper, it became clear that there was far more to say than that. Finn and friends: I owe you. I'm tempted to add that you owe me for the last two or three years! But it has been a great project.

Many have been a great help and encouragement. The nature of the subjects in the book is that their life and implications grow by chatting with people who have also noticed them as blind spots. These people are invariably friends who enthuse about their discoveries. There is always the danger of getting so carried away and caught up by exciting topics that you lose sense of perspective. Other friends have kindly given honest feedback for one chapter or another, helpfully sharpening thoughts and being excellent second pairs of eyes. I am so grateful for such friends as Chris and Anna, Doug and Helen, Lizzie, Dominey, Russ, Jam and Melissa, and Ben. I also want to thank members of my church for bearing with me; I have tried not to get obsessed by the subjects in this book, but inevitably they have probably come into my preaching and teaching a little too much.

Wipf and Stock were willing to take a gamble on me and have been very helpful and encouraging through the whole process. Special thanks are due to the editorial team for not only spotting all sorts of things that needed tweaking and clarifying, but for making the whole process fun.

Lyndsey, my favorite (and only) wife, has not only co-written one of the chapters, but has been a constant sounding board. She possesses not only the beauty but also the brains of our marriage. As chapter 4 will tell, this book has been written in the aftermath of her cancer diagnosis. You will see from that chapter the difficult experience has resulted in spiritual growth in both of us that would not have been possible otherwise. God is good. Even—perhaps especially—through the tough times, he pours out his blessings. All praise, thanks, and glory to him.

Finally, and under God, I would like to thank the people I don't know and will never meet: the shadowy characters behind the COVID-19 crisis and other related threats to a peaceful world order. Were it not for the events of 2020 onward, I might have remained a little more inclined to pootle along in life without really recognizing the seriousness of the battle the Bible speaks about so plainly. I might have continued to exist in my tribe of the church, looking down on the other tribes and enjoying feeling that I was vaguely right about most things. I thank God that he shook things up and showed what is worth living for, fighting for, and where we must truly fix our hope.

Introduction

All Scripture is God-breathed.

2 Tim 3:16

There are more things in heaven and earth, Horatio,
Than are dreamt of in your philosophy.

Shakespeare, *Hamlet*

THE WEST IS WONDERFUL! Those who live in the West have so much to be thankful for: its heritage of Christian-shaped culture that has made its society flourish in so many ways. The church in the West, too, has so much to celebrate: God has blessed it with centuries of learning and structures, resources, and influence across the entire world.

But there's also something that doesn't sit easy with the church these days. Have you felt it?

There was a long time when the church knew its place. Yes, there have been many struggles and strains. But Western society was like a well-bred schoolboy with a bit of a wild streak: sometimes quite a rebellious nature, to be fair. But the church was the kindly schoolteacher, steering him right (or perhaps the stern aunt, nagging him back into line). The church has floundered and struggled at many times and in many ways down the years; but it knew its place, its role. Recently, however—in a generation or two—the society has changed. It's gone wild, mad. It's lost all sense of boundaries, limits—in fact, it's lost all sense, period. People are debating points of total insanity, and experimenting with the foundations of human existence. Society is seeming less like a schoolboy and more like a rabid dog staggering along the road. And the church is not quite clear where it belongs any more. It hasn't rediscovered the missionary spirit of existing in utter paganism, new and despised with nothing but the Spirit of God for protection. Neither has it come to terms with not being thought of as important by most of the people around.

The church in the West has a lot going for it, but it's kind of frozen in the headlamps, unsure what it's allowed to say, where it belongs. In fact, at times the Western church feels like someone struggling with a low-level fever, someone who has forgotten what it's like to be really well.

Stories from Christians elsewhere in the world can leave those of us in the West slightly bewildered. What do you do with reports from China that in some networks pastors are only appointed if they have first served a term in prison for their faith, or that they have to recite the Psalms off by heart to prove they are genuine? I have heard of South Sudanese Christians who walk hundreds of miles to cross the border into Uganda so they can access Bibles; together they learn a book of the Bible off by heart and return to teach it to people back home. Christians in my own church, fresh from Nigeria, are astonished that we don't routinely see miracles. However you react to these sort of things, there ought to be something within you that feels exposed, which at least raises questions of a concerning nature.

Rather than referring to "the persecuted church" as if their experience was exceptional, we have to see that it is Christians in the West who are the anomaly. Perhaps it is we in the West who should have a prefix—but which would you use? Even if we were simply known globally as "the unpersecuted church," it would be saying something uncomfortable. I know there are many exceptions—but as a general impression, the Western church does not seem particularly battle ready.

Decades of trying it have taught me that vague feelings of guilt or denial do not really help. Those who have been placed in the West seeking to serve Christ need to get beneath the skin of what has gone wrong if there is to be change, and if we are to "fight the good fight" in this quickly changing world. There may be many factors at play, but this book addresses just one of them: the cultural unwillingness of Western Christians to look beyond their own received categories—in other words, to engage with bits of the Bible we've never really taken seriously.

I am now middle-aged. I know I am middle-aged because on the road I no longer get annoyed with slow, older drivers only—now I get annoyed with fast younger drivers also. Before too long, I will only be bothered by the young and energetic. One day I will not be fit to drive at all. If the church in the West is experiencing something like a midlife fear of danger, doomed to cripple itself with the self-fulfilling reluctance to get up and live, I want to help. If you are part of that church, I want to help you to rediscover the excitement of growing in Christ.

Horatio

You might not be a particular fan of Shakespeare. I have to admit to being a bit uncultured on that front. (Yes, I think I "did *Macbeth*" at school. I guess I didn't feel the need to listen.) But with my own kids actually *learning* stuff at school, I've discovered more recently why people get so excited about Shakespeare. It was truly a jaw-dropping moment when I understood about "iambic pentameter." "What? *Every* line in his plays has ten syllables in pairs of alternative emphasis?" "Yep, pretty much." " . . . Nooo!" I couldn't stop telling people about it for weeks. It was mostly met with blank or pitying faces, in spite of my enthusiasm. But at least now I know it's not called "bionic parameter."

But it's not just his use and influence on the English language for which Shakespeare is recognized. His understanding of human nature and character is profound. Take Horatio, for example. Horatio is a model of rational thought. Like his friend Hamlet, he's a student of the University of Wittenberg, a bastion of Protestant philosophy. His whole existence is founded in science and logic, things that are reasonable and sensible. When he barges into Hamlet's conversation with his dad's ghost, it is beyond Horatio to possibly comprehend.

And so, that well-known quote from Hamlet:

> There are more things in heaven and earth, Horatio,
> Than are dreamt of in your philosophy.[1]

Perhaps Shakespeare, through Hamlet, has a point. Can a character like Horatio open his mind to the possibility that there is so much more to existence than the categories of his own thought? Or, true to his Protestant self, perhaps he will (begrudgingly) accept it as a reasonable point of logic—but keep it in a safe compartment of his mind, certainly not allowing himself to get too excited or carried away by the thought.

Well, it's only a story—a play. In real life, of course, there is no such thing as ghosts. We all know that.

Except not all people do know that. In fact, to most people in the world outside of Western Protestantism, ghosts are an accepted reality. But not just out there—in Africa, Asia, Latin America, or those "backward" parts of Europe (as we might secretly think). Even in the ordinary British town

1. Shakespeare, *Hamlet*, 1.5.187–188.

where I live, most people believe in ghosts. These are the sort of people who don't go to watch Shakespeare plays, don't have discussions about Protestant philosophy, and don't get knotted up by what Shakespeare wanted us to think anyway. Those who believe in ghosts usually say they do so for one simple reason: they've seen one. Or they know someone who has.

What is our reaction to that? Perhaps some of us would dismiss such people because they are just poor, ignorant souls who are easily led, not educated at a university (such as Wittenberg). We, on the other hand, know better. We know the Bible. It's all we need. But we certainly wouldn't want to get too carried away by the thought that even Jesus's own disciples—some of the Bible writers—also seemed to have had a worldview that included ghosts (Matt 14:26).

Ghosts are not one of the things I particularly want to write about. But in his portrayal of Horatio's reaction, perhaps Shakespeare understood something about some Protestants that those of us who carry that label don't recognize about ourselves. We have a certain, rigid set of beliefs. Whether we call it Protestant, Calvinist, conservative evangelical, traditional, orthodox, or biblical, we tend not to be willing to shift or entertain anything that appears to threaten them. There might be good reason for that; after all, the Bible is the word of God. "All Scripture is God-breathed and is useful for teaching, rebuking, correcting and training in righteousness, so that the servant of God may be thoroughly equipped for every good work" (2 Tim 3:16–17). It's one of our favorite texts, and it gives us a wonderful foundation to life and understanding.

My aim in this book is not to question that in the slightest. Actually, it's sort of the opposite. I've discovered how reluctant Western, Protestant Christians are to really believe it. I write about the church cultures I know; you must decide for yourself how much this applies to your own church culture. But it's the word *all* that is the problem. Aspects of Scripture that don't fit into accepted categories of thought are often quietly dismissed or explained away. The plain reading of the text—even when those preaching are keen to be biblical—is too often killed by caveats, or dulled by a dreary two-dimensional flattening of texts that are supposed to blow our minds.

It is hard to see one's own blind spots; but having a fixed mindset produces spiritually lame disciples. It can sap character and courage and weaken engagement with the world, a world that increasingly finds God irrelevant, and—worst of all—it can shrink a clear vision of God and all his glorious works. Exposing some of these blind spots can only help us regain—or gain—spiritual vitality and health. More on this in a moment.

This is not a book about finding obscure parts of the Bible in an attempt to make people gasp at new insights. The seven subjects covered are simply ones where people in our context and in our time are weak, assuming we know better than those who have gone before us. But the weakness does not have to be terminal. Sometimes, grasping straightforward truths that have been staring us in the face can bring bounds of new energy to our lives. Simply repenting of the sin of dismissing God's teaching on some point or another brings refreshment like water from God's well, reviving Christians, churches, and whole church cultures.

It is possible, of course, that you will reach the end of this book without having changed your mind on much. But I hope you will at least be willing. Because a willingness to change our views of God, ourselves, and the world according to God's word is healthy, right, and what Jesus's disciples should be doing all the time.

How We Got Here

The patterns of our thought and logic are based more on the *Enlightenment* than we tend to realize. You can read good summaries of the Enlightenment in any history of philosophy or theology. But in an all-too-simplistic nutshell, in the eighteenth century, Western culture had begun to feel that people didn't have to just accept the existence they were born to—they could better their lives and do good to all of society by that.

It was the age of discovery, science, and optimism for a better world. It rethought forms of government, structures of society, and economics. Similar to the present-day terms *woke* and *awake*, the very term *Enlightenment* had the idea of being in the light now—seeing what others have never been able to see before.

Reason, evidence-based knowledge, scientific discovery: such exciting things! They encouraged the individual to have the freedom to choose and to have an openness to new ideas, with the results of invention, technological advance, progress of thought and life and society. It aimed for knowledge as a good in itself, with a belief that it led to increased happiness. All well and good, perhaps. But where does it lead?

A dog can be so focused on the ball he is chasing that he pays no attention to anything else—by the time he notices the river bank, or the beautifully arranged picnic table, it is too late! In the same way, the Enlightenment has shaped Western society as it pulled the culture toward rational thought, without awareness of what that society was losing in the process. Even the ability for rational thought itself has been lost, as the very foundational principles of right and wrong, truth and lies, have been questioned into oblivion.

The real shock of it all is this: Enlightenment thinking hasn't just shaped Western society—it has shaped the Western church. What else explains the vast plethora of church denominations, or the ease at which some people flit from one church to another, or our readiness to claim "spiritual abuse" rather than receive hard teaching, if not the *think-for-yourself* attitude? In much of Western thought, traditional beliefs themselves are suitable subjects for mockery simply because they are traditional—such as the topics in this book that were, after all, widely-held beliefs at one time. There were dangers with the pre-Enlightenment way of simply accepting what "the church teaches." But can you see the problem when Christians, like their surrounding world, are quick to dismiss previously assumed realities, mocking the old in favor of the current?

Tribes and Subcultures of Twenty-First Century Churches in the West

Let us think for a moment more about the way our more specific church cultures affect our thinking. There are various titles some of us use to define our churches as *good* ones. Yours might be *Reformed, evangelical*, or *Protestant*. Or maybe for you it's *Catholic, Orthodox, Spirit-filled* or something else that helps you to feel like you're in safe hands on a Sunday. It's a shame we can't just call ourselves Christians. But we have to have definitions to distinguish ourselves from those who are in serious error in some way, don't we? The downside, of course, is that it's too easy to side with our trusted tribe over *truth*—like sports fans booing the referee just to support our team. We are not always objective observers.

In my own English context, mixed in with the church tribes is the British class system, which further defines each of us quite deeply. It has certainly evolved a lot over the last century. The wealthy no longer rule from drafty castles or manor houses with servants who live in underground basements and feed off turnips (in case you imagined that). However, a hierarchy is still fairly deeply ingrained in society. It's more complex than the old feudal system, where you could judge someone by the size of their mansion or straw hovel. Yet a British citizen will probably have pigeon-holed you into a category such as "posh," "common," or "a wannabe of some sort" the moment you open your mouth, if not before.

All of this affects our willingness to be challenged. Every identity and subculture has things that are received as fact, as *gospel* truth, that are not actually part of the gospel and are not shared by Christians elsewhere in the world. That's a problem, because it probably means we've got stuff wrong.

Our cultural instincts shape our securities, attitudes, and approaches to how we process information and relate to others. But as Christians, we need to be willing to question our deepest assumptions if we are to live lives that truly honor Christ.

Bits of the Bible We Barely Believe

When it comes to Scripture, there are parts we tend to dismiss or brush over, simply because they don't fit with our assumptions. And that matters. It's not that we have to thoroughly understand every part of Scripture perfectly to be saved. But resisting God at any point is a serious mistake, with consequences.

I would like to lay down a ground rule at this point. I hope you'll agree to it; if you don't, I'm not sure we'll be able to go much further together. The rule is: no more talk about "secondary issues." It is all too easy for someone to dismiss something as *secondary* the moment they realize they don't want to think about it. I don't think that's an acceptable way to treat God's word.

There are certainly such things as *debatable* issues (e.g., Rom 14:5—"One person considers one day more sacred than another; another considers every day alike"). There are things open to discussion and disagreement, issues where there is room for people to reach different conclusions or apply in a variety of ways. As the same verse concludes, the rule in such cases is "Each of them should be fully convinced in their own mind." But that is quite different to being indifferent, to disengaging or dismissing.

On top of debatable issues and cultural blind spots, we all have things we find *personally* difficult to understand or accept: particular areas that our sinful natures repeatedly resist or from which our past hurts cause us to recoil. But to take any part of Scripture, however small, and brush it aside is to tell God we know better—even if we happen to agree with most of what he says. It is not enough to relegate things as secondary, as an excuse to close our minds. "*All* Scripture is God-breathed."

Do you believe that? If so, what do you think are the consequences of dismissing or explaining away parts of Scripture—whether particular texts, or more general ideas within Scripture? What does God's loving discipline look like, for us as individuals or whole wings of the institutional church? And even if we are foolish enough to risk God's discipline ourselves (which suggests we don't know much about God), what of the effects it will have on others? Or for our relationship with God?

Growing Through Scripture

So how should we approach Scripture? Of course, it's always easier to point the finger at others than to notice our own errors. And it's right that we identify things that are wrong with other groupings of the church, so we know what to avoid and can cling to the truth more closely. But it is much harder to recognize and accept that *we* might be wrong. And as a general principle of Christian living, it's better to consider our own faults first. That means it is always healthy for us to come to God's word with the expectation that *we* will be exposed in some way—that we have something to learn and will be changed by it. We can always depend on our loving Father for that change to be a good thing for us. Unsettling, yes; humbling, yes; but always good.

I often return to one of the simple and vivid diagrams that was explained at the superb Cornhill training course in London, which I attended twenty-five years ago.

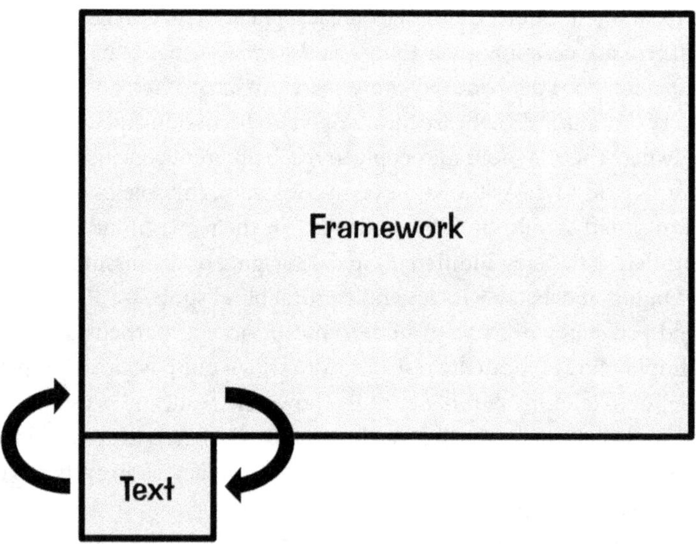

The idea is that you need a good framework to approach any given text in Scripture. The framework is the sum total of our knowledge of the Bible—our biblical theology, if you like.

The arrow on the right says our framework of thinking, our understand of the Bible as a whole, not only *will* but *must* strongly affect the way we approach an individual text. If you were to read a text with no reference to the wider body of Scripture—in other words, just pluck a text out of context—you would come up with all manner of wacky ideas. We've probably all seen people do that. People can easily find a "proof text" to justify almost anything. So we have to apply a good, biblical framework to every text we read. In the church networks I know, I think we tend to be reasonably good at that part. There may be a small dollop of arrogance in thinking we have a better biblical framework than anyone else, but on the whole we have learned to be fairly good at reading texts in the context of a fairly decent biblical frame of reference.

But the arrow leading from the text to the framework is equally important. Each text we meditate over must in turn shape our framework, each enlarging and correcting it. The more texts we read, study, and meditate on, the better our framework becomes.

Maybe sometimes it is unsettling to take this process seriously. Take, for example, a text like Exod 4:11: "The LORD said to him, 'Who gave human beings their mouths? Who makes them deaf or mute? Who gives them sight or makes them blind? Is it not I, the LORD?'" It is easy to jump to the caveats insisted upon by our framework: "God only ever does good things; he doesn't *directly* make people mute, deaf, or blind—that came through the fall, etc." But one can quickly lose the whole weight of the verse by explaining it away like that. What if we rather take it at face value, even if it challenges our understanding? What if God does actively blind and deafen people? In fact, there are biblical examples of God doing precisely those things.

Taking the time to meditate on a text and allowing all the possibilities of it to soak in is the only way to enlarge our framework—which is ultimately our view of God. But we often fail to develop our frameworks as we ought in this way. And usually our frameworks are not as big, and solid, and correct as we thought in the first place. Our cultural assumptions play a bigger part than we admit in shaping our framework of thinking, and we assume those assumptions are biblical—because we don't allow texts of Scripture to penetrate our framework. It's a chilling thought, but many Christians are having their framework of thought expanded rapidly and daily by news outlets, secular education, and social media rather than texts of Scripture. You can easily assume such things as "Russia is bad" or "Aliens are probably real" or whatever current affairs there may be without ever grappling with Scripture to the point of having a framework that can seriously think biblically about them.

The Consequences of Taking "All" Scripture Seriously . . . Or Not

There are three wonderful results of continually repenting by engaging with the Bible afresh:

It creates in us character and courage

Like so much of today's architecture, our whole existence in the twenty-first century Western world can be soulless and bland. In fact, architecture is a good indicator of a society in general, and many new developments in our country (at least) smell of greed, indulgence, and recluse. It mirrors a society that likes to grab what's mine, shut the door, and have as little to do with other people as possible. There is little that people would fight for, and there are few who are driven by a cause beyond their own comfort.

Sadly, the church mirrors much of society's malaise. My wife, Lyndsey, and I have far too often led small-group Bible studies in the past where long-established Christians seem to want to hear only what they already knew. If it's familiar territory, all well and good; if unfamiliar or stretching, it creates unease. Life is ok, they plod on as Christians, they don't upset the apple cart by suggesting too much change. But where is the sense of adventure? The yearning for growth?

The Christian life should be the life that is really living, "the life that is truly life" (1 Tim 6:19), as we hear the words of Jesus and put them into practice (Matt 7:24). Through faith, through suffering, through seeing the living Lord at work, we discover more of the abundance of the Life-giver. I hope you will see, in the pages that follow, how growth in our knowledge of God's word opens up the possibilities of new horizons—ones that surpass the growing horizons of the Enlightenment age and their new discoveries. I hope you will find something that grabs your imagination—because with hope comes energy, energy to explore ever more of God in his creation, in his health-giving renewal, and in his subversive values that save us from the satanic banality of what the Western world has tragically become.

As our culture grows darker, we as Christians should shine brighter. That's not just because of the growing contrast due to the darkening, but also because of the brightening on our part. Seeing more clearly that the world of false comfort is not worth investing in, and tasting the foulness of its values, we will flee to the sweetness of Christ. As we discover more of the infinite depths of his goodness, we will find our resolves for godliness strengthened, our purposes crystallized, and our zest for life overflowing.

My own church is situated within a social housing estate. Whenever people escape the character-crushing existence of life confined by the estate and discover the great outdoors, a world of size and beauty far beyond the narrow limits of the neighborhood, it is a beautiful picture of the way the life of new discoveries in God's word lifts us to vast new vistas.

It strengthens our engagement with the world

With political unsettledness and the race for more extremes in morality and in public thinking, an increasing number of people are looking for something more. They are waking up to the fact that there must be more to life than the ideologies or agendas imposed on them. Many people are acutely conscious of spiritual forces behind the politics and upheavals of the world. The New Age movement has become quite popular.

One Sunday, two visitors came to our church—unknown to each other—with almost identical stories: "I have been a New-Ager for a while. I sense deep evil in the world; I know there is a devil, so I figured there must be a God. I found a Bible and I know there must be truth in it. I've come to find out what that truth is."

There are people crying out for answers, for good news! They are seeing things in the world around that they perceive as great, powerful lies. They are looking for *truth*—but the issues that are so pressing to them are things that the church at large hasn't begun to think about. We don't think their issues are big issues—so we don't bother to notice that the Scriptures we read actually address them at all. We too easily reduce all texts to our six-picture summary of the gospel,[2] as if that is all you need. No wonder people find us to be an irrelevance. And that is very hard for us to understand, when we know the gospel is exactly what people need. As it is, the closest they can often get to satisfying their curiosity is slightly off-the-wall YouTubers and a vaguely Christian spirituality. I'm discovering that there are many people around who now call themselves Christians, but are not connected to any church—because they think churches are blind to the realities of the world. That is not a good state of affairs.

How different it could be if we happened to be discovering parts of the Bible that ring true to people's intuition, like Paul and his explanation of the

2. "Two Ways to Live" is perhaps my favorite tool for explaining the big-sweep message of the gospel; see https://www.twowaystolive.com. It's important to add that those who developed it have a healthy biblical framework and significant depth of thinking behind it. The point here is that it is easy to be lazy and simply reduce our whole gospel to a summary.

"unknown god" in Acts 17. If, with our own journeys of discovery, we could enthuse about dragons, healing, or the blindness of intellectuals and institutions, we might rediscover the joy of our social interactions with people as we seek by any means to "win as many as possible" (1 Cor 9:19).

It enlarges our vision of God

My friend Geof was converted through a builder he used to work for. They once had a lad on the team who thought he knew everything. Whatever topic of conversation came up, he already knew all about it. I'm sure you can picture how that worked out: it was a daily game of seeing if he would take the bait and spout his superior wisdom on any and every obscure subject. One day, they downed tools and asked him straight: "Of all the knowledge in the universe—of all the stuff there is to know—how much of it do you think you know?" An awkward pause. Then he replied, "About 4 percent." So that became his nickname from then on: *4 percent*.

I sometimes remember Geof's story and smile to myself when I read those awesome chapters at the end of Job. After all has been said and done, the Lord speaks. For four long chapters, he asks Job dizzying rhetorical questions about the vast unknowns of his creative powers: oceans and mountains, planets and sea monsters, ecosystems, good and evil. *Job, how much do you really know of me and my works?* I cringe as I imagine for a moment Job answering, "Hmm—about 4 percent." The thought is utterly blasphemous. God and his works are so infinitely beyond anything we can imagine, that Job can only collapse before the living God in humility and repentance.

Those with any concept of God and the gospel would not dream of saying we know 4 percent of all things. But in practice, there does seem to be a flavor within some church circles of thinking we've got knowledge of God pretty much wrapped up. It is sometimes clearest among the young bucks at theological seminaries or in church leadership, driven by the hierarchical flavor of the church culture to assume themselves to be the great leaders of tomorrow. But it can have an influence across the church. Question: *Who is God?* Answer: *He's like me, but a bit bigger.* If we think our framework is pretty much complete, then we will not cry out with the psalm writer, "Open my eyes that I may see wonderful things in your law" (Ps 119:18). And so we settle for an understanding of God that we can contain.

One of the most memorable evenings of my life was spent with a friend who (it turned out) was something of a world leader in his field of astronomy. He took a couple of us up to the giant telescope where he spent many of his hours. It wasn't so much the views or even the amazing Victorian engineering of the telescope itself that I remember most—it was the conversation. After describing at length, with the excitement of a true enthusiast, exactly what his team had been discovering in recent years about the mathematics of clusters and superclusters, I asked him, somewhat flippantly, "Does it make you feel small?" He answered immediately, with wide eyes, "It gives me vertigo."

On another occasion with the same friend, I asked if he thought there was life on other planets. As a Christian I fully assumed he would say no. But he surprised me by saying with the same wide-eyed enthusiasm, "I don't doubt it." "Nothing equivalent to humans," he added, "but everything new we discover is so vastly beautiful, complex, abundant, it would utterly fit the nature of God to fill the distant ends of the universe with incredible things we will never see."

With a view of God like that, now let us approach the Bible again—his self-revelation to us. I'm not suggesting we look for things to contradict the gospel foundations we already know and destabilize ourselves and others. But when we find things that blow our minds, and in fact *do* challenge what we thought we knew, then our view of God is rightly magnified. We get another tiny glimpse of the majesty of the God who has chosen us to call him our Father.

King David knew about the stresses of life. He spent much of his with his back against the wall, his life hanging by a thread. When he grasped afresh the greatness of his God, he wrote, "With your help I can advance against a troop; with my God I can scale a wall" (Ps 18:29). It is by the refreshing of an ever-enlarging vision of God that we will be transformed. Instead of the nervous and cowardly existence we are familiar with, we will rise up as warriors with our King.

"Open my eyes that I may see wonderful things in your law" (Ps 119:18). That would be a good prayer for each of us as we read through the chapters that follow. God's law is full of wondrous things. What better desire could there be for us in life than to have our eyes opened to more and more of what he has revealed? Instead of being crushed from the oppression of clinging to our limited vision of God, let us stand tall and fill our lungs with the fresh air of truth, our blood with the health-giving word, and our eyes with the breathtaking vision of God and his works.

1

Land Is Living

The spirits of the hills are not what they were, Master. They are losing their power. Ten years ago they would have killed you all for coming to them in that manner.

Samutchoso
Laurens van der Post, *Lost World*

The battle spread out over the whole countryside, and the forest swallowed up more men that day than the sword.

2 Sam 18:8

It all starts in the mountains. They do something to you. You might spend your working days in a city skyscraper office, or have a routine job in some urban industrial estate. You might have had a religious upbringing, or have been subject to philosophical options displayed side by side in school assemblies. It all makes little difference: it's mountains that reveal the hidden realities. When you are in the mountains, you know.

The 1993 film *Alive* (remember the one where they eat each other?) starts with narrator John Malkovich describing the experience of finding yourself in the middle of the Andes.[1] Similarly, in the movie of Heinrich Harrer's *Seven Years in Tibet*, the trailer begins with Brad Pitt's character narrating the dizzying experience of life in the Himalayas.[2] The wonder of time and space, stillness and absolute aloneness—they express what others have felt when all else is stripped away. In the mountains there is the true sense of perspective: there is the smallness of one's own being and the vastness of God, experienced and felt, not just learned about. The senses are filled; spiritual realities, hidden by civilized life, become clear. Crystal clear.

It all starts in the mountains. But oceans, hills, and plains can have a similar effect: a sensation so rich it lifts you from the mundane and the busy and the merely material. It's physical, but it's more than physical. The land itself has a life force, a meaning beyond itself. Yes, a pointer to God, but somehow more tangible than just a lifeless pointer. It is a living witness. It speaks. It breathes. It rejoices and it grieves. It relates to its creator.

I believe the significance of land is an instinct shared by all who live on it and by it. The instinct is lost by industrialization and urbanization. These things are not bad in themselves; it's just that those of us in the industrialized age have lost language, connection, and meaning from the land. That has not made us wiser about God. It has diminished our knowledge of God. We accept our existence as normal. But something is profoundly missing from our outlook, such that people who know nothing of Christ yet know things about God just from his creation. And these things are lost on us, his children.

Back to mountains; Lord Robert Baden-Powell, founder of the Boy Scout movement, puts it like this:

> There is to me something sacred about their calm isolation far far above the world where it would be presumption for puny man to make his footmarks.[3]

He goes on to quote an unnamed source:

> One becomes a kind of Yoga in the mountains, where you can only walk and sleep and think.
>
> I do not know what it is; nine-tenths of the people who live higher than 1400 feet are Buddhists. The mountains almost talk you into it. In the quiet of the night you listen to their voices; you are drawn into the brooding intensity all round you. Then, as the slough of immediate cares and preoccupations slips away,

1. Marshall, *Alive.*
2. Annaud, *Seven Years in Tibet.*
3. Baden-Powell, *Lessons*, 108.

> the spirit expands and wider cycles of consciousness are opened out.
>
> In warm cities where men huddle together, one must have something to cling to, a personal Saviour, a lantern in a sure and kindly hand, comforting voices in the dark.
>
> But here you do not seek—you know. Self vanishes. There is a mystic purpose in Nature with which you are concerned—remotely not individually.[4]

Some Westerners do turn to Buddhism and practices of Eastern religions because such things appear to provide a deeper understanding of life than Christianity. Buddhists and the rest seem connected to the world in a way Western Christians are not. They claim to have found "a mystic purpose in Nature." And it's not that they are merely seeking something: "You do not seek—you know."

By contrast, in Western Protestant circles, it can be quite ordinary to hear comments like, "I'll enjoy nature in the new creation; for now, there's a gospel to preach." Just pause and take that in. What do you think of it as a statement? Yes, it's all right and true. It's definitely well intentioned—more than that, it's correcting the idolatry of ecology that has invaded many churches. It sounds very godly. (Certainly more godly than you, the one it was addressed to.) But if the land we live on has, in fact, deep spiritual significance—and that is something people *know*—then such a statement isn't quite as godly as it seems. It's a bit like saying, "I'll be nice to her when we're married; for now, I've got better things to do."

My guess is that many readers will be anxious at this point. Are we saying that Christianity is wrong, and pagans are right? Are we establishing *fact* around what people apparently *know*? Is the Bible just *one* part of God's revelation, and—Buddhism, here we come!—there are other great mysterious ways to discover God, as the quotes above imply?

I want you to see from this chapter that there *is* some sense in which the land we live on has emotion, feeling joys and pains, as an extension of its Maker. But I want to show you that that is not a pagan view: it is the *Bible's* view. We don't need to deny it, avoid it, or be afraid of it. It is a wonderful thing that many people, ignorant of Christ, sense profoundly. It is a glorious opportunity to connect with spiritually aware people and point them to their loving Maker and Savior. (Yes, their *personal Savior*.)

But Enlightenment thinking has its own instincts, and will dismiss the whole idea as obviously untrue, and certainly of no importance. If this Enlightenment thinking clouds our vision and our reading of Scripture—well,

4. Baden-Powell, *Lessons*, 108.

it would be a shame, wouldn't it? We'd be missing out on something pretty special. And our gospel would appear irrelevant to many.

Before we even get to the Bible, I think it would be helpful to start by thinking about the things that our Western culture—and the church within it—has lost from our understanding of the land.

What Have We Lost?

Language

Have you ever noticed how some modern-day governments and institutions seem to base their plans and behavior on sci-fi movies and dystopian novels? The movies and books were made to predict worst-case scenarios. I imagine some high-powered meetings where they study one of the classics together, as if it was a operation manual: "*Hey guys—this is a great idea! If we mapped everyone's DNA, we could control the world!*" "*If we made people half human, half robot, we could have an excellent police force!*" "*There's an idea—if we give people soft drugs and a life of ease, they'll do anything we want!*"

George Orwell's *Nineteen Eighty-Four* is about a government's over-control that is out of control. The main character is called Winston. His job is to trawl through back copies of newspapers, cutting out and destroying news that is no longer in line with "truth." ("*Hey guys—that's a great idea . . . Make sure it's only on the internet, so we can erase it at will!*") The dictionary in *Nineteen Eighty-Four* has become a fraction of what it used to be, because with fewer words there is reduced ability to understand, imagine, and even think. Concepts disappear.

It is the same in relation to the land we live on. When we lose language to describe it, we lose understanding of it. And we have already lost a lot.

> Once upon a time, words began to vanish from the language of children. They disappeared so quietly that at first almost no one noticed—fading away like water on a stone. The words were those that children used to name the natural world around them.[5]

Thus begins the beautifully illustrated book *The Lost Words* by Robert Macfarlane and Jackie Morris. What it describes might not be as deliberately sinister as the language erasing of *Nineteen Eighty-Four*—but there is a

5. Macfarlane and Morris, *Lost Words*, 1.

similar result. By losing language, we lose meaning. "What we cannot name, we cannot in some sense see."[6]

Macfarlane and other authors (such as Dominick Tyler) have compiled lists of words that have fallen out of use in the English language. *All* the words are to do with the "natural"[7] world, often found in older dictionaries but removed in newer editions. By contrast, newer words added to dictionaries are most often to do with ideologies, or the technically shifting and morally experimental world—such as *cisgender, anti-republican, cosplay.* Some of these newer words leave a bad taste in my mouth. Contrast some of the lost ones:

Zawn—It's an arch in the cliffs.[8] Doesn't it give you the sense of a yawning gap, making you feel dizzy as you look down into the crashing waves?

Ryme—The buildup of feathery white frost in high winds when droplets of water in fog or low cloud hit cold surfaces.[9] How delicate! It takes staring, being drawn in, to have names for different types of frost.

Swang—Low-lying piece of ground liable to be flooded.[10] I reckon if local government authorities knew the word *swang*, they'd cancel half their new-build planning permissions on the spot.

So, lost language empties us of meanings; we become unaware of the significance of things. The controversial building of giant wind turbines on the Isle of Skye, in Scotland, has been opposed by members of the local population by pointing out they had tons of local words for parts of the landscape and plant life[11]—it wasn't just a bunch of moorland like any other after all, as the developers and their research documents assumed. Scientific study has its limits. And of course it does—because the scientific society has lost the language to understand the land. And the loss is not just academic: it's spiritual. Things intrinsic to who we are are lacking.

New words fill our minds with other meanings instead. If you have a word for something, you notice it. Take the example of names for colors. The Himba tribe from northern Namibia do not have separate words for green and blue. But they differentiate between shades of green that look the

6. Macfarlane, *Landmarks*, frontispiece.

7. I put the word "natural" in quotation marks where it refers to God's creation as a reminder that we are not referring to something that is simply innate rather than created.

8. Tyler, *Uncommon Ground*, 11.

9. Tyler, *Uncommon Ground*, 52.

10. Macfarlane, *Landmarks*, 53.

11. For example, John Muir Trust, "Why We Love Bogs."

same to European eyes—*because* Europeans have no words to distinguish them.[12] With a name comes a meaning. So when most children are more familiar with words like *app*, *gym*, and *homophobia* than *beech tree* or *lichen*, it tells you plenty about their society, what they do and don't understand, what is important to them.

No wonder the average Western Protestant Christian does not get what so many other people get.

Connection

"Earthing" (or sometimes "grounding," for Americans) is an increasingly popular therapy initiated by Clint Ober. In 1998, after a successful career grounding systems in the cable television industry, the earthing pioneer began investigating the potential to improve human health with grounding.[13]

Growing up in rural Montana, many of Ober's childhood friends were from the Native American reservation. Yes—his friends were from a community well known for herbal medicines, spiritual places, and talking to wildlife. He was used to their alternative (to Western eyes) ways. Once a girl in their community was very sick with scarlet fever. The girl's grandfather dug a hole that he partially buried her in, lit a fire, and stayed by her. After several days, she was lifted out, her health restored.[14]

Another time, arriving home from school, the mother of Ober's friend told him to remove his shoes—"They will make you sick," she said.[15] Later in life, he observed how we insulate ourselves from the ground with our rubber-soled shoes. Just as domestic electronics need earthing—not just for safety, but to prevent build up of static and electrical interference—so our own brains and nervous systems operate through electrical transmissions and need earthing for healthy operation.[16] The earthing movement ascribes many of our developed-world health problems to this regular build up of stress/charge.

Ancient people groups, such as Native Americans, Indigenous Australians, and the Bushmen of southern Africa, have an attitude to land that those of European descent have notoriously failed to appreciate. In each case, a crass pseudo-Christian outlook has justified disdain, even wholesale murder, of such people on the basis that they are sub-human, living

12. Visagie, "How Do Namibian Himbas."
13. Ober, "About Clint Ober."
14. Ober, "About Clint Ober," 1950s.
15. Ober, "About Clint Ober," 1950s.
16. Ober, "About Clint Ober," 1998.

like animals from the land with only the most basic technology. To those who blame Christianity itself for some of the inglorious aspects of White expansion, it is worth pointing out that among the frontiersmen of each European advance, there were brave Christians, such as David Brainerd, John Paton, and David Livingstone, who fought the cause of the indigenous peoples, seeking to befriend, equip, and evangelize. Yet today, even among those Christians most sensitive to historic racism, there is still commonly an unwittingly patronizing view of "natural" peoples: *their* traditional views are of little worth—simply pagan, pantheist nonsense to be swept aside for the gospel.

But suppose such people actually understand some important things that we don't? Suppose that even some of the hippie, tree-hugging types from our own society have got a point when it comes to "nature"? If there is anything deep and mysterious about the land we live on, then our uglifying of the world is not just to do with our disconnect with the land. It is also a reflection of our relationship with God, as revealed in the glorious intricacy of his creation. And all without considering whether the Bible has anything to say on the matter. Interest in the spiritual significance of land is dismissed all too quickly as merely being a shadow of the new creation or something. But I'm not sure we ought to dismiss it. After all, we don't dismiss marriage, food, or homes just because they are shadows of the new creation. Land is not in the biblical category of things that have been fulfilled in Christ and therefore no longer directly apply. Perhaps connection with the land should be an important part of our lives now, a means of relating to the wondrous ways of the Almighty.

Meaning

Missionary Kids (MKs) have to recognize the great danger of not belonging in any particular place. They can often feel rootless, especially if they grew up living in many different places. In the best cases, MKs grow into adults who are particularly able to hold the things of this world loosely, recognizing their true home is in heaven. They are flexible in their preferences, socialize easily with all sorts, and settle quickly in new environments. But some find great difficulties, feeling they do not belong *anywhere*. People they have lived among somehow appreciate *who they are*, in a way the MKs themselves are denied. These people they see—their national, tribal, or family identity is rooted in a place. Even nomadic people know where they belong.

I grew up in a part of London known for its Indian- and Pakistani-dominated population. Particularly for the second generation of immigrant families, it can be hard to know where you fit in. You are not quite the same as the "native" English kids, with your ethnic difference and your parents' value system. But also, the visit to India to see relatives quickly shows you're no longer one of them, either. It's the theme of Alex Haley's famous novel *Roots*—the longing to fit in, to find meaning in who you are, where you belong. If there is any deliberate, sinister agenda behind the mass migration into the West at present (beyond simply Islamic expansionism), it could be to do with the way movement undermines the sense of meaning about where you live. A national or regional identity becomes less possible. The question of *who we are* becomes less clear. Unrooted or displaced people often don't respect the place they are in: it has little intrinsic worth to them. The whole population becomes less settled, with a reduced sense of identity and belonging. That makes other changes easier to impose.

The gospel of Jesus Christ is, of course, the glorious answer to finding meaning and belonging. We are rescued from the world, with all its uncertainties, to find fullness of life and an everlasting home. But dismissing the importance of land in this life is not the solution to understanding that better. Instead, the more we appreciate concepts of *home*, identity with a place, and the almost *magical* experience of being in forest, riverside, coastline, hills, farms, gardens, desert, or moor, the *more* we will understand what it is to belong to the great God and Father of our Lord Jesus Christ.

The Spiritual Earth

Ok, so it's harder for most evangelical Christians in the Western world to grasp any concept of a spiritual connection with the earth. But for many people in the world it is second nature. I reckon those people find certain parts of the Bible much more straightforward.

In his book *The Lost World of the Kalahari*, Laurens van der Post tells the story of his expedition to find remnants of the near-extinct Bushmen, the first people to inhabit southern Africa. He had heard that small groups of them still existed deep within the Kalahari desert. This was in the 1950s.

As his team, in their Land-Rovers, advanced into territory never before explored by people of European descent, strange things started happening, especially in the Slippery Hills—an area sacred to Bushmen. You may have heard similar stories in other accounts: he and his team members all had a great feeling of unease; there were strange attacks by bees; their cameras all inexplicably failed to function; and so forth.

Van der Post was not a Christian, but of strong Afrikaans Dutch Reformed heritage. After detailing all the bizarre events that eventually drove them away from the hills and the clear interpretation from his guide Samutchoso, Van der Post states in his own cool and reasoned way that this is simply an account of what happened. No more, no less. He himself was not attempting to interpret or judge—just recount, for the reader to reach his or her own conclusions. (Or not.) Were they actual spirits? Were they *evil* spirits? Were they perhaps *good* spirits, or were they just *neutral* spirits in the hills? Did Samutchoso really hear their voices? Readers simply needed to accept some facts as the author told them—this was not just the imagination of those who were there, and it was all too much to be simply a series of mere coincidences. And one more thing: with the passing of time and more Christianized (if not Christian) Europeans arriving in the area, and some settling there, the strange spiritual activities stopped happening.

I wonder what you make of that sort of thing? This account raised some very interesting questions for me when I read it several years ago. The idea of *neutral* spirits had never occurred to me, nor had territorial spirits been something I had ever taken too seriously. "Gods" of regions or nations, perhaps—the Bible often refers to the gods of the nations. It says they are no gods at all, and we know there is but One True God. But on the other hand, there is clearly some sort of reality and significance there.[17] But here was something far more local and tangible—the sort of thing African friends of mine have talked about quite freely, as if it were obvious. Here was something simply told as an experience, without the cultural divide that would otherwise invite me to dismiss it with a mental wave of the hand (and no doubt written on the face): "Of course you think that. That's your outlook on life, your language for things we don't understand." But perhaps my outlook wasn't *right*—just *Enlightenment*. Not *biblical*.

Now here's what first blew me away. Very soon after reading Laurens van der Post, while preaching through 2 Samuel, I was stopped in my tracks by the narrative of chapter 18. Verse 8, in particular, undid me:

> The battle spread out over the whole countryside, and the forest swallowed up more men that day than the sword.

This is the Bible, now. Did you take in the language? "The forest swallowed up," or "devoured" (ESV). It's not passive, as in, "They died in the forest." It's not even just cause and effect, as in, "The forest caused more deaths than the actual fighting." It's loaded language: "The forest *devoured*." It *ate up*. It deliberately evokes feelings of passion, savagery, anger. This is not J. R. R. Tolkien or C. S. Lewis. This is the Bible.

17. For a helpful investigation into all of this, see Heiser, *Unseen*.

The context is within the long saga of King David's rise to the throne of Israel and the establishment of him as king. David, like the reader, knows God has destined him to rule over his chosen people. But his experience is lots of frustration and opposition, with one setback after another, at many times feeling as if his life is hanging by a thread. The latest attack against him is from his own son.

Absalom had his own griefs in life, but was a real charmer—and used it to become the darling of Israel. He conspired against his own dad, the true king. This treachery against God's chosen king is so unfitting. And so was the civil war within God's chosen nation. Such is the danger to David's life that his generals persuade him to stay behind while they advance with the troops. God gives them a decisive victory. And in the end, Absalom himself is caught—by a tree. His girly long hair, pride of the town, is his downfall.

What is the significance of verse 8? It's not essential to the story, except perhaps so that we are not surprised to read about Absalom's accident as his mule crashed through the thick lower branches of a big oak tree. The more I chew over the verse, the more I can find no other reasonable way to take it than as a poetic expression of the very land rising up against the enemies of God's king. It really comes across very much like Tolkien's *Lord of the Rings* or Lewis's *Narnia*. The writers of those classics were very fond of incorporating animals, mountains, and trees as living, conscious beings into their literature. Perhaps they didn't get that idea just from their love of ancient folklore; perhaps their keen understanding of Scripture fell entirely in line with a world like that.

In 2 Sam 18, I felt I had stumbled upon a world previously unseen in the Bible as I had been taught it. Like the children stumbling through the wardrobe into Narnia, here was a world of life and possibilities I'd never thought to consider, for all my love of "nature." The Lord's creation was far bigger than I had dared to believe. There was something far more mysterious, spiritual, and *alive* about creation. And therefore the Lord's ways of relating to us and his world were far bigger than I had recognized.

The Language of the Bible

Second Samuel 18, it turns out, is not a one-off. The Scriptures are loaded with language of a conscious creation. Perhaps it is no more than poetry—use of metaphor to paint pictures that stir the emotions. But if you just open your mind to the possibility that other cultures in the world might just understand something we don't, then perhaps Scripture is simply speaking in terms that are obvious to others—just not to us. After all, wherever you go in the world, from Japan to Africa, Australia to Scandinavia, "traditional religions" all believe pretty much the same things: trees, mountains, and stones are not merely inanimate objects. They have spiritual life. Yes, all such people need the gospel. Yes, they take created things and turn them into idols. But does that make them wrong in everything they believe? Is it possible that deep down in their history and consciousness there is a common root in reality?

Take the trees, while Absalom and his flowing locks are fresh in our mind. In Gen 1, God said, "Let the land produce vegetation: seed-bearing plants and trees on the land that bear fruit with seed in it. . . . The land produced vegetation: plants bearing seed according to their kinds and trees bearing fruit with seed in it" (vv. 11–12). It is not just that God stuck plants and trees on the earth, like he was building Legos or creating a Minecraft world. No, expressed in the very account of creation, the earth itself is given the power and means to produce, and the plants and trees do just that. There is a will and purpose within the things created.

It is called *anthropomorphizing* when we talk about inanimate objects or nonhuman life-forms as if they were people. (It's a good word. Write it down.) Expressions like, "Plants want to reach the sunlight," or "The oxygen wants to find a hydrogen"—it's making out that the things have desires of their own. But while the scientist loves to explain the mechanisms behind why things look that way, the fact remains that they do: things *do* seem to have a will, much as we humans do. Even Richard Dawkins's atheistic masterpiece is betrayed by its own title: *The Selfish Gene*. The thing has a will to live. The Scriptures are unashamed to speak in these terms. These are the terms of the majority world view—that the land, and the things in it, have a life of their own, as ascribed by God.

When David brought the ark of God home to Jerusalem, he sings a psalm (1 Chr 16). It is a great appeal to all people to praise the LORD, who has done wonderful things. Yet David seems to get a bit carried away by verse 23:

> Sing to the LORD, all the earth;
> proclaim his salvation day after day.
> Declare his glory among the nations,
> his marvelous deeds among all peoples. (vv. 23–24)

"All the earth"? Obviously it means all the people of the earth. Except the same word comes again in verse 31:

> Let the heavens rejoice, let the earth be glad;
> let them say among the nations, "the LORD reigns!"

It's less obvious there that *the earth* means people. In fact, it seems to be explicitly speaking to the created things, and telling them to rejoice and proclaim the Lord's sovereignty to people.

The song goes on:

> Let the sea resound, and all that is in it;
> let the fields be jubilant, and everything in them!
> Let the trees of the forest sing,
> let them sing for joy before the Lord,
> for he comes to judge the earth." (vv. 32–33)

Ok, it's a song. There is poetic license there. Just as there is with Isaiah's celebration:

> The mountains and hills will burst into song before you,
> and all the trees of the field will clap their hands. (Isa 55:12)

In my experience, my church culture, the typical preacher of this verse would try to express the intense celebration of the event Isaiah speaks of. He might say, "It is *as if* all creation is singing and dancing." Well, there is certainly metaphor there. Trees don't have hands. But suppose it's not just *as if*? Suppose it's more than *just* metaphor, and the hills will sing out, and trees actually dance? Is it really too hard to imagine?

When Jesus entered Jerusalem on a colt, an atmosphere broke out similar to what Isaiah foresaw. The multitudes of Jesus's disciples rejoiced and yelled out praises to God for Jesus. The grumpy Pharisees were offended. They told Jesus to set the people straight. He was having none of it, however; it was inevitable that people would praise the coming king. But his choice of language is quite breathtaking:

> I tell you, if they keep quiet, the stones will cry out. (Luke 19:40)

Just pause on that. Pause and imagine being there, in the heated moment. What is Jesus's tone? Angry, exasperated? Firm? In control, and crystal clear? "You Pharisees—here's a fact . . . " It is impossible for stones to cry out. But they would, if the people didn't. They would. Because it is *more* impossible for Jesus not to be praised.

Jesus then turned and *spoke to* the city of Jerusalem, in tears, as he foresaw its downfall. Culturally, I can find it a little awkward speaking or singing to inanimate objects. "O Christmas tree, O Christmas tree, how lovely are your branches" just doesn't do it for me. Perhaps I just need to soften up a little. But even with my callous, English heart, "O Little Town of

Bethlehem"[18] can't help but draw deep emotions—how beautifully natural it seems to address *the town*; how powerful to sing the words. How much more for Jesus to address dear Jerusalem.

This idea of speaking to things was not a new concept for Jesus at this point. Up till now, yes, Jesus spoke to people. He also spoke to demons (living, conscious beings). He spoke to dead people, and brought them to life—as God spoke things into life in the beginning. And Jesus spoke to inanimate objects, as if they had ears to hear. Apparently, they did:

> He got up and rebuked the wind and the raging waters; the storm subsided, and all was calm. "Where is your faith?" he asked his disciples. In fear and amazement they asked one another, "Who is this? He commands even the winds and the water, and they obey him." (Luke 8:24–25)

> Seeing a fig tree by the road, he went up to it but found nothing on it except leaves. Then he said to it, "May you never bear fruit again!" Immediately the tree withered. (Matt 21:19)

Let's also meditate on Rom 8 for a moment. This glorious chapter speaks of the coming glory for God's children. We, the "children of God," cry out for our liberation. God's Spirit within us cries out to the Father. But which modern-day, Western, evangelical Protestant would have written what Paul did next?

> I consider that our present sufferings are not worth comparing with the glory that will be revealed in us. For the creation waits in eager expectation for the children of God to be revealed. For the creation was subjected to frustration, not by its own choice, but by the will of the one who subjected it, in hope that the creation itself will be liberated from its bondage to decay and brought into the freedom and glory of the children of God. (Rom 8:18–22)

Groaning in pain. Aching for the joy of freedom it will feel. When it comes to the land we live on, the biblical worldview seems to invite a more natural connection from pre-industrial thought and attitudes than our own. We need to get in line.

But why does it matter?

18. Brooks, "O Little Town."

What's the Big Deal?

Allowing yourself to accept that there is more to *land* than just something for our pleasure, for our use, and to occasionally inspire awe of God will affect things deeply.

In a vital sense, it restores a *poetry in our soul*—an empathy with the world that we, in the industrial West, often lack, which causes us to sing in tune with creation. Such poetry is essential to our humanity, and only with it can we engage with a large part of Scripture. Accepting the deeper significance of land helps us find our proper place in it, with all the joy and awe-inspiring wonder stirred by that. Then, in turn, we can find a connection with other people that we otherwise lack. But above all, we discover vastly more of the deep wonders of our God himself.

Our Place in Creation

Understanding land as we ought, as a living entity, pulsating with the passion for God's glory—it makes the whole eco/green debate very straightforward. Both sides are badly wrong. On the one hand, to trash the environment on the basis that it's all passing away anyway is a pretty cold and soulless way of reasoning. More sensitivity is needed. It's like the kid who squishes worms or burns ants for fun: there's something wrong with cruelty and its lack of empathy. Yes, there are times, perhaps in the brutality of war or with the need for infrastructure, where environmental destruction must happen. But to do it callously is to disregard the fact that *in some sense* God has made the land living.

On the other hand, the virtue-signaling of green politics makes an absolute mockery of the concept of care. Of course, there are many who genuinely believe that sustainable protection of the "natural world" should be the number one priority for us all. That has a fundamental problem of its own: it is exalting creation above its creator and also inevitably reduces the worth of people to below that of tigers and squids, which is to overturn the order of value God has declared. But most of green politics is about vaguely appeasing guilt rather than having any real benefit to the environment we live in. It is far from clear that lithium mining is ecologically and socially more noble than fossil fuel production, or that wind or solar farms really have less impact on the environment than fossil fuels, for example. In his book *Fake Invisible Catastrophes and Prophecies of Doom*, Greenpeace founder Patrick Moore exposes the corruption of the multi-billion dollar eco-charity industry. Sin becomes a worse thing when you make out you are doing right, and it is easy to justify materialism and greed by using "greener fuel" or because the packaging claims to be recyclable. The same old Western sins of greed, comfort, and indulgence are given a green veneer. That's all.

There is a much better approach to our relationship with God's wider creation. It is about harmony and respect. God blessed his image-bearers, mankind, in Gen 1:28. He said to them, "Be fruitful and increase in number; fill the earth and subdue it. Rule over the fish in the sea and the birds in the sky and over every living creature that moves on the ground." Can you picture what it means to rule over the earth in love?

As a child, I was always fascinated by jungles. I stared at the world map on the wall by my bed and imagined adventures in the vastness of the Amazon. But it turns out Disney's *The Jungle Book*[19] is not completely accurate, and that, in fact, jungles are extremely hostile environments. Everything in them snags, cuts, stings, or bites. Where people live in jungles, those people have to some extent tamed them. And that is the picture of Genesis's opening chapters—a garden is better than a jungle. The land is made to be tamed. I do still love the idea of wilderness, and I have seen a little. It is breathtaking in its beauty, and I'm glad it's there, whether I personally see it or not. But nothing compares to places where people are part of that landscape—such as the English Lake District National Park, or rural village life in the fertile hills of Kenya, with its lush, multilayered gardens producing abundance and variety.

One of the most fascinating studies I have ever read on this subject of relating to the land is from Kenya: *A New Earth* by Elspeth Huxley. It is simply an account of the work of the British Colonial Government's agriculture and forestry policies in the 1950s. I realize that might not sound particularly fascinating to you, but don't judge too soon if you haven't read it. It has much to teach us. Some of the things she describes were failures. But many were astonishing successes of the honest, hard-working civil servants who were simply seeking the best for the population they served.

Take, for example, desertification—a huge environmental issue in northern Kenya. I remember being taught in school about the inevitable southward spread of the Sahara, and that most of Africa was virtually doomed to become desert in the next decade or so. But in Huxley's account, the process was thoroughly reversed in areas where rotational grazing was introduced. (For the uninformed, that is not about cows turning in circles. It is the practice of limiting grazing to one area a year, then moving on to the next.) This sort of simple, caring respect for the land meant grasses were allowed to become established. They, in turn, trapped moisture, and allowed

19. Reitherman, *Jungle Book*.

for soil improvement. Land was protected against erosion and soon supported more livestock overall—as if the land was happy to be properly cared for. In other examples, vast irrigation structures turned desert into farmland, and reforestation even reversed local rainfall patterns. It is a wonderful example of the land *rejoicing* over being looked after properly.

Conversely, I still don't know what to make of the astonishing accounts of wild boar running out of the forests and goring ISIS soldiers to death in Iraq in 2017.[20] It is hard not to see a stark expression of anger against these particular evildoers. Pigs against Islamic terrorists. Animals against foul men who dared to inflict such horrors upon God's children and other innocents. Whose anger was expressed? God's, yes. But were the boar indifferent? Or did the boar from the forest express the very anger of God themselves? To anyone with a glimmer of poetry in their soul, there was certainly something more than "natural" at play.

For those of us who are not in the fields of agricultural development work or government policy making, this still has a day-to-day impact on us. Christians know the satisfaction that comes from doing something that's right. There is a great sense of harmony by simply *leaving a place better than you found it*. Was my house more pleasant to look at and to live in when I sold it than when I bought it? Did the extension add beauty and charm or only monetary value? Did the garden become more peaceful or more soulless? Even on a day-trip somewhere, did my presence leave the place a little tidier or sadder-looking? In my shopping and eating choices, am I blessing the land or pillaging it? Am I restoring it or poisoning it? With disregard for land, these things will rarely enter our minds, let alone make any actual difference.

A concept of *beauty* is to do with what fits nicely with God's creation. If we allow ourselves to delight in beauty—the beauty of what the Lord has made—it will affect everything about us on a daily basis: our work patterns, our stress levels, our sense of proportion, and our own importance. Why should those who live above fourteen hundred feet, having the most spacious vistas, be Buddhists? Why should they not be Christians, rejoicing in the living land—and its glorious Creator?

Relating to People

I should come clean about some of this eco stuff. My own parents were well ahead of the trend, and for all the positives and negatives of their values, some of this encouraged me to go to university in Wales, where I studied

20. See, for example, Mendelsohn, "Wild Boars."

agroforestry. Most of my course mates were sponsored by their governments to be trained in the much needed land management in their developing countries. One such friend was Dhorji.

Dhorji is the only properly Buddhist friend I have ever had. He is from Bhutan. Dhorji worked for the Forestry Department. His brother was a saffron monk in a monastery in the Himalayas. I never knew him particularly well—we shared some course modules together, and occasionally played basketball with other international course mates before work began in the mornings. But we had enough of a friendship that he came to some of the events run by our Christian Union, where the gospel was clearly preached. He heard it. We chatted about it. But he never connected. I remember him saying on one occasion, "Yes, I heard that Jesus is the only way to God. And there are other ways."

I didn't understand why it wasn't getting through to him, and I have often looked back and wondered. But here's what I now think happens, not just with Buddhists, but with many people—followers of the New Age movement, paganism, and even occultists, but particularly people who live in close relationship with the land. They have their particular worldview. They are ignorant of Christ and have various things wrong and confused. But they know something. (Remember that word, *know*?) However they might express it, they know the land is spiritual. That is something they understand, experience, and highly treasure. Our attempt, then, to engage them with the good news of Jesus can go badly wrong. We might start with a little of listening to their point of view. We hear them say, "I know something." But then we say, in effect, "No you don't. You don't know. You're wrong. Here's the truth."

What is so devastating about that is not only our inability to understand someone's genuine experience. It's that we're not even speaking from a biblical worldview! Instead, we are speaking from an Enlightenment, reductionist worldview. I'm sure it would be better if we began by understanding, by appreciating reality as the Buddhist (or whatever) friend sees it. They *know* stuff; they don't have to deny it. Perhaps a little more of the "Paul in Athens" (Acts 17) approach would help: "Yes, that's really interesting; I can see what you're on about. Look, the Bible says something similar, and I feel it too. What I loved about discovering Jesus is that he gives hope over the destruction of the world. There's a real solution to that feeling of grief, and the whole issue of the human heart."

Jackie Morris, illustrator of *The Lost Words* mentioned above, is an example of someone with a wonderful sense of *beauty*. She writes, "I would like my garden to be consumed by the hillside, to grow heather and foxgloves and all things wild, where snakes and spiders live with butterflies and birds."[21] (Would you not describe that as a sort of Eden picture? Back here in the fallen world, I have seen spiders that catch both butterflies and birds. Fascinating, but as scary as the giant man-eating spiders from old Tarzan films, designed to make children lose sleep.) Apparently, Jackie Morris came from an evangelical Christian family. But alongside her discovery of "nature," she engages with Tarot. I wonder what has happened there? Perhaps the Christian culture she has known does not understand her deep connection with God's creation, because its own view of the land is diminished. I imagine that only someone who shares her spiritual view of "nature" could begin to engage her in conversation about sources of good and evil, creation, and the destiny of the earth. And I'm not sure that is just for Christians who happen to be interested in that sort of stuff—specialists, if you like. If we know God as revealed in Scripture, we will all be able to engage.

Knowing God

The sinful nature is always prone to limit God and exalt ourselves. In much of the church culture of Western Evangelicalism, there is a readiness to explain away any hint in Scripture that there is more to land than physical matter. This is a sin of the church culture—we limit our view of God, because it fits with our systematic theology approach of having everything in categories we can understand.

But here are things that *are*—yet that are far beyond understanding. Mysterious, non-scientific things. Talking donkeys did not originate with *Shrek*.[22] Singing trees were not conceived by *The Muppet Show*.[23] Fairy tales and folklore and the magical imaginations of children are shut down—not by Scripture, but by the rigid outlook of (Western) adult Christians.

Anyone who has done any real study of science (or any other field, for that matter) knows the experience of finding how every discovery simply opens the eyes to the vast amount of what is still undiscovered behind it. Is that not the delight of exploring God's creation? As we become willing to accept the idea of spirits, unseen forces in the created world—in short, that *land is living*—we find that much more of Scripture comes alive to us. There is that glimpse of how infinitely beyond our understanding is our God and Father. He is terrifyingly great in all his ways; yet has chosen to lavish his love upon us.

21. Morris, "Biography," para. 12.

22. Adamson, *Shrek*.

23. Henson, *Muppet Show*.

Great is our Lord and mighty in power; his understanding has no limit. (Ps 147:5)

He alone stretches out the heavens
and treads on the waves of the sea.
He is the Maker of the Bear and Orion,
the Pleiades and the constellations of the south.
He performs wonders that cannot be fathomed,
miracles that cannot be counted. (Job 9:8–10)

2

Giants Are No Joke

The Nephilim were on the earth in those days—and also afterward—when the sons of God went to the daughters of humans and had children by them. They were the heroes of old, men of renown.

Gen 6:4

You have conquered the lion; conquer also the dragon.

Augustine of Hippo, *Exposition on Psalm 91*

THE EARLY CHAPTERS OF Genesis have a lost-in-the-mists-of-time feel about them. It's like a forgotten world, a bygone era of civilization. There are cities we can't picture, technologies that are not spelled out, personalities we can't know—with strangely long lifespans. There were people the same as us, and yet somehow not the same. And then in chapter 6 we discover there were giants. It is distant, and mysterious.

Perhaps for that very reason such chapters are a playground for theological eccentrics. There are people who seem to spend all their time in either Genesis or Revelation. They ignore most of what's between those books, but read much of what's between the lines within them—more than the lines themselves. Those pre-flood days offer a world ripe for guesswork.

And the story of Nephilim, sons of God and daughters of man with mighty offspring—that is a juicy opportunity for your wildest speculations.

What a shame. Because that sort of approach is one reason the more level-headed types back right away from it. It's *wacko* territory! In my experience and observation, here's what often happens: a typical good, respected, evangelical preacher gets to a passage like Gen 6:4 (quoted above) as he faithfully preaches his safe, sound series through chapters 1–11. His steps of logic as he thinks it through go something like this:

- Starting point—There is no such thing as actual giants, apart from the occasional very big person, and angels can't have babies with people. It must mean something else.
- Other explanations seem to fit well enough—such as powerful chiefs ("sons of God") having all the wives ("daughters of humans") for themselves, or perhaps it's something to do with the descendants of Cain and Seth. A commentary said that, and it kind of made sense.
- Anyway, it's obscure, so I don't want to get too into it. People brainier than me have reached different conclusions; who am I to say I understand it?
- Also, I've got quite a big chunk to cover on Sunday. Best skip over that bit, and focus on the flood. Much safer ground.

Aside from the irony of the flood story providing solid ground, something very sad has just happened. For fear of being counted among the nutjobs, and without questioning his baseline assumptions, our preacher has dismissed a pretty big theme—a fascinating one at that. It might not have been the *biggest* point of his passage—if he's taking all of chapter 6 as a whole. It may never be the central point of any chapter of the Bible. But without it, he's missing something important that ought to shape other points he makes.

Here's what's important: the appearance of giants is where the heavenly battle between good and evil becomes most tangible and close to home. Bad heavenly beings do something dreadfully evil. God responds in terrifying judgment, destroying all life on earth, and starts again with a single ark-full of animals and a single human family. It's that serious. The serpent of chapter 3 came and tempted the woman. Now in chapter 6, evil spirits come and marry women—and produce freakish, evil offspring. These offspring are human, but somehow more than human. They are notorious, mighty monsters of men. God-like beings (referred to as "sons of God," yet rebels against the True God)[1] have come to live on earth—among men and in men.

The term *demigod* is likely to turn your thoughts to myths of the ancient Greeks—or to Disney's *Moana*,[2] depending on your cultural leanings. Well, that in itself is interesting: that both Polynesians and Greeks have demigods in their folklore. (How far do you have to go back to find their common history?) But what should really make the hairs on the back of your neck stand on end is that this is the Bible: Christian Scripture has the same folklore of divine-human hybrids.

Those strange, distant days of old! And yet one chilling phrase stands out in Gen 6:4. It's like a close-up of an alien spawn at the end of a scary sci-fi episode, showing us the horror is not over after all, that there will be a sequel. It's the phrase, "and also afterward." The tangible, demonic evil on earth carried on after the flood! Demon gods' human offspring walk the earth *after* the flood too. They walk *our* earth, the earth we know. The cosmic battle between Jesus and his angels, on one hand, and the devil and his, on the other, is raging—at least in part—on earth, among men.

Maybe this has revealed something even worse about our imagined preacher than his Bible handling: his starting point has revealed his heart. Just think about his assumption: "There is no such thing as giants." Can you see how he has defined *truth*? He makes an assumption based on his cultural, materialistic worldview and holds to it without a thought. It is unmovable. Had that occurred to him, he would be shocked; but his parameters of *truth* are so defined by his worldview that the very word of God has to give way to them. He has robbed himself of the imagination that Genesis is appealing for him to have. And so he has failed to see—and teach—how close to hand *the battle* is. He has left his people unready to face it.

What a gamble he has taken, by leaning on his assumptions! But what if he is wrong? What if giants are real? Actual giants, in the real world, in people's actual experience? What if the "enlightened" viewpoint is actually blind to reality?

Here's the result—and what I hope this chapter will help the Western church to escape: if we don't engage with the Bible's teaching about giants, we will remain spiritual dwarves. We may be wise and strong in our own eyes, but oblivious to the strength and closeness of our enemy.

Welcome to the Western church of today.

1. For a study of angels, "sons of God," gods, and heavenly beings, see Heiser, *Unseen Realm*.

2. Musker and Clements, *Moana*.

Whatever Happened to Folklore, Anyway?

I live in the UK—the United Kingdom of Great Britain and Northern Ireland. Northern Ireland is connected to the mainland by a geological phenomenon called the Giant's Causeway. (The eighth wonder of the world, according to the visitors' center. Big claim indeed.)

Great Britain itself is made up of the countries of England, Scotland, and Wales. Wales has a dragon on its flag. England's patron saint is St. George, the dragon-slayer. Scotland's national animal is—of all the animals on offer—the unicorn. Maybe everyone just loves myths that much. But giants, dragons, unicorns: there seems to have been a time, in the not-too-distant past, when people took these things seriously.

Actually, even today there is a fair amount of curiosity around mythological creatures—a fascination with the paranormal. Sure, for some people it's a symptom of rejecting the living God and his gospel, seeking spiritual connection in the murky world of unseen powers. But for others, it is a simple awareness, a vague sense, or a suspicion that folklore is not completely made up. Some even have a conviction that the weight of evidence is in favor of there being, or having been no so long ago, the likes of giants and dragons on earth.

About those two things—giants and dragons: I wonder if it has ever struck you that every single culture on earth includes them in its folklore. At least, I have looked at many, and have not yet found one that doesn't. From Indigenous Australia to the Aztec kingdoms, China to the Congo, India to Ireland, from the Babylonians to the Scandinavians—*everyone* seems to have taken these things as realities.

That is quite a staggering thought, is it not, from a Western mindset? *All* ancient cultures have stories of things that do not exist according to the all-knowing West. In fact, to broaden the point, diverse cultures include equivalents of the likes of faeries, nymphs, will-o'-the-wisps, auks, elves, dryads, ogres, and various hybrids. Some are good spirits, some are malevolent, in a fairly consistent way across cultures. Isn't that strange, if they are all just a fiction?

To the typical Western mind, if something can't be seen, it probably isn't real—unless it can be proved by clever math or science. We are taught to be materialists, in the sense that the physical is what is: that's it, and there is nothing more. But the devotee of Western materialism lives a contradiction in that respect: in practice we all operate with realities that can't be seen or proved, such as love or humor. Such things are some of our highest values. And many Westerners have a strong sense that in the race of progress of technology and science, something has been lost along the way. Life has become sadly disenchanted.[3] In response, some dabble in the occult or take hallucinogenic drugs to seek connection beyond the material. (Perhaps they actually find it.) But while it loves to dream of spiritual realities, today's secular world at large denies the plethora of (usually) unseen spiritual beings.

This being the air we breathe, even some Western *Christians* are effectively materialists in their outlook. They make an exception for God, of course, plus the devil (usually), a few angels, and the miracles of Jesus—some of them at least. But beyond that, most things are explained in material terms.

But how can our society be so sure? More than that: why does it insist on dismissing the evidence of other people's accounts? That doesn't seem very scientific.

The Bible does not have too much interest in faeries or unicorns.[4] But giants and dragons do feature. In fact, I hope to show you they are part of a single theme. First, however, I want to invite Western readers to open their minds, by means of a brief world-tour of dragon, and then giant, accounts. Some may seem far-fetched to us. But other people evidently had no doubts at all. With all the caveats that myths can have questionable origins and evolve into the parabolic or ridiculous, it is still quite compelling to read a short compilation of evidence.

Dragons

> The just reward of him that is accustomed to lie, is not, to be believed when he speaketh the truth. . . . Let not our present truth blush for any former falsehood sake: the country is near us, Sussex; the time present, August; the subject, a Serpent; strange, yet now a neighbor to us; and it were more than impudence to forge a lie so near home, that every man might turn in our throats; believe it, or read it not, or read it (doubting) for I believe ere thou hast read this little all, thou wilt not doubt of one, but believe there are many serpents in England.[5]

Thus begins a pamphlet published in 1614 titled *True and Wonderfull: A Discourse relating A Strange and Monstrous Serpent, or Dragon, Lately*

3. For a hefty study on the process of disenchantment and on the atheist cultural mindset, see Taylor, *Secular Age*.

4. Although the King James Version has several unicorn references. Even if the translation has been shown to be wrong in that, it is still interesting that the translators thought it perfectly legitimate and reasonable.

5. A. R., *True and Wonderfull*, 1.

Discovered and yet living to the great Annoyance and divers Slaughters both Men and Cattell, by his strong and violent Poyson. In Sussex, two Miles from Horsam, in a Woode called St. Leonards Forrest, and thirtie Miles from London, this present Month of August, 1614. Pithy, no. But intriguing, yes. The author is known only by initials, though eyewitnesses are named at the end. He goes on to describe the creature's slimy trail, appearance (with "on either side of him . . . two great bunches so big as a large foot-ball, and, as some think, will in time grow to wings"),[6] venom, behavior, and favorite food (rabbits). Believe it or believe it not, says the author—but people saw it.

There are hundreds of accounts of dragon sightings in Britain alone. Most are too vague in terms of dates and details to cite with any authority. They are described variously as having bat-like wings, claws, scales, teeth, and poisonous or fiery breath. Some hoard treasure; some dwell in caves; some are kept at bay by tributes of meat or milk. Some are described as simply great reptiles; others have spiritually sinister qualities. But all are terrifying. No wonder the likes of St. George attained hero status: what a man, to fight and kill such a monster as has eaten the children in the village and the young women at the well.

Oftentimes dragons appear in connection with other great terrors and, perhaps, judgments from God. By the eighth century AD, the English church had long been dabbling in heresy, watering down the gospel of grace by the teaching of Pelagius, an Englishman of a former generation. Pelagius rejected the scriptural teaching that God predestines and elects his children. Instead, human free-will was held paramount, so that the gospel effectively became a message of salvation by being good enough. The church was not in a healthy state, and the nation was dark and floundering. Then, in the year 793, northern England was unsettled by strange and disturbing phenomena. The skies seemed filled with anger and foreboding: "immense whirlwinds, flashes of lightning and fiery dragons" were seen flying in the air, according to Anglo-Saxon writers.[7] A great famine followed. But all these were but the first pangs of birth pains; the worst was yet to come. On June 8 of that year, a horror of unimaginable proportions arrived in the form of Vikings. They came first upon Holy Island, Lindisfarne, on the Northumbrian coast: an attack on the very heart of Christian influence. And they came with their dragon-headed longboats.[8]

6. A. R., *True and Wonderfull*, 5.

7. Story, "Lindisfarne," para. 2.

8. For an excellent analysis of this, and the general subject of dragons in history from a biblical perspective, listen to the podcast episode by Garrett and Sauvé, "On Dragons."

If details of many dragon accounts are blurred with the passing of time, they have still left their mark. Britain has many place names with dragon references, such as Wormbridge, Wormhill—or Wormingford,[9] formerly known as Withmundford until the early thirteenth century when a terrorizing dragon was slaughtered by Sir George Marney.[10] Coats of arms, stained-glass windows, and inscriptions on walls all testify to *something* in history.

In the year 1240, Bishop Jocelyn of Wells is said to have personally killed a dragon in the woods.[11] (And yes, bishops are supposed to be brave warriors for Christ.) The imposing Wells Cathedral was built there shortly afterward, now merely featuring a dragon mosaic and play area. However, a tradition remains that residents of the nearby village of Dinder do something dragon-y every fifty years, lest they forget—the most recent ceremony being in 2001, where they paraded and then burned a giant model dragon.

Similarly, if slightly further afield, the Basilica of Santa Maria e San Donato in Morano, Italy, is partially named after St. Donatus, who slew a dragon that had poisoned the local well. The remains of St. Donatus are buried behind the altar. But his remains are not there alone: four rib bones from the dragon are displayed hanging from wires—each more than three and a half feet long. They can be seen today.[12]

To those who are skeptical about the physical existence of dragons, it is a bit of a mystery as to why creatures that can only be described as dragons appear in cave paintings in places as diverse as France and Utah.[13] Perhaps they could be termed *dinosaurs*; but that simply means "great" or "dreadful lizards," and the word wasn't coined until 1841.[14] Many children go through a phase of fascination with dinosaurs, the great monsters that roamed the earth millions of years ago. But before that theory was invented, such creatures were simply called *dragons*. They were not *discovered* in 1841; they appear in art preserved from long ago.

Dragons are built into the history of vastly varying civilizations: a dragon/dinosaur carving was famously uncovered on a wall of the Angkor Wat temple in Cambodia, having been buried by jungle for five centuries.[15] Why would the artists have depicted what looks like a perfect stegosaurus

9. *Wyrm* is derived from the old Norse word for dragon.

10. AdOYo, "Wormingford Dragon Window."

11. Dunning, introduction to *Jocelin of Wells*, 1.

12. Cusumano, "'Dragon Bones' of Santa Maria."

13. See, for example, Varga, "Dinosaur Rock Art."

14. Osterloff, "Dinosauria," para. 1.

15. Ilbonito, "Dinosaur of Ta Prohm."

before "dinosaurs" were even conceived of, were it not a familiar creature? Why, in China, would the ancient zodiac of years, with the rat, ox, tiger, and so on include the dragon alongside eleven normal animals? In human memory, dragons are a living reality.

In fact, as you explore ancient writings, texts (otherwise) respected for historical reliability, you find dragons appear all over the place. Claudius Aelianus (third century AD) writes:

> When Alexander threw some parts of India into a commotion and took possession of others, he encountered among many other animals a serpent which lived in a cavern and was regarded as sacred by the Indians who paid it great and superstitious reverence. Accordingly Indians went to all lengths imploring Alexander to permit nobody to attack the serpent; and he assented to their wish. Now as the army passed by the cavern and caused a noise, the serpent was aware of it. (It has, you know, the sharpest hearing and the keenest sight of all animals.) And it hissed and snorted so violently that all were terrified and confounded. It was reported to measure 70 cubits although it was not visible in all its length, for it only put its head out. At any rate its eyes are said to have been the size of a large, round Macedonian shield.[16]

Pliny the Elder, in his first-century work *Natural History*, mentions dragons freely. For example:

> It is India that produces the largest [elephants] as well as the dragon, which is perpetually at war with the elephant, and is itself of so enormous a size, as easily to envelope the elephants with its folds, and encircle them in its coils.[17]

> Æthiopia produces dragons, not so large as those of India, but still, twenty cubits in length.[18]

Pliny was not talking about crocodiles, by the way. It's easy to assume, as many do, that something has been lost in translation—or that people in the old days were not that smart, and got muddled up between truth and fiction. But he writes about crocodiles in other sections—various types of them, in fact. Also, he describes dragons swooping down from trees upon elephants (bk. 8, ch. 12). There comes a point where the *crocodile* theory and other attempts to explain away dragons become more far-fetched than

16. Aelianus, *Animals*, bk. 15, para. 21.
17. Pliny, *Natural History*, bk. 8, ch. 11.
18. Pliny, *Natural History*, bk. 8, ch. 13.

some of the wilder dragon accounts themselves. Perhaps the plain reading is the right one.

Another great zoological work appeared in the 1550s, when the Swiss Protestant Conrad Gessner produced his *Historia animalium*, a whopping encyclopedia of every animal. Volume 2 is for the four-legged animals. Alongside familiar mammals like the cow, rat, porcupine, and various species of dogs is the unicorn, with no apology, and with illustrations. In volume 5, on snakes, page 700 starts a *seventeen-page* description of dragons, again with illustrations. Why not!

Mundus subterraneus was another epic work, written by Athanasius Kircher and published in 1678. (It doesn't even feel so long ago any more.) It is largely a geological study, describing the inner workings of volcanoes and the like. But he writes about underworld creatures, such as dragons, as just part and parcel of the world as it exists.

The modern secular world insists that dragons are a fiction. But it was only in the eighteenth century that scientists and historians began to suggest that dragons do not exist. The secular West will now fight tooth and nail for its theories and speculations around ancient dinosaurs and chance evolution over millions of years rather than consider any evidence for the reality of creatures like dragons. If old myths are accused of being mere allegories to promote certain morals or explanations for how the world works and what life is about, they have merely been replaced in the modern West by other myths—teachings about the origins and meaning of life with little grounding on solid fact. Christians ought to recognize this. As for dragons, their reality, on physical earth, should not be seen as just in the abstract. If we can accept that real dragons have appeared in time and space and human history—or even, as some claim, still do[19]—or have appeared at times of particular evil, distress, and judgment, then we can recognize that the spiritual and physical realms are not so separate after all. Great, evil monsters can engage in physical human history.

Giants

The internet age may have reduced the production of printed daily news, but it has made old newspapers so much more easily accessible. Search functions make it easy to browse countless editions and articles from long ago of almost every local, as well as national, newspaper. You may wonder about the worth of spending time reading news of yesteryear—especially if you are not over-bothered by today's current affairs. But it can actually

19. For example, Freeman, *Dragons*.

be quite fascinating—even eye opening. For example, a single copy of the Cardiff times from 1908 contains news of the Belgians annexing the Congo, New York police brutality, the introduction of daylight savings—and this article, tucked away on page 12. To quote in full:

> **PETRIFIED GIANT. RAILWAY COMPANY'S QUEER STORAGE.** "To storage of Irish giant, £200," is an item which appears in the books of the L. and N.W. Railway at the Worship-street goods depot. The story is a peculiar one. Nearly 32 years ago a coffin-like receptable [*sic*] of stone arrived at the Worship-street goods depot, consigned from Manchester. It contained the mortal remains of a petrified Irish giant, weighing close upon three tons, and it took a dozen men and a ten-ton crane to shift it. This gigantic skeleton is 12ft. 2in. in height, has a chest girth of 6½ft., one foot has six toes, and the length of the arm is 4½ft. It was accidentally dug up many years ago in County Antrim by a Mr Dyer, who made a considerable amount of money by exhibiting it in Manchester and Liverpool. A showman named Kershaw afterwards obtained a partnership in the exhibition, but owing to some disagreement the giant was sent to London without his knowledge. While it was still on the railway company's premises Kershaw brought an action in Chancery and obtained an injunction to prevent the company delivering it until the ownership was satisfactorily settled. Nothing further was heard, and the coffin with its grim contents was moved to the Worship-street goods depot, where it still remains, and the company have opened a fictitious account, in which they pay, theoretically, several shillings a week for storage.[20]

Again from Wales, shortly before events that would plunge the world into the Great War, this article appeared:

> **GIANT SKELETONS UNEARTHED.** A skeleton which, it is stated, appeared to be that of a person 10 ft. in height, has been discovered at Dysart, Co. Louth. It was one of three unearthed by two men who were digging the foundations for labourers' cottages. Each skeleton was in a separate grave completely encased with stones. The skull of the giant was in a state of perfect preservation, and measured 18 in. from the crown to the chin, and the leg bones were abnormally large. The remains are supposed to be those of a prehistoric age.[21]

---

20. Duncan and Sons, "Petrified Giant," 12.

21. Morgan, "Giant Skeletons," 2.

Intriguing. The small country of Wales, however, is awash with stories and legends about giants. To clarify, this is not about people with the condition known as *gigantism*, who happen to grow abnormally large due to increased levels of growth hormone. This is about people, or beings, of a different type: the giants of legend and folklore. Claire Barrand, a paranormal researcher and author, has collated a large collection of stories from Wales. They include the account of a "huge burley naked man covered from head to toe in thick red fur"[22] spotted by a shepherd from the village of Nant Gwynant, whose residents had been suffering losses of livestock and food for some time. Eventually, a woman struck the creature with a hatchet as he was squeezing himself through a window into her cottage. Villagers followed the blood trail from his severed hand back to a cave in the woods, behind a waterfall, where they assumed he had died, but didn't dare to venture in.

Such stories of giants appear from all over the world. The old West African kingdom of Benin is famous for its demigod prince Aruan.[23] In Australian Indigenous folklore there is the giant Wadaba, who lurks in the mangroves,[24] and Thardid Jimbo, the cannibal giant.[25] Even the early European settlers in Australia had tales of giant *wildmen*. The first Europeans to discover Patagonia also reported giants. Antonio Pigafetta recorded Magellan's circumnavigation, 1519–1522. He reports, "One day we suddenly saw a naked man of giant stature on the shore of the port, dancing, singing, and throwing dust on his head."[26] In 1615, Dutch explorers Willem Schouten and Jacob Le Maire found graves with human bones of beings that appeared to be ten or eleven feet tall.[27] Similar tales were brought home by Sir Frances Drake (in 1628) and Captain John Byron (1766).[28]

Many Solomon Islanders believe giants are still living on the island of Guadalcanal.[29] We may be used to thinking of our world as small, in these days of modern travel. But its largeness is evident when we consider what it would take to explore such regions to prove the claims one way or another. The forest is dense and inaccessible; the forest-dwelling people can be hostile and resistant to threats of intruders upsetting the giants within. Some islanders claim they are themselves of part-giant descent.

22. Barrand, "Welsh Giants," para. 27.
23. Uyiedos, "Aruan of Udo"; Edoworld, "Arhuanran of Udo Deity."
24. Konishi, "Formidable Giants."
25. Smith, *Aborigine*, 273.
26. Pigafetta, *First Voyage*, 76.
27. Patagonia Cascada, "Truth About Patagonia's Giants," para. 5.
28. Archeology World, "Magellan's Strange Encounter," paras. 8, 10.
29. Barrand, "Welsh Giants," para. 7.

Myths, artwork, carvings, and skeletal and other archaeological remains can be found across the world, including the Japanese horned giants and African, Irish, and Russian six-fingered giants.[30] But some of the most striking examples are from the United States of America.

Diverse Native American tribes have stories of "white-skinned" or "red-haired giants"[31] who lived alongside them many years ago. It was popular at one time for American newspapers to publish the latest giant findings. For example, *The New York Times*, on May 4, 1912, included the headline "STRANGE SKELETONS FOUND.; Indications That Tribe Hitherto Unknown Once Lived in Wisconsin." Scientists were baffled by the discovery of eighteen skeletons of people nine feet tall with enormous heads and unusual facial features. To quote:

> The head slopes straight back and the nasal bones protrude far above the cheekbones. The jawbones are long and pointed, bearing a minute resemblance to the head of the monkey. The teeth in the front of the jaw are regular molars.

Discoveries of giant remains "tend to have a double row of teeth, 6 fingers, 6 toes and like humans [come] in different races. . . . Heads usually found are elongated believed due to longer than normal life span."[32]

Over two hundred giant excavations have taken place in America, but here's a strange thing: none have made the headlines since the 1950s. In fact, a controversy has arisen over whether the Smithsonian Institute has hidden or destroyed thousands of giant remains. My experience with such things is that after wading through the acres of internet articles on the matter, you are simply left believing whichever side of the story you were inclined to believe at first. Either the whole matter of finding giant remains is a hoax, promoted by those who wish to bolster a supernatural point of view, perhaps even a biblical one. Or else the scientific institution has indeed hidden evidence that contradicts its evolutionary-atheistic worldview. For the amateur investigator, it is so hard to say.

Nevertheless, we are left with countless old newspaper reports.[33] We have folklore from an extraordinarily wide range of cultures, and a similarity of accounts from such cultures. It may be that none of this exactly *proves* the existence of giants beyond all reasonable doubt. But perhaps it should

30. Van Dorn, *Giants*, 294–95.
31. Cited on Garrett and Sauvé. " Giants in Myth."
32. Quoted in Archeology World, "18 Giant Skeletons," paras. 6–7.
33. For a good collection see Dahl, "Old Newspaper Articles."

not be surprising, at least to the Bible-reading Christian. After all, "The Nephilim were on the earth in those days—*and also afterward*."

The Bible and Giants

As we turn to the Scriptures, then, we will try to discover why the subject of giants matters to us, as Christians today. We should begin in Genesis chapter 6.

Nephilim

God does not like the Nephilim. Their existence in Gen 6 is mentioned right alongside the wickedness of mankind—wickedness that is so great God will wipe humanity from the earth, save one small family. There is clearly something really ugly going on.

Some language scholars seem to get quite anxious around the word *Nephilim*—which is why it is generally left untranslated in our English Bibles. But the translators of the King James Version of the Bible simply used the word *giants*, in keeping with the Septuagint (Greek) translation that was familiar to Jesus and the apostles, which used the Greek word *gigantes*, the root of our English word. The word *Nephilim* is rare in Hebrew, but (for those who are interested) it was likely borrowed from the Aramaic word *Naphila* (meaning *giant*) "during the final editing of the Hebrew Bible in Babylon (where Aramaic was the lingua franca) and then the ending was corrected to Hebrew rules of word formation."[34]

If we wonder why Gen 6:4 seems so obscure to us, perhaps it is because the details did not need spelling out to the original readers. What was described was something they were familiar with from their own experience, or at least their folklore and other texts.[35] Enoch, in the seventh generation from Adam, wrote much about angelic beings and giants in his apocryphal book 1 Enoch. It may be popular today to dismiss it as strange nonsense—but Peter and Jude are both quite comfortable to quote from it in the New Testament. Likewise, later apocryphal writings spell out what is not so clear in the original text—such as Jubilees 5:1:

> And it came to pass when the children of men began to multiply on the face of the earth and daughters were born unto them,

34. Heiser, "Nephilim," para. 5.

35. A point argued in the excellent episode "Land of Giants" on *The Lord of Spirits* podcast by Fr. Andrew Stephen Damick and Fr. Stephen De Young.

> that the angels of God saw them on a certain year of this jubilee, that they were beautiful to look upon; and they took themselves wives of all whom they chose, and they bare unto them sons and they were giants.[36]

It is the same thing, but slightly more explicit. But objections to the idea of angelic beings producing giant offspring may, for some, be more practical or scientific: *how can angels mate? How can there be crossbred offspring?* In order to think through what it might actually look like, accounts from unearthed Sumerian texts may be a great help. Ritual rites of passage are spelled out in graphic detail, including temple rituals in which a pagan king would invoke his tribal spirit-god to infuse him. Part of the ceremony involved sex with a temple prostitute on a ceremonial bed (like that of Og—see below—examples of which have also been unearthed). If the encounter resulted in pregnancy, the offspring was reported to have had some superhuman properties. Such a person would be referred to as two parts divine (the king being considered divine as well as the god) and one part human.[37] They are similar to the demigods of Greek, Norse, Celtic, or Polynesian mythology with their spiritually mixed parentage. In one sense, they are physically human with two human parents, counting the king as a man. In another, they are spiritual beings, charged with demonic power—but physically they lived on earth.

The Bible's account puts the emphasis on the desire of "the sons of God" rather than the whole thing being initiated by human agents. But still, you can see, with information about these occult rite practices, how this realistically might have come about. And if this sort of ritual was familiar in the world of the first readers of Genesis, it would explain why the writer felt no need to spell out the details. In fact, such practices are said to be common across many pagan cultures, including among Japanese emperors until the twentieth century.[38] So the phrase *and also afterward* in Gen 6 suggests that the practice continued after the flood, in spite of the judgment on it—in much the same way as the whole matter of sin carried on. The giants continued to be conceived—*the heroes of old, men of renown.* In fact, they themselves formed whole terrifying groups and tribes.

36. Charles, *Book of Jubilees*, 43.

37. Damick, *Lord of Spirits*, 185.

38. Damick and De Young, "Land of Giants."

Og

Thus, the story of giants continues through Scripture. Meet Og. He first appears in Num 21, where he starts a fight with the wandering Israelites at Edrei—a bad idea on his part. But only in Deut 3:11 during Moses's replay of the event are we given an aside about his sleeping arrangements:

> (Og king of Bashan was the last of the Rephaites. His bed was decorated with iron and was more than nine cubits long and four cubits wide. It is still in Rabbah of the Ammonites.)

Nine by four cubits is fourteen feet by six (or four meters by 1.8). He was a big boy. And, thanks to God's victory, he (and his sons) were the last in a line of big boys, feared by many. Again, a fact our Bible translators have put in parentheses:

> (The Emites used to live there—a people strong and numerous, and as tall as the Anakites. Like the Anakites, they too were considered Rephaites, but the Moabites called them Emites.) (Deut 2:10–11)

Can you just imagine what the Israelites were up against? Can you picture the people God empowered the Israelites to defeat? After all, the details are given exactly so that we would imagine them, in their colossal power.

Exploring Canaan

But that was not the last of all giant tribes. Trying to picture such peoples might give us at least a little understanding of why the explorers sent into Canaan alongside Joshua and Caleb were so scared and faithless, in Num 13. Not only were there descendants of Anak, but at least a part of the exploration reads a little like an expedition into giant land from a fairy tale. In the valley of Eshcol, the Israelite spies couldn't believe their eyes. In fact, they knew the people back in camp wouldn't believe the stories of what they saw. So they stole a bunch of grapes as material evidence. What was so special about the grapes? The bunch was so massive, *two of them had to carry it between them on a pole*, like a dead gazelle after hunt! We're told they also took some pomegranates and figs. Presumably a wheelbarrow for each one.

I have often tried to imagine that bunch of grapes. And how are we to picture the vineyard it was growing in? I can believe the cities and farm houses of the inhabitants were supersized, but the actual produce seemed to match. What was going on there? Was the land supernaturally affected by the presence of giant landowners? I don't understand that, and the text is pointing out what a *good* thing it is in its impossibly great abundance, a picture of heaven itself in a way. But for the explorers, it must have been a surreal experience.

And so, returning to camp (with sore shoulders and plenty of fruit), they gave their infamous report. While Joshua and Caleb knew the Lord's power to fulfil his promise, the rest were suffering a bit of PTSD, just at the sight of what they'd seen. They said,

> "The people who live there are powerful, and the cities are fortified and very large. We even saw descendants of Anak there. . . . We can't attack those people; they are stronger than we are." And they spread among the Israelites a bad report about the land they had explored. They said, "The land we explored devours those living in it. All the people we saw there are of great size. We saw the Nephilim there (the descendants of Anak come from the Nephilim). We seemed like grasshoppers in our own eyes, and we looked the same to them." (Num 13:28–33)

Were they exaggerating, out of fear? The grapes say otherwise. They had had my experience of high school sport—going on to the pitch against another school team, and staring into the kneecaps of the opposition, wondering what on earth had been put into their school dinners. The explorers were genuinely terrified. They shouldn't have been, knowing the Lord's track record with them and promises for them. But they were terrified simply at the size and strength of the current residents of Canaan. Oh, and not just their size: also their behavior, apparently—it is a land that "devours those living in it." Yikes.

We are not supposed to sympathize with the faithless spies. The Lord is exasperated with them—ready to wipe them out, and in fact condemns the whole generation to wander and die in the wilderness at this point for sharing the spies' fear. Joshua and Caleb say "do not fear." Far from the land devouring its inhabitants, "the people of the land . . . are bread for us" (Num 14:9 ESV), they say. I am only trying to help you imagine the reality of what they saw.

Conquering the Land

As the story unfolds, it is clear that the people of Canaan are not all giants; in fact, giants are pretty rare. All we hear of the Anakim after this is in the book of Joshua, where, without any great drama, the few sons of Anak are killed or driven out by—guess who?—Joshua and Caleb. "There was none of the Anakim left in the land of the people of Israel. Only in Gaza, in Gath, and in Ashdod did some remain" (Josh 11:22).

But it is worth pausing here to mention a couple of big issues—ones that can become real sticking points for Christians if not understood. The first is to do with the law that was given through Moses. The modern reader can easily be confused by the many commands to not mix stuff—fibers in clothing, crops in fields, breeds of animal, certain foods. Why were such things so important for the nation of Israel? Part of the answer must be to illustrate and remind God's people that *they* are set apart, they are not to intermingle with the ways of the inhabitants of Canaan when they settle there. But there is also in it the fundamental reminder that God abhors blurred boundaries. In Creation, God brought order out of chaos. Order makes things distinct, distinguishing one thing clearly from another. What the bad angels did was blur even the division between heaven and earth. Some of the inhabitants of Canaan were the product of these unions—and God's people are to be opposed to that at every level.

The second big issue our understanding of giants helps with is the command for genocide in Canaan. It makes sense once we realize the inhabitants were not just ordinary people. Four hundred years previously, God told Abraham that the land would be given to his descendants only when the iniquity of the Amorites was finally complete (Gen 15:16). Who were the Amorites? The Lord reminds his people many years later:

> Yet I destroyed the Amorites before them,
> though they were tall as the cedars
> and strong as the oaks.
> I destroyed their fruit above
> and their roots below. (Amos 2:9)

It is not that every citizen of Canaan was a giant. But the society was governed by absolute monsters with monstrous behavior: people sacrificed their own children and all sorts. After the flood, when God gave the go-ahead on eating meat, he made the point that it doesn't include people (Gen 9:3–6)! That seems so obvious; why did it need stating? Is that what the descendants of the Nephilim did? Does it describe the society of Canaan? Genocide was the command—as brutal, if not as universal, as the flood—because these beings cannot remain.

David and His Men

Mention of the Philistine cities of Gaza, Gath, and Ashdod reminds us of a more familiar giant story. Perhaps it's so familiar that it fits more easily into the category of myth than Bible; we don't take in what Scripture is actually describing—a *giant*! But before we think about Goliath, let us picture the times by the glimpses we're given in 2 Sam 21 and 1 Chr 20, which include snippets of some of the amazing exploits of David and his brave men.

First, in 1 Chr 20:2, Joab defeated the city of Rabbah, and the crown of the king was placed on David's head. It weighed a talent. To get some perspective, the heaviest crown of the crown jewels of the British royal family is a little over two kilograms. Queen Elizabeth II practiced wearing it around Buckingham Palace to get used to the great weight, so she wouldn't topple over on some formal occasion. But the gold crown of the king of Rabbah weighed a *talent*—that's thirty-four kilograms! Putting it on David must have been a sort of macho challenge. Who *was* the king of Rabbah?!

A few verses on, we meet Sibbekai:

> At that time Sibbekai the Hushathite killed Sippai, one of the descendants of the Rephaites, and the Philistines were subjugated. (1 Chr 20:4)

More stories follow:

> In another battle with the Philistines, Elhanan son of Jair killed Lahmi the brother of Goliath the Gittite, who had a spear with a shaft like a weaver's rod. (1 Chr 20:5)

In still another battle, which took place at Gath, there was a huge man with six fingers on each hand and six toes on each foot—twenty-four in all. He also was descended from Rapha.

> When he taunted Israel, Jonathan son of Shimea, David's brother, killed him. These were descendants of Rapha in Gath, and they fell at the hands of David and his men. (1 Chr 20:7–8)

At a time when David was exhausted,

> Ishbi-Benob, one of the descendants of Rapha, whose bronze spearhead weighed three hundred shekels and who was armed with a new sword, said he would kill David. But Abishai son of Zeruiah came to David's rescue; he struck the Philistine down and killed him. (2 Sam 21:16–17)

Ishbi-benob was descended from giants. But mention of his spearhead at three and a half kilograms, the weight of a small sledgehammer, says he was no midget either.

Now let's meet Goliath himself, in 1 Sam 17. He appears on the front cover of my edition of *The Beginner's Bible*, laughing with the rest of the cast for some sort of cartoon group photo. But he was no laughing matter. At nine foot nine, he overshadowed King Saul, who was himself a head taller than anyone else. I have to wonder whether the description of the champion Goliath's weaponry and armor is a little lost on us today. His bronze mail jacket (weighing fifty-eight kilograms!), bronze this and bronze that—was he someone brought out from a previous age, as some people have suggested—a relic from a past era? The man was so terrifying the whole Israelite army quaked in their little boots.

Picturing him properly is important to the story. He is not just an oversized warrior, like Saul but even bigger—the sort of role that would be played by Brian Blessed in a drama. He is far more than that: a descendent of Anak, one of the Nephilim, the product of an unnatural union, a demonic giant. David, too, must be understood in terms of the whole-Bible narrative. The boy is not just an example of a brave little shepherd-soldier. By 1 Sam 17, he is the secretly anointed king—the messiah.

Here's what happens: God's anointed king destroys the mighty enemy, the great champion of those who oppose God's children. David rescues God's helpless people from an enemy far too strong for them to overcome. The great demonic power is brought down. Does that remind you of anything? When David slaughtered the giant Goliath, it was a shadow of the work of Jesus on the cross.

After Goliath, there was still plenty of mopping up to do by David and his men—just as there is still mopping up to do by Jesus and his church following the decisive victory at the cross. The battle against Satan is won—but not over.

The Great Dragon and the Cosmic Battle of Today

The imagery of Revelation does get a bit confusing in places. Anyone who says otherwise should be politely avoided, because the whole point is that it is straining to express heavenly things in terms that people on earth can understand. So it uses images familiar to us—frogs, lampstands, a harlot: things to provoke an appropriate reaction within us, making us squirm, feel comforted, repulsed, secure, and so on—because these things are the most appropriate earthly pictures of deeper realities. Satan is pictured as a dragon—because we all know what a dragon is like and how we should feel about one.

> The great dragon was hurled down—that ancient serpent called the devil, or Satan, who leads the whole world astray. He was hurled to the earth, and his angels with him. (Rev 12:9)

Yes, the dragon is one and the same as the serpent of Gen 3. And what is he doing now? He is at war against the forces of good:

> Then war broke out in heaven. Michael and his angels fought against the dragon, and the dragon and his angels fought back. (Rev 12:7)

So war is raging in the heavens. But John's Revelation was given to the churches so they could understand their experience on earth. You see, they—we—are in the battle:

> Then the dragon was enraged at the woman and went off to wage war against the rest of her offspring—those who keep God's commands and hold fast their testimony about Jesus. (Rev 12:17)

The woman's child (Jesus) is snatched up to heaven (ascended), and *the rest of her offspring* (faithful Christians on earth) come under horrific attack from the dragon who was cast down to earth. Chapter 13 describes the horrible powers of two beasts, agents and manifestations of the dragon on earth, which I understand to represent great evil regimes and ideologies.

The good news of Revelation, of course, is that *God wins*! That is what the church must hold on to, because for century after painful century, that is not how it feels on earth. There are times in history when Satan inflicts appalling injuries even to God's people.

When you recognize that the great dragon is behind such things on earth, you will not be surprised when monstrous powers manifest themselves—even if they were to appear literally as monsters. For the ugly creatures described in Revelation are not in a remote realm. They are integral to human life on earth.

The Ordinary Church in Ephesus

Are you beginning to wonder what all this has to do with giants? I believe the New Testament Letter to the Ephesians shows how the ordinary church of today relates to such things.

A little context, from Acts 19: the city of Ephesus, on the coast of modern-day Turkey, was a hot-spot of the occult. Much of the identity and culture of its citizens revolved around the temple to the goddess Artemis, some of which can still be seen today. Through the preaching of the gospel by the apostle Paul, the church was born. It caused uproar in the city, because the whole economy around the Artemis tourist industry was threatened—as was witchcraft itself. It is no coincidence that in Ephesus, of all places, "God was doing extraordinary miracles by the hands of Paul, so that even handkerchiefs or aprons that had touched his skin were carried away to the sick, and their diseases left them and the evil spirits came out of them" (Acts 19:11–12). There were Jewish exorcists, who got a hiding from evil spirits when they tried to use the name of Jesus, ending up being chased down the street naked and bleeding! And when people who learned to fear the name of Jesus then publicly burned their spell books, someone there calculated that the value of the burning mass was truly a small fortune. Giants don't feature; but it was a place where the spiritual realm was stark, and the spiritual battle felt keenly. It was an exciting place, to put it positively; but being a Christian there was not for the faint-hearted.

Paul's letter to the church, some time later, reflects the vibe of the place. The first half, chapters 1–3, is loaded with cosmic spiritual language: "spiritual blessing," "heavenly realms," "rule and authority and power and dominion," and so on. "Power" is a common word, and the Christians are reminded of how much they've got of it!

The second half, chapters 4–6, then tell the church what to do with this great power they have, and all the other mind-boggling blessings they have in Christ. And to the observant reader, it's a shock. Because in the context, you might have thought they would be charged to do more "extraordinary miracles," even take down Artemis and the powers that oppose and oppress them. Yes, it is all about how to live in the mighty power of Jesus. But what that looks like is so down-to-earth it feels almost bland: work at marriage, tell the truth, stop stealing, and so on.

This is so important to our discussion, because on one hand, it recognizes the tangible work of the devil, right here in our faces, in our community, lives, and surroundings. Satanic work on earth—as with the grotesque form of giants—is not something that belongs to another planet, an imaginary world. Demonic opposition is real, and it's here. On the other hand, we don't have to go weird about it, as if we're tapping into another dimension. The way we do battle is by everyday choices, by godly actions, by the way we behave in our private lives.

Ephesians 6:12 is a well-known and well-loved verse by many. But it's one we get subtly wrong, and therefore almost miss the whole thrust of it:

> For our struggle is not against flesh and blood, but against the rulers, against the authorities, against the powers of this dark world and against the spiritual forces of evil in the heavenly realms.

If we are skeptical about giants existing, perhaps it is because we are skeptical about the idea of the spiritual world manifesting itself in physical terms. The Christian with a Western-world mindset might believe in the spiritual realm, but imagine it somewhere "out there," in a separate dimension. Therefore, Eph 6:12 becomes a command to not get too involved with presenting issues. Politics, current affairs, difficult or threatening people: don't waste your efforts on those things. After all, our battle is not against flesh and blood. Just preach the gospel, we're told. But that's utterly missing the point. And the result is to take a verse about our wrestling, our fighting, against great forces of evil, and turn it into something so vague it ends up meaning nothing. If the "spiritual forces of evil in the heavenly realms" are a whole separate realm, what does fighting them even amount to, apart from perhaps a little more prayer? But if, in fact, those "cosmic powers" are manifest in evil people, political moves, societal changes, temptations, "accidents," sicknesses, and frustrations—then we understand the verse to mean that behind the "flesh and blood" manifestations we should recognize spiritual forces at work.

With this understanding, the "armor of God" verses that follow make far more sense. The fight is real and tangible as we strive for righteousness, battle for truth, and so on. It is written to make us into soldiers—not pacifists. We are to join the fight against evil—and recognize just how deep the evil goes.

Joining in the Fight

In the West, giants belong only in fairy tales. If your worldview doesn't accept giants, dragons, or associated things, you won't ever rise up to slay them, or even think well of those who do.

I appreciate that there are burning, unanswered questions here: *Why do we not see giants today, if they are truly a reality?* And, *How can you talk about slaying them if they don't exist any more?*

The truth is, I don't know why we don't see them today. Nor can I personally speak to the claim of the Solomon Islanders and their like, mentioned above, that giants still exist in pockets of the world, here and there. But the Bible's testimony is clear and powerful. The way that David and his mighty men slew the last of them—or virtually, seemingly, the last—tells us that giants are a live issue for us today. Why? Because David and his men deliberately serve in Scripture as a picture of Jesus and his faithful followers.

David is the Christ-figure, the original messiah and prototype of Jesus. As he and his men exterminated those great enemies, it was an impossible-looking achievement. So today, Jesus and his brave followers fight against evil, and ultimately see the God of peace "crush Satan under their feet" (Rom 16:20). If there are not literal giants, then there are other manifestations of demonic presence on the earth. And that is not just limited to the demon possession of unfortunate individuals. If giants of old were hybrids of human and demon-god unions that led peoples and nations in untold evil and opposition to the Lord, the suggestion is that there are some sort of equivalents at large in the age of the church. Great, murderous forces and figureheads opposed to the truth of Christ have sometimes been labelled with the New Testament term *antichrist*. Perhaps that is the fitting description for demon-infused opponents of our King.

It is also worth returning to the point that the world is big, and there are many things beyond our knowledge. The modern West might assume the world is small, that we have explored it and understood it now. We have the world mapped out, and any speck can be viewed on Google Earth—there's nothing more to see, we may suppose. So let's explore space! But that viewpoint is all wrong. The world is large. There is much we do not know. We don't know what monsters lurk in the deep oceans, or what creatures exist in the forests or caves of the many "God-forsaken" regions of our globe. You can see a blur from aerial photos—but there are vast places that remain unknown. There are laws of physics we don't understand or haven't discovered (or have been discovered and are now forgotten). And the modern Western *church* thoughtlessly accepts the arrogant assumptions of the culture.

Meanwhile, the New Testament is telling us there is more going on than we can imagine. There are angels fighting it out in the heavens, there are great forces influencing life in heaven and earth. Actual giants on earth today or not, the principle remains: we need to recognize the nature of our enemy. That is uncomfortable to Western sensitivities, but let's name some of the big examples of our day. Islam is not about people innocently believing something wrong: it's a mighty move of Satan to cause misery, death, and damnation to great swathes of humanity. Politicians are not just well-meaning buffoons making some bad decisions: bad policies are of spiritual significance, works of the Dragon resulting in horrific muddle, suffering, and death of the innocent. The Hollywood industry is every bit as sordid as the revelations of recent years. Can you see some of the battle fronts? Can you see how it changes our outlook? Instead of making a rule about not watching "18" rated movies, when you see the work of the entire industry for what it is, it makes the fight for righteousness a little more engaging.

To illustrate further, in the last few years I have come across two people who have had experience in two well-known secret societies—ones that appear clean on the outside. But the inner workings involve horrors you might struggle to believe: ritual sexual abuse of sedated children, the drinking of human blood (cannibalism), trafficking of children on a global scale—things we would rather not think about. But perhaps that is the point: to some in the relatively peaceful West, the world looks largely harmless. But what satanic monsters lurk behind the façade—perhaps literally?

There is much discussion in recent years around the hidden powers behind governments and industries and the elites of this world. It is easy to become sucked into endless and obsessive speculation, and for that reason many, understandably, prefer to avoid ever engaging with the subject. But in just my own country, it is common knowledge that there are vast networks of tunnels beneath the Parliament buildings, Liverpool city center, Blackpool Winter Gardens (where political conferences have been held), and other such places—and no one quite knows why. It chills the bones to even wonder whether an Epstein Island–type existence is darker and deeper than any of us suspected; and who would want to dwell on such things? But what we do know is that whatever evil we recognize, the reality is far deeper, far worse—and far closer—than we dared to imagine.

I found it a shock to discover, from time to time, what schoolmates from high school were really up to: things I didn't want to believe or know about, things that chilled the blood. That same reality is the case in relation to the cosmic powers around us. Ephesians 6:12 is not inviting us to explore the depths of what is happening; but it is telling us to not be naïve. The likes of giants and dragons lurk around us; true horrors are never far away from us. Who knows under what circumstances they might reappear in those age-old forms? But even if they don't, such spiritual monsters are at large. The Son of David and his small band of mighty men are not living in the false comfort of denial: they are fighting them today.

People who talk about giants might sound to you like spiritual eccentrics, the sort of people who bring a bad name to the church, who make life difficult for the rest of us by stirring up trouble when we were enjoying peace. But by the very act of reducing monsters to fairy tales, we place ourselves within the story as the villagers who turn a blind eye, who accept the status quo of girls being snatched at the well, because angering the giant or dragon is a risk too great to take.

The Western Christian believes in the spiritual realm in theory, but he is a functional materialist. As such, the spiritual battle can be fought without getting his hands dirty. Real courage against the devil and his allies is not necessary; engaging with demons is for some people in other cultures. For the Westerner, success in the Christian life and the growth of the church comes without the risk of pain, suffering, or the spilling of blood.

But everybody else seems to know that's not how battle works. It's not how victory is achieved. It's not how you withstand an enemy.

It is easy to read about giants in the Bible in the same way children hear accounts of war. Children can even play games about war harmlessly enough. But we are not playing a game; we are in the church of God and we are in a real war. Some of our churches need to wake up.

Typical Anglican baptism vows include questions and answers such as these:

> *Question*: Do you renounce the devil and all the spiritual forces of wickedness that rebel against God?
> *Answer*: I renounce them.
> *Question*: Do you renounce the empty promises and deadly deceits of this world that corrupt and destroy the creatures of God?
> *Answer*: I renounce them.[39]

Would this be a good time for you to review your baptism vows? To think about what they really mean? Would it be good to consider how tangibly demons affected life on earth, from those hazy days of Gen 6 onward? Ought you to take a moment, now, to think about what it means to define the spiritual battle as the normal Christian life?

If it all feels rather scary, the good news of Rev 12 is that Michael and his angels win. Perhaps it is time for the Western church to do better than just name schools or churches after St. Michael.[40] Perhaps it's time to become dragon-slayers with him. How? It's quite simple, really: you start by recognizing the enemy, the reality of giants and dragons, of monstrous workings of our monstrous enemy. You then take courage to stand your ground, to speak up against him. (That will require all the armor of God—prayer and the rest of it.) Then you accept whatever suffering results, with joy alongside the pain. Finally you celebrate the victory with the words of he who is seated on the throne of heaven:

> Those who are victorious will inherit all this, and I will be their God and they will be my children. (Rev 21:7)

39. Anglican Church, *Book of Common Prayer*, 164.
40. Cary, "St. Michael."

He who would valiant be
'gainst all disaster,
let him in constancy
follow the Master.
There's no discouragement
shall make him once relent
his first avowed intent
to be a pilgrim.

Who so beset him round
with dismal stories
do but themselves confound
his strength the more is.
No foes shall stay his might;
though he with giants fight,
he will make good his right
to be a pilgrim.

Since, Lord, thou dost defend
us with thy Spirit,
We know we at the end,
shall life inherit.
Then fancies flee away!
I'll fear not what men say,
I'll labor night and day
to be a pilgrim.[41]

41. Bunyan, "He Who Would Valiant Be."

3

Poverty Is Privilege

Bonhoeffer knew that something of this unwillingness to speak out with boldness had to do with money. The state provided financial security for the pastors of Germany, and even pastors in the Confessing Church would jeopardize their incomes only to a certain point.

Eric Metaxas, *Bonhoeffer*

Blessed are you who are poor, for yours in the kingdom of God.

Luke 6:20

In Matt 5:2, Jesus starts his famous Sermon on the Mount:

> And he opened his mouth and taught them, saying:
> "Blessed are the poor in spirit, for theirs is the kingdom of heaven." (Matt 5:2–3 ESV)

His opening words are the fundamental first step of the gospel: the kingdom of heaven belongs to those who are *poor in spirit*—humble, morally bankrupt before God, those who recognize they have no right to God's kingdom. They may feel broken, but they are *blessed*. Because the heavenly kingdom, the great unseen, ultimate reality of everlasting goodness, is for people who come empty handed, in need of a Savior. It is the subject of many a cracking hymn, part of any good evangelistic sermon, and the greatest news for those who "get it."

That's why Matt 5 is such an easy out when we come to Luke 6.

From verse 20, Luke 6 appears to be very similar to Jesus's Sermon on the Mount in Matt 5–7. Some people assume that it is simply Luke's record of the same event. Others are convinced that it is a whole separate episode, using some of the same teaching. I think it doesn't matter. Sure, you can argue it either way. But the point of Bible study isn't to produce interesting arguments about who said what, when. It's to hear the voice of the Lord through the various authors. Even if Luke 6 is a second account of what Matthew wrote, Luke starts by conspicuously—and, if we take the Bible seriously, deliberately—missing the words *in spirit*. "Blessed are you who are *poor*," he says.

It is not ok to assume Luke was being less clear or made a mistake. He didn't just forget to add the words *in spirit*, expecting his readers to figure that's what he meant, and kicking himself when he discovered Matthew's much clearer version. No, he's drawing out a point in Jesus's teaching, and is not expecting us to need Matthew to interpret it.

In Luke, Jesus is talking about physical poverty: "Blessed are you who are poor"; "Blessed are you who are hungry now" (Luke 6:21). He confirms the point with the opposites:

> But woe to you who are rich, for you have already received your comfort.
> Woe to you who are well fed now, for you will go hungry.
> Woe to you who laugh now, for you will mourn and weep. (Luke 6:24–25)

Luke 6 is not just Matt 5 in shorthand. He is saying something far more uncomfortable to Western Christians like me. It can be so uncomfortable, in fact, that it is very easy to skim over it, assuming it can't mean what it says—or even rushing straight past it as quickly as possible hoping the Bible has something else to say to us on this particular day. Can Jesus really be saying that the poor receive the kingdom of God and the rich don't? There's got to be another explanation!

It is, in effect, a bit of the Bible we don't believe.

Why Do We Find It So Hard?

I think there are three main reasons that Jesus's words in Luke 6:20 are uncomfortable.

We Dread the Implications

We dread the thought of what those words might mean for us. We wonder whether taking Jesus seriously here would mean we have to give up our wealth.

Let's have the courage to sit with that for a moment, to think through why we find it so unpleasant, or unbearable. Why do we fear it so much? Because there are probably some good reasons to fear it. For example, perhaps our wealth is something that others have worked very hard for—parents or grandparents maybe. It would be insulting, to say the least, to despise the gift they have given us. Or perhaps we would be letting others down by giving our wealth away—failing to give our children or others the help we should responsibly give them.

Perhaps giving up our wealth would simply be too much of a shock to the system—such a radical change to our lives would be asking something more than our faith would allow, too big a thought to possibly follow through on.

You may occasionally see videos of people flinging themselves off high cliffs into deep pools below. How do you react to that sort of thing? For some, given the opportunity to try it, the thrill would be too much to resist. ("Wow, falling through the air, hoping there are no sharp rocks under the surface! Woo hoo!") Most people would find it a silly idea, even if all the cool kids *are* doing it. Sooner or later you're going to land on someone else. Or belly flop. And Jesus's statement about the blessing of being poor may feel like that—an extreme sport, an adrenaline rush: "Sure, some people are so brave, they give it all up in a moment, and do seem to have a great time of it. But I don't think I could. I'm not that sort of person. It feels a bit too extreme for me."

But while we are thinking about the possible meaning of Jesus's words for us, and our fear that it might mean becoming poor—let's just play though the possibility in our minds, and ask a question that I find helpful in all sorts of situations: *What's the worst that could happen?* Suppose you gave all your wealth up—or lost it for reasons beyond your control—as a Christian: is it really the worst thing imaginable? Sure, life would be hard. You probably can't imagine how hard. But would God not provide, somehow? Would we not get through somehow, with his help? You know that in reality, even if the effects of poverty killed us, God still has us safe in his hands. So the fear of what Jesus's words might cost us should not make us dread them—even if it did mean something so extreme. But that is the first big reason for our discomfort.

We've Heard These Words Taught Badly

There is certain teaching around some fringe parts of the church about giving up all wealth, apparently based on Jesus's words in Luke 6, that is just wrong. We don't want to join some commune or cult where we give up everything we own because some charismatic, all-powerful leader persuaded us. We're not that stupid.

Even the less extreme outworkings don't seem quite right. Occasionally you might hear of a young couple, known by a friend of a friend, who gave away all their inheritance and belongings, and live on bare floorboards, cook over a candle, and feed off dandelions and vermin—all because they're taking Jesus more seriously than the rest of us. But isn't that just avoiding responsibility and calling it godliness? Or am I too cynical? My wife and I used to know a couple who refused to own a car on the principle of shunning wealth. They were always scrounging lifts off everyone else, with the sad, wide eyes of their multiple small children letting you know how much they would miss out on the fun that everyone else was having if you didn't oblige.

When earnest Westerners become wannabe Mother Theresas it feels a little like Marie Antoinette playing at shepherdess in her cottage at Versailles. A Christian student group might gain something by spending a night, or a week, sleeping rough with the homeless, as some occasionally do. But it is always going to be a thoroughly different thing when there is the option to go home at the end. I also wonder if that sort of thing is pretty insulting to homeless people too—"Do you mind if we join in with your homelessness?" It's playing at poverty, not embracing it. It somehow feels like *pretending* to obey Jesus, or feeling noble by going beyond the obedience of others.

Is it even possible to voluntarily become poor? If you choose it, there's always some sort of safety net (friends, family, skills, qualifications) to fall back on if necessary. But genuinely being poor is to lack any such luxury as that. From Luke 6, at least, it doesn't seem right to conclude that poverty and hunger are things you *can* choose, let alone ought to choose. It doesn't seem quite workable.

Jesus's Statement Seems to Challenge Common Sense

More than that—the words *Blessed are you who are poor* seem to plainly contradict other parts of Scripture—for example Prov 10:15: "A rich man's wealth is a strong city; the poverty of the poor is their ruin." That's the world we experience and understand. Our framework of biblical thinking is not just enlarged by Luke 6:20—it feels shattered. And it is not ok to simply say that the New Testament outweighs the Old. The relationship between the two is not so simplistic; besides, both have far more to say on the subject than the two isolated texts, Luke 6:20 and Prov 10:15. The point is that we know, and the Bible confirms, that wealth, even with all its dangers, is a good thing.

One reason for the prosperity of the West is our inherited *Protestant work ethic*—a fair wage for a fair day's work. A man puts in his work, earns his keep, and provides for his family. He has the dignity of not living off the charity of others, and of being in a position to help others in need. It's the beauty of the Christian way of life, and it's a way of life that has been so dreadfully undermined in the sort of community in which my church ministers, where handouts have become the accepted way of life. It is good that people in need are cared for—but being in such a position should not be an aspiration.

Actually, it is only with this common-sense viewpoint that Jesus's words have any impact at all. If common sense told us that having nothing is nice, Jesus's words become nothing more than a bland political statement. Poverty is horrendous, and Jesus knew it! His words are meant to shock, to turn our common sense on its head and make us see it all from a very different point of view.

It is exactly at this point that Jesus's words should become exciting to us. If, as a Christian, you are reading the Bible devotionally, quite often what you read confirms what you know. That's good. Sometimes it makes you think a bit harder; it puts things in a way that surprises you. But on reflection, you discover you're reading familiar truth from a fresh angle. That's good and healthy too. But when Scripture seems to completely grate with your framework of thinking, that should be a great day in your devotional life! It's a day for cracking open the party poppers, and announcing to the world what you've found. If your style of church allows, you could be that person who stands up on Sunday morning to share the great insight from your week for once, instead of leaving it to the same one or two who always do it. The reason it is so good is that God is changing your framework of thinking. He's enlarging your grasp of his ways, and correcting your life to be more in line with his.

So don't skip over Luke 6:20. Don't explain it away. Let's chew it over properly, and enjoy the thrill of God changing our minds in some way.

The (Now) Confusing Word *Privilege*

We need to know in what sense the poor are *blessed*—privileged. And what *privilege* even is.

In ancient civilizations, in Bible days, through the medieval era and the last few centuries—in fact all through history up until about the late twentieth century, *privilege* was a straightforward concept. Some people had more, and for them it was good. Where social mobility allowed, that was something to aspire to. Where privilege included any sense of humility or obligation, the blessed one became a blessing to all. All through its own history, the church understood that those who were somehow privileged helped those who were not; the relatively rich helped the poor.

That has been our cultural understanding for a long time. There is a grand Tudor house near where I live, now open to the public. Apparently Shakespeare stayed there while he wrote one of his plays. Back in the day, the ornate great hall would not only serve as the dining and meeting room, but as sleeping quarters for all the workers, on the stone floor around the huge fireplace. The balcony at one end was where the lord of the manor and his family would sleep—apart from the common people, but able to look down on them. That way, he could check they weren't stealing the silverware; but also he could have his protective, watching eye over them. His privileged position carried responsibility.

The waters have now become a little muddied as far as definitions go. The word *privilege* carries quite a negative vibe in much of the modern West. If you happen to have more, in terms of wealth, education, stability, or opportunity, than others because of your ancestry, ethnicity, location, or even the good choices of your parents, you are supposed to feel a little ashamed of it. Privilege is bad. Lack of privilege is noble. It is a socially complex issue, of course; but that is the general feeling the word now carries.

The culture Jesus lived in understood what it was to be *blessed* in a more straightforward way than many of us today. We need to be careful not to read our own very strange and unusual culture of guilt into Jesus's statement. So let's not read it through the lens of our perspective, but let's clear up some of the things Jesus did *not* mean by *Blessed are you who are poor*:

Jesus Was Not Being Sentimental

He was not saying that there is something nice or refreshing about being poor.

There was a visiting missionary to a church I belonged to many years ago. She showed pictures of the poor children she worked with, as missionaries sometimes do. After her presentation there was a chance to ask questions. One lady piped up with the question—or statement—that makes the rest of the church cringe on such occasions: "They're poor, but happy . . . aren't they!"

She'd seen their bright little smiling faces on the slideshow. And she'd reached a conclusion: *How nice for them to be free from all the trappings of our stressful existence! What a blessing to live the life of simple poverty!* Perhaps there is something of a point lurking somewhere in her statement: perhaps there is a certain freedom in the uncluttered simplicity of life in a poor country. But it's also a conclusion with some disturbing—and convenient—implications. First, it means we don't really need to do anything for them. They're the lucky ones. Perhaps toss some spare change in the collection basket at the end toward a new pair of shoes for one of them. But really, they're doing all right.

Second, and more seriously, such a viewpoint is turning Jesus's words into sentimental mush, like a fundraising celebrity jetted into a poor village with a camera crew. Can't you see Jesus's eyebrows raised earnestly in the middle as he looks at the group of half-naked paupers in front on him? In the sentimental televised adaptation, Jesus would say, "Blessed are you who are poor! So free from the frantic strivings of the modern world, the futile existence of the materialistic fast-lane, the hamster-wheel of worldly success! This—*this* (hands outstretched) is where the kingdom of God is found, not in the monstrous skyscrapers of the wealthy. No, cursed are they! The rich are the ones who have ruined the world! But you poor ones—you are the good people who enjoy the true blessings of life." But that is not Jesus's tone nor his teaching.

Jesus Was Not Being Naïve

The lady's question to the missionary showed she had no concept of what being poor is like. So often we compare ourselves to people with bigger houses and assume we are living humbly. But if you can afford to replace your broken TV—or toaster—you are stinking rich on a global scale.

There is nothing nice about being poor. Jesus knew that. Being poor means having one meal a day, if that—and usually a meal of just plain rice, potatoes, or maize flour. It means disease and infection, because you have no access to clean water or basic hygiene products, or physical resilience. It means watching your child or sibling die because you can't afford hospital fees, and have no means to get there anyway. It means having no security, no one to protect you, no money for emergencies.

My wife's great-grandfather set out by foot from Cornwall to Lancashire when his wife died, because he heard there was work to be had in the Victorian cotton mills of the north. He left his children in the workhouse while he travelled to find slave-labor employment to support them.

My wife's father keeps his living-room boiling hot, because he knows what it's like to be cold, having spent his childhood sleeping in the freezing attic under bare roof slates through Yorkshire winters.

My own grandfather was one of eighteen siblings growing up in a Victorian terraced slum in the East End of London. (My grandmother was the nineteenth kid in her family.) My father considered himself well off in his three-story East End terrace, shared with two other families. He and his three teenage brothers shared one bed, two at each end. After World War II, the family were wandering the streets of West London hoping to stumble upon a house to live in, along with other refugees. My mother was a wartime baby. Their family house was bombed in an air raid. By daylight, anything of value had been looted by neighbors. (Oh, that wartime spirit, where we all looked out for one another . . .) They were left with nothing.

Barry, from our own church in Leyland, grew up in Birmingham. He would get an orange for Christmas—but only some years, as he remembered. As a teenager, he escaped from the "lunatic asylum" he was in, bribing police with cigarettes, and walked north a hundred miles to Preston in his pajamas in the snow to find his brother who had a house. A few years ago, a very old-looking man in his sixties, he received his government winter heating allowance of £200. He promptly bought £200-worth of cigarettes, smoked the lot, and died.

This is Great Britain in the recent past! We don't have to go far to find poverty. There is no excuse to be naïve about what poverty is like, or to read that into Jesus's words. He knew what it was like to be born homeless, and to be a refugee in a foreign country. He was not saying poverty is nice in any way.

Jesus Was Not Being Communist

Neither is Jesus advocating any form of communism, pseudo-communism, or the anti-capitalist "race to the bottom" that is becoming fashionable in some sections of the modern West. John the Baptist said, in Luke 3:11, "Anyone who has two shirts should share with the one who has none, and anyone who has food should do the same." He didn't say, *Whoever has four should give one to the person with two, so they both have three.* John, Jesus, and Luke are not campaigning against material success, nor are they advocating the supposed and oft-quoted teaching of the World Economic Forum: "You will own nothing and be happy."[1] Jesus's statement in Luke 6 is not a political statement, and is not designed to manipulate the masses. But Christians caught up in the mindset of seeking to level all wealth can find justification in Luke 6:20—*Rich is bad. Poor is good.* But that is not Jesus's teaching; his blessings and woes are not because the states of poverty and wealth are themselves moral standards.

Jesus's teaching is not sentimental, naïve, nor communist. But neither is it a mistake. It sums up a big theme in the rest of Luke (and his sequel, Acts, and the wider Bible). While knowing that wealth is truly a gift from God and cause for thanksgiving, it is so important to see that it comes with some very real problems—problems from which the poor are spared. The gift of wealth can cost you your life, your salvation. Woe to you who have it! Blessed are you who do not—and, lacking the corrupting, deceitful hold of wealth, flock to Jesus and receive his words of life.

The Problems with Wealth

It is time to explore the good news of what Jesus is teaching. I should point out that with an issue as sensitive and blinding as money, it will only be of any worth if you explore it with me prayerfully and humbly. If we are to receive Jesus's true blessings, let's not look for excuse and caveat, like so many of the people do in Luke's record, and like so many of his recorded parables warn against. By listening to and trusting Jesus, we'll find we have more than we ever knew.

Are you ready? Here are some of the major problems with wealth that Luke exposes.

Wealth Is Tarnished

The majority of the time, wealth is gained and maintained on a morally dubious basis. Most money is dirty money, to a greater or lesser degree. If we see it as that, it helps us see its true worth.

The parable of the dishonest manager in Luke 16:1–15 is so matter-of-fact on this point. As the story goes, the man has been caught in his long-term financial irregularities. He's called to the boss's office, and he knows

1. See, for example, Wikipedia, "You'll Own Nothing."

that when he gets there, the game's up. Too late to make amends. So he acts quickly and uses his final moments to prepare for the next step of his career—redundancy, later that day. What does he do? He phones round the company debtors and makes bargain repayment deals. He rips off the boss with his final act in employment, so that he'll have friends to give him a sofa to sleep on in his sudden early retirement.

The shock of the story, to those expecting a moral lesson, is that when the boss finds out, he gives a wry smile and tilt of the head to the man and says, "I've got to hand it to you for your shrewdness." Jesus agrees:

> I tell you, use worldly wealth to gain friends for yourselves, so that when it is gone, you will be welcomed into eternal dwellings. (Luke 16:9)

Tut tut. The man was crooked. But this is not a parable for Jesus to teach us to be good boys and girls and to always do the right thing. Jesus is making a point about priorities. In the process, he says: see money for what it is (namely, unrighteous) and use it for what it's for (preparing for the hereafter). He's not teaching us to get knotted up in the ethics of trade and business. Quite easily, we can get so concerned about misusing money it's as if we are worried about offending money itself. As it is, "The sons of this world are more shrewd in dealing with their own generation than the sons of light," says Jesus (v. 8). Money is just a tool. The problem for Christians, living by our noble Protestant work ethic, is that we can be so careful with it we end up serving it.

Money is nearly always a dirty business. You can't completely avoid that; you can't buy everything completely ethically; you can't escape the corruption that all society is built on. But you can avoid falling in love with money, and see it for the corrupt thing it is.

I know an older man who has made it from rags to riches through hard work and business. I once gave him a copy of Eddie Stobart's autobiography.[2] There were so many similarities with Eddie's life and his own, I thought he would really engage with it and hear the testimony of Eddie's faith in Christ in the process. Some time later, I found he had got a couple of pages in and given it up. "It doesn't ring true," he said. I didn't understand—Eddie's story is true. "No," he said; "No one makes it that big by playing by the rules."

I don't doubt Eddie Stobart's integrity. (And all credit to the many Christian businessmen who have generated wealth honestly.) But what an interesting statement, still: by and large, the rich don't get rich by being

2. Stobart et al., *Only the Best*. Eddie Stobart became one of the biggest road haulage companies in the UK, and Eddie himself was well known to be a Christian, funding various ministries through his business.

completely honest. Others are mistreated along the way. For you to grab and keep and hoard, others have suffered. So don't serve money. Don't see it as ultimate, the thing to lose sleep over, or to dream about. Rather, *despise* it. Use it for God's kingdom. It's not everything—in fact, wealth is tarnished.

Wealth Terminates

Here's another problem with wealth that brings woe to those who have it and makes poverty a privilege: it's temporary. It has a use-by date. It terminates.

> Sell your possessions and give to the poor. Provide purses for yourselves that will not wear out, a treasure in heaven that will never fail, where no thief comes near and no moth destroys. For where your treasure is, there your heart will be also. (Luke 12:33–34)

These words of Jesus come in the context of comfort to the disciples. God feeds the wild birds; God clothes the wild flowers with incredible beauty. Why should we, God's beloved children, worry about provision, since we are worth tons more to God than birds and flowers?

Jesus might have stopped at verse 31: "But seek his kingdom, and these things will be given to you as well." But that could be misunderstood. I have heard a very wealthy Christian say, "You can have the best of both worlds!" That doesn't seem quite Jesus's tone, even if he had stopped at verse 31. But he doesn't stop there; he spells out the implications, because it's a fact that wealth terminates—thieves steal, vermin destroy.

The true wealth that God gives is so much better than what money can buy. So act on it! Teach yourself to do it by getting rid of money and possessions. The more money and possessions you have, the more your heart is drawn to them. Why would you allow that to happen, when worldly possessions don't last?

Jesus's point here is not to help the poor—it's to help *you*. To cull your possessions is to teach yourself a vital lesson about the value of material things compared to the true, lasting wealth of his kingdom. Things we own are often useful. But you need to find a way to teach yourself what matters. I heard the Australian preacher David Cook urging this sort of self-discipline. He said he made it his habit to teach his wallet who's boss by, every so often, *halving* his bank account. That seems to be the kind of thing Jesus is talking about. It's a simple truth, but we need to slap ourselves in the face fairly often to remember it: wealth gives the illusion of security. But it isn't secure. It can be lost in an instant.

There is another side to this too. What has come immediately before all this, in Luke 12, is Jesus's parable of the rich fool. Jesus tells his story about a farmer who has bumper crops and therefore the lovely problem that he hasn't got enough storage facilities. He builds bigger barns, thinks he's got his future all smoothed out, dies that very night, and gets told by God he's a fool. Why? Because not only can wealth be snatched from you; *you* can be snatched away from *it*. And your wealth is worth nothing to you then.

> This is how it will be with whoever stores up things for themselves but is not rich toward God. (Luke 12:21)

In one sense, you can't help accumulating things through life. You get given presents every Christmas. You buy something that's useful, and keep it for next time you need it. You might even find it economical to buy higher quality items that last longer. With a relatively stable life you end up with so many things it's a pain for your children to have to clear them out when you die. But Jesus's point is that we so easily stress and strain to get more, and it's worth nothing in the end. And if you are not *rich toward God*—if you are not investing in him, his kingdom, his purposes—you will find, for all you thought you'd achieved like the farmer in the story, in the end you miss out in an appalling way. So don't live for money. Live for God. Wealth terminates. God's kingdom doesn't.

Now the statement "woe to you who are rich" (Luke 6:24) becomes more clear-focused. Jesus adds, "For you have already received your comfort." I don't suppose Jesus did a slow, sarcastic hand clap with that statement. But he might have done, and added the word *bravo!* too. *You got what you were aiming for. Congratulations. But what you were aiming for was worth nothing.*

Wealth Tricks

Jesus's parable of the great banquet in Luke 14 is spoken to people who are embarrassed when the gospel gets too extreme. (Yes, Jesus does make it all quite extreme.) It's supposed to be a polite dinner party, but Jesus talks about the day of resurrection. One man blurts out, "Blessed is the one who will eat at the feast in the kingdom of God" (Luke 14:15). It's the kind of thing people say when they want to show they're a fan of Jesus, but also want to deflect the real implications of his teaching.

People in the story make excuses for not turning up at a party (representing heaven):

> I have just bought five yoke of oxen, and I'm on my way to try them out. Please excuse me. (Luke 14:19)

These are people who had generally warm intentions. They like Jesus and want to go to heaven when they die. But what happens? They end up missing out—all because, when push comes to shove, they like the things of this world.

Wealth is *deceitful*, as Jesus says.[3] You can know what you want, what is of real worth, what really matters. But wealth plays you. It is more tangible than the kingdom of God and lures you to destruction, like the Sirens of Greek legend luring sailors onto the rocks.

We can become so accustomed to a certain standard of living that it is unthinkable to exist any other way. The invitation of Jesus makes demands on us. But we don't spot those demands. We assume they don't apply to us. Our wealth tricks us into thinking it's the important thing round here, and obviously we have to attend to that rather than running to the banquet of God.

Wealth Traps

Wealth is like a banana-in-a-jar-type monkey trap. When people have it, they won't let go—even though it costs them their life.

The episode of the rich ruler in Luke 18:18–27 is multilayered. The real punch line is that *no one* can enter the kingdom of God by their own merits (their goodness, evidenced by their God-given wealth, or anything): "What is impossible with man is possible with God" (Luke 18:27). Only God's grace can bring us in. That's the heart of the gospel. But in the discussion, Jesus gives a stark command to the man:

> Sell everything you have and give to the poor, and you will have treasure in heaven. Then come, follow me. (v. 22)

Have you ever put yourself in his shoes, and wondered how you would have reacted had Jesus looked you in the eye and said the same? A few answers spring to my mind:

- "You don't mean it." It was kind of a trick question to explain the gospel—getting into heaven is all about God's grace. I don't have to give up my money. The man just asked the wrong question to begin with.

3. In the parable of the sower, Matt 13:22 and Mark 4:19 use the expression "the deceitfulness of wealth." Luke 8:14 simply says, "They are choked by life's worries, riches and pleasures."

- "It's not a good use of money." Just giving poor people loads of cash doesn't help the deeper issues.
- "But I need this stuff—for my gospel work." Seriously, if I gave it all up, then I'd need charity from someone else in the same way. As it is, I'm in a position to do the work you've given me to do.

There are all sorts of complexities when we take Jesus's command to *him* as a direct one to *us*. Rather than asking, "Is Jesus saying that to *me*?" the better question is, "Why did Jesus say it to *him*?" (And by they way, when Jesus does address you directly, you are left in little doubt.) But the man's response still exposes us for the hold wealth has over the rich. And the richer you are, the harder it is to give it up.

And most of us in the West, like the man in Luke 18, are *very wealthy* (v. 23). We might look at ourselves as average; there are always wealthier neighborhoods not too far away. But as Richard Garnett pointed out,[4] you only need a (British) annual income of £30,000 (in 2024) to be in the richest 1 percent in the world.

How are we to respond? You can't exactly make yourself poor. In Luke 6, Jesus looks out at the crowd of his followers in front of him, and most of them *are* poor—while the rich look on and make excuses not to follow. The same is true today—most Christians in the world *are* poor. Christians in the wealthy West clearly need more than the common response of vague guilt when it comes to this issue. What are we to do with the truth that poverty is privilege?

What Are We to Do?

It is all too easy to jump to simplistic conclusions, or demand one-dimensional responses from one another. Yes, some of Jesus's commands on the matter are brutally simple; but they are not for everyone at all times. When he told the rich ruler to give away all his wealth, he did not expect (or instruct) the entire watching crowd to dash off and divest themselves of all worldly possessions. If they had done, they would have been missing the point. But neither is it an issue to do nothing about. So, no rash shortcuts; but no standing still either. Let me conclude by suggesting a four-part response to Jesus's teaching that poverty is privilege, for Christians in the relatively comfortable West.

4. Inspired Podcast, "Generous Living."

Enjoy what you have . . .

When the apostle Paul wrote to the Philippians to thank them for their generosity toward him, he was at pains to say he didn't depend on their money. Instead, he says,

> I am not saying this because I am in need, for I have learned to be content whatever the circumstances. I know what it is to be in need, and I know what it is to have plenty. I have learned the secret of being content in any and every situation, whether well fed or hungry, whether living in plenty or in want. I can do all this through him who gives me strength. (Phil 4:11–13)

Contrary to the classic Christian posters with a picture of a mountain climber or victorious athlete, that last sentence (v. 13) is not about God giving his people superhero powers if they have faith. It's really about contentment, and specifically contentment about your current financial situation. Plenty or hunger, abundance or need, says Paul: I'm comfortable with it.

Different people will be challenged by that in different directions. For some, lacking resources is extremely stressful. In fact, for most of us the idea of being content to be *without* sounds like a very godly but distant aspiration. Being without money doesn't necessarily free you from the love of money; the poor can have just the same love for money that the rich have—only longing for it rather than actually having it. The idea of being content to "be in need," to *not* have, is a big challenge.

But for other people, learning to be content *with* wealth can be very difficult too—because with money comes responsibility. It is sometimes easier to have little than have to manage much. Life can become demanding when you are entrusted with much.

An observation sometimes made about people in poorer communities is that they share the little they have. You might hear it said at a funeral, for example: "She had nothing; but she'd give her last £10 to someone in need." It's a nice epithet. But part of that way of life can be because having money feels awkward. Having money gives you responsibility you'd rather not have. It's why lottery winners fall apart at the seams.

But for Paul, receiving an inheritance or unexpected windfall is not a cause of guilt or anxiety (assuming it's been received ethically). He says he has *learned* contentment. It didn't come naturally; he had to teach himself. And, in and of itself, it's ok to *have*. There have always been wealthy disciples of Jesus, just as there are wealthy people of God mentioned through Scripture, Old and New Testament. They are often leaders, especially those who have inherited wealth or status; some people are bred to lead and handle responsibility. Moses grew up in Pharaoh's house. Daniel was a gifted young man picked from the nobility. Paul (Saul) was from a highly educated Pharisee family. Aquila and Priscilla hosted a church in their house (1 Cor 16:19)—I imagine it to have been a fairly plush Greek-Roman villa with mosaics and bunches of grapes all over the place. There is no sense of that being inappropriate or wrong.

How lovely that some Christians are wealthy, even by Western standards—either by successful business or inheritance. It is a beautiful thing that the church is made up of all sorts. Do you suppose unbelievers could comprehend the breadth of friendships that we enjoy? The same church fellowship can include both lords and ladies and people from some of the poorest places on earth. Bloom where you're planted, as they say. Enjoy what you have, what God has entrusted to you, at this moment, at this time.

. . . but recognize the anomaly

> Brothers and sisters, think of what you were when you were called. Not many of you were wise by human standards; not many were influential; not many were of noble birth. (1 Cor 1:26)

The Countess of Huntingdon, Lady Selina Hastings, was the great eighteenth-century benefactor behind much of the ministry of John Wesley and George Whitefield. She is often quoted as saying she owed her salvation to the letter *M*—1 Cor 1:26 doesn't say "not *any* of you" but "not *many* of you." There were some in Corinth, even if just a few, who were from a wealthy background.

Whether or not she did actually say it, the quote attributed to Lady Selina is delightful. It not only expresses her assurance in the grace of God but, as one of noble birth and influence, that she is unusual in the kingdom, an unlikely guest at the party. The great revival of the eighteenth century in Britain and the American colonies saw many thousands of people turn to Christ. There are towns in Wales with more chapels than pubs (many funded by the countess), such was the need for meeting places for believers. Christians gifted with wealth funded much for the church. But the vast majority of believers were poor—miners, tenant farmers, and, in the American colonies, slaves. Wealthy believers were an anomaly.

Two and a half centuries on, that is not so apparent in the West. The church is not viewed as being primarily made up of poor people (though it is, globally). Perhaps that is because the West has prospered and there is less poverty in general here. Perhaps it is because converts from poor backgrounds began to prosper as they gave up drinking and such, so they're no longer the poor ones. Perhaps it is because wealthier (influential) people are generally more confident personalities, and therefore seem to dominate, even if they don't numerically. Whatever the case, there is rarely the sense that to be a wealthy believer is extraordinary.

The eighteenth-century hymn "Amazing Grace" is as popular as it ever was. When we sing the opening lines today,

> Amazing grace (how sweet the sound)
> that saved a wretch like me![5]

how many of us include the concept of *rich* in the word *wretch*? Sure, a *wretch* is a poor person, in scruffy clothes, who smells. Easy to think about God stooping to save scruffbags—and that *is* amazing. But what about how amazing it is that God would stoop to save even rich wretches, the really unusual ones, in his plan of salvation, the ones to whom he once said "Woe to you"?

If we understood a little better this idea that wealthy believers are an anomaly, it would change us deeply. The increasing prosperity of our society at large has not stilled our souls, has not reduced our anxieties. We are not a more rested or balanced society as a result of becoming wealthier, but have become more insecure in who we are and what we exist for. Overworked and tunnel-visioned, we have become like the Cyclops, the one-eyed giant of Greek mythology: our sense of the value of material gain under Western democracy has grown to gigantic proportion, such that we can appreciate no other way of existence, having only a single eye to promoting more of the same. Even in the church, the wealthy Westerner typically (and unwittingly) has a patronizing manner toward those from poorer societies; he calls him brother and wants to serve, but doesn't understand why the relationship is still strained.

Perhaps Laurens van der Post, discussing this dynamic, provided the answer in conversation with the Dutch leaders in Java at the end of the colonial era, who were confused by the desire of the Indonesians to see them leave their country once and for all. He recounts:

> I remember the Governor-General turning to me and saying: "I cannot understand it. Look what we have done for them. Look at the schools and the hospitals we have given them. A hundred years ago the population was only a few million, today it is nearly sixty millions. We have done away with malaria,

5. Newton, "Amazing Grace."

> plague and dysentery and given them a prosperous, balanced economy. Everyone has enough to eat. We have given them an honest and efficient administration and abolished civil war and piracy. Look at the roads, the railways, the industries—and yet they want us to go. Can you tell me why they want us to go?" And I felt compelled to say: "Yes, I think I can: I'm afraid it is because you've never had the right look in the eye when you spoke to them."[6]

Why, in the church in the West, can we mean so well and yet understand so badly? It is because we have forgotten that we, the wealthy, do not set the norm in God's kingdom. We are the anomaly.

At a large meeting of Anglican church leaders from around the world a few years ago, the gathering was given accounts of the murderous persecution Nigerians are suffering in the north of their country. Western delegates were, rightly enough, shocked and moved, eager to support in any way they were able. But one Nigerian leader announced, "We are praying for *you*! We are concerned for you, and the state of the church in the West. You are the ones we worry about."

It is a wholesome thing to be on the receiving end of that sort of statement. We assume that our financial security contributes to our spiritual security. But quite the opposite: wealthy Christians are unlikely candidates for the kingdom. Realizing that changes our relationship with wealth.

Hold it loosely

"Earthly goods are given to be used, not to be collected," wrote Bonhoeffer.[7] The early church (with the exceptions of Ananias and Sapphira, Acts 5) modelled this by having "all things in common," according to Luke's sequel (Acts 2:44). The Christian writer Tertullian (AD 145–220) confirms it: "So we, who are united in mind and soul, have no hesitation about sharing property. All is common among us—except our wives."[8] It's helpful that he clarified that last bit. But rather than imagining a central possessions dump, where every Christian family took an entire inventory of all earthly goods as if filing a corporate tax return so anyone could help themselves to anything at any time, I suspect it was more the general sense that nothing was considered exclusively *mine* any more. Whatever one owned, it was all for the

6. Van der Post, *Dark Eye*, 90–91.
7. Bonhoeffer, *Discipleship*, 155.
8. Tertullian, *Apology*, 177–79.

common good, for the kingdom. When there was some need for the church or individuals within it, people gladly sold goods to help out:

> All the believers were one in heart and mind. No one claimed that any of their possessions was their own, but they shared everything they had. (Acts 4:32)

> All the believers were together and had everything in common. They sold property and possessions to give to anyone who had need. (Acts 2:44–45)

Many Christians stick to the Old Testament idea of *tithing*. 10 percent of one's income (that's *before* tax[9]) should be given to the church. It's certainly a good habit to set aside a proportion of your income for giving (1 Cor 16:2). But the danger of a tithing mentality is to think that 10 percent is for God, and 90 percent remains mine. In reality, all riches come from the Lord, and all we have is to be used for him and his kingdom. Whether it remains in our savings account, is spent on domestic use, or is given to a church fundraiser, all is for the Lord—not 10 percent; not 20 percent; but 100 percent. That is to be expressed in holding all we have loosely, ready to let go, to pass it on as there is need.

After all the characters and stories through the book of Luke who serve as warnings against the grave dangers of wealth, we finally meet Zacchaeus in chapter 19. He is the Lord Farquaad[10] of first-century Jericho—little, but minted. But when Jesus calls him by name and invites himself to tea, Zacchaeus is a changed man:

> Look, Lord! Here and now I give half of my possessions to the poor, and if I have cheated anybody out of anything, I will pay back four times the amount. (Luke 19:8)

His attitude to wealth is changed in an instant. Yes, he has defrauded people. ("If," indeed.) But if they form an orderly queue (British style), he'll repay fourfold. As for the rest of it—he teaches his wallet who's boss. Half is given straight away.

He takes a big financial hit. It's not *all*, by the way—but *half*. Who knows, possibly he is still reasonably comfortable. Maybe not. But either way, he takes drastic action. Why? It is an expression of his overwhelming joy in receiving Jesus. He hasn't necessarily become poor (though he has become poorer)—but he knows that the poor are blessed, because getting ahead in this world, as he has been doing, is ultimately worth nothing.

9. As emphasized by Reverend Lovejoy from *The Simpsons*. Groening, *Simpsons*.

10. Shrek's antagonist. You know the one. Adamson, *Shrek*.

There is Luke's picture of the response of the wealthy to following Jesus. When those who are relatively wealthy (say, in the top 1 percent) receive Jesus, they count their hard-earned wealth as of little value, and give it liberally as an expression of their joyful new life with its new priorities. They have something worth infinitely more than rust-bound, moth-bound, thief-bound, landfill-bound goods.

That is the teaching for richer Christians throughout the New Testament. First Timothy puts it like this:

> But those who desire to be rich fall into temptation, into a snare, into many senseless and harmful desires that plunge people into ruin and destruction. (1 Tim 6:9)
>
> Command those who are rich in this present world not to be arrogant nor to put their hope in wealth, which is so uncertain, but to put their hope in God, who richly provides us with everything for our enjoyment. Command them to do good, to be rich in good deeds, and to be generous and willing to share. In this way they will lay up treasure for themselves as a firm foundation for the coming age, so that they may take hold of the life that is truly life. (1 Tim 6:17–19)

There are rich Christians. But they know the dangers of wealth (their hearts easily follow it), and they know the value and certainty of what they have in Christ. Live for that.

Grasping this will be expressed in various ways. For some, it will mean joyfully refusing a promotion or accepting a pay cut in order to use their time more for the better things of the kingdom. But it's not necessarily saying that Christian businessmen should not get ahead. Some absolutely should—for the kingdom. Those gifted with ability to earn lots may well do so—in order to give lots.[11] But they will do so with a sober realization: *It is the poor who are blessed. Lucky them. What a privilege. As for me, I need to walk the hard road of managing wealth.*

John Wesley, mentioned above, ended up earning plenty of money by his gospel work. But seeing how zeal for the gospel faded in converts to Christ the more they grew in wealth, he resolved to never increase his own standard of living but to give away everything beyond a basic threshold.[12] Wise money-earners in the church will do the same. Greater possessions might enable good ways to bless the church. But it's very easy to convince

11. If this is for you, read Rinehart, *Gospel Patrons.*

12. White, "Four Lessons on Money."

yourself it's for the kingdom, when it's really for your own gratification and comfort. That does not serve you—or your children—well.

After visiting a men's breakfast hosted by another nearby church recently, a few of us were driving home together. One made the comment, "I see those sort of people as *serious* Christians." He wasn't insulting our own church. What he meant was that, in contrast to most of the comfortable Christianity we see, here were people who were principled. They made bold decisions, knowing what it means to follow Christ. Even if you don't agree with everything they do or think, you know you are in the presence of people who take discipleship *seriously*.

Attitudes to wealth are the great telltale sign of whether we belong in that category or not. Christians can speak boldly (talk big), teach Scripture with great insight, and have very busy church programs. But it can still come across as somehow superficial. When, on the other hand, they make decisions, on principle, that *cost* them financially—then their Christianity carries weight. Too many Christians in the West stop short.

Accept loss

The question of how much a rich person should give away to be obedient to Jesus is always going to be elusive. Is it *everything*, like the rich ruler, or *half* our possessions, like Zacchaeus? And what about if our church, corporately, is rich? Never mind the individuals; we might be part of a church that has a plush building compound, state-of-the-art tech, and an operations manager, while other fellowships have nowhere to meet and nothing to pay a pastor. That's an imbalance that doesn't always seem to sit right either. What do we do about it?

Sometimes that question doesn't need answering. Circumstances force choices that reveal our true hearts. Consider the early Hebrew Christians:

> Remember those earlier days after you had received the light, when you endured in a great conflict full of suffering. . . . You suffered along with those in prison and joyfully accepted the confiscation of your property, because you knew that you yourselves had better and lasting possessions. (Heb 10:32–34)

Get Luke 6 clear, and it helps you behave like the people of Heb 10—*joyfully accepting the confiscation of your property*.

It does happen that church property is confiscated by authorities—and is happening in the West today. When the leaders of St. John's Church, Vancouver, made a bold stand to disassociate from the apostate Anglican Church of Canada in 2008, their denominational authorities claimed ownership of the church's $13 million property—leaving the congregation to start saving again for another place to meet.[13] When the Church of Scotland similarly changed its doctrine of marriage in 2014, many churches that could not remain within the denomination had to leave their precious buildings, some of which had been built with their own hands and money.

More usually, the choice to stand for Christ or hold on to wealth will happen in small, subtle increments. The kind of thing is not too hard to imagine:

- An international crisis is an excuse to ban church meetings—just for a while. The church stops meeting together to avoid paying a fine.
- The Charity Commission (or equivalent) threaten to remove charity status, with its tax perks, unless churches sign up to its diversity agendas.
- The risk of accusations of homophobia or Islamophobia involving police investigations, court action, and fines threaten clear teaching on such issues.
- Before long, taxes are actively *added* for noncompliance on certain matters.
- If a church has still refused to compromise its teaching and way of life, full on brutal loss of corporate and even private property follows. Bank accounts are frozen, investments confiscated, mortgage lenders repossess homes, church properties are seized.

At every step, the temptation is to make excuse: *It's just a small matter; it's just for a short time; we can find a way round this one.* Perhaps it's true; perhaps it is ok to find a way out, a loophole through the regulations, though some other churches have made a costly stand. To use popular euphemisms, perhaps this is not the hill to die on, perhaps the red line still lies just ahead.

But red lines always do stay just ahead, like a mirage on the road. Before you know it, the line was crossed miles behind, years ago, and you missed it.

At some point, you have to choose to follow Jesus at financial cost. It's best to make that choice very early on.

Bonhoeffer was so frustrated with the majority of church leaders in 1930s Germany. One small compromise after another; excuses not to pay a cost: *the church shouldn't get involved in politics; we can quietly just get on as before; taking a stand would cause division in the church.* The bottom

13. Anglican Church, "Largest Anglican Church in Canada."

line was that pastors didn't want to lose their income.[14] We can see the error of churches who compromised under National Socialism. I wonder how future generations will view our reactions (or lack of them) to the social and political changes of our own time? In their analysis, will they say that *money* was the bottom line for us, compromising our discipleship, jeopardizing our salvation—or, at least, the salvation of the generation that follows?

The truly privileged are not the rich, the comfortable, the well fed, the settled, or the steady. The truly privileged are the poor. They have the kingdom of God.

14. Metaxas, *Bonhoeffer*, 282.

4

Confession Can Cure Cancer

Therefore confess your sins to each other and pray for each other so that you may be healed.

Jas 5:16

"It happens rarely, but there are cases of self-induced healing." You see how it's worded? Not recovery through treatment, but actual healing. See?

Aleksandr Solzhenitsyn, *Cancer Ward*

This is a highly sensitive subject. Many of us have known the awful experience of a loved one on the journey of symptoms, diagnosis, and the highly unpleasant series of treatments that follow, be it surgery, radiotherapy, chemotherapy, or amputations. Some will have known the roller coaster of hopes raised and then dashed again, remission, and then secondaries. Some will be haunted by the memory of dreaded words such as *cancer . . . prognosis . . . I'm sorry*. If so, thank you for being brave enough to read this.

This chapter is not only about something sensitive, but personal—to me. Lyndsey, my wife, was diagnosed with breast cancer several years ago. It has been the time of biggest spiritual growth in our lives, especially hers. Through the chapter I will include parts of our story, so you can see the principles worked out in real experience.

The chapter title is not meant to be provocative. It is certainly not flippant. By writing it, I am not claiming to cure cancer.[1] What I am wanting to do is persuade you to take Scripture seriously.

Taking Scripture seriously on this subject is a big ask. Because when it comes to healing, be it cancer or anything else, it takes enormous courage to question whether there may be more to consider than medicine. It takes courage to even ask whether there might be things the mighty Western medical system does not understand.

Perhaps you are already on high alert as you read this. What sort of interpretation of Scripture is coming? Are we about to receive medical advice from a non-medic? (A shock surely too great to bear!) Will this be the ravings of a self-taught skeptic, spouting wild ideas that have been debunked by actual science?

If you *are* in a concerned frame of mind, I would thoroughly encourage you to remain so. Because one of our biggest cultural dangers with a sensitive issue such as healthcare is that we are conditioned to be unwilling to think for ourselves. *Trust the experts*, we are told. Nevertheless, let me give you some reassurances:

- I am not offering a formula for recovery, a secret new method of self-healing;
- I am not assuming each disease is the result of specific sin. We won't be going down that road;
- I am not suggesting a new and novel way of reading a part of Scripture.

What I am saying is that the subject of confession and healing has become one of our cultural blind spots. But I want you to take it as seriously as Christians outside our own particular moment in time and space have done.

There is an assumption in the back of the Western mind that we are now brighter and more informed than all who have come before us. Without putting it into words, we can assume that even Scripture was written by people who were pretty ignorant in some ways: after all, they lived before science existed. Had the writers of Scripture understood what we understand today, they would have written it differently . . . wouldn't they?

I'm saying, no, they wouldn't.

1. In many countries, my own included, there is a law against making such claims, presumably to protect us from cruel scams. So let me be clear: I never have cured anyone of cancer. This is not about techniques or brazen claims.

Our Story

Over the years, Lyndsey has had a number of small lumps, as many women have—lumps concerning enough to have them checked out. We were expecting the results of this particular lump to be much the same as others, a simple explanation relating to tissues or hormones, and instructions not to worry but keep an eye on it. And so it was a shock to be told this one looks like cancer.

It was done badly—she received the call over the hands-free connection of the phone, while she was driving on the motorway (freeway) with our youngest son. The follow-up explanation of things was not forthcoming; she had to seek it out. Then somebody did call, by phone, while she was walking the dog. She sat on a tree stump at the end of our road to receive the news, called me, and I met her in the park. We sat on a bench together. She cried. We prayed. That was the beginning of many appointments, waiting rooms, and clumsy conversations by busy medical staff about prognoses, procedures, and pathways. "What's in this medicine?" "Don't worry, it's fine." "What if I say no to this treatment?" "Then we'd insist on a mastectomy."

In the face of illness, the Lord God (alone) offers us the most wonderful good news. I would like you to join me on an amazing journey of discovery. But let's start with the basics.

God

Is God real? If you answered yes, and I hope you did, then ask yourself again: Is God real? Because if he is, then this means that everything in your life, everything outside of your body, and everything inside of your body, is being influenced and monitored by the one whose power and love are both supreme. Do you know that as a fact? Is this the God you know? Or do you sometimes think that God will not see something, or that something has happened outside of his interest and work?

What kind of God do you believe in?

These are important questions. They become essential questions when a big diagnosis comes your way. If that hasn't done so yet, it will happen, probably to you, at some point in your life. Almost nobody lives their entire life without something serious being written on their medical notes.

So what is God teaching you when this happens? Lots of incredible intellects and great believers have written about God's work through suffering.

Yes, to all of it. (Or most of it.) What do we need to know about God when it comes to *non-persecution* suffering—and what is God teaching us when it comes our way?

In a sense, it is easier to think of God's sovereign rule over distant galaxies or breathtaking phenomena of nature. Such things are *out there*, way beyond my life, my personal concern, my responsibility. As King David wrote,

> Such knowledge is too wonderful for me, too lofty for me to attain. (Ps 139:6)

It is comforting to think of God's majestic works in his vast creation. But that psalm, Ps 139, is not talking about *out there* stuff; it's talking about God's sovereign rule over one's own body, thoughts, and movements. Have you praised God, recently, for his intricate, detailed care over every aspect of your life, body, soul, and circumstances? Do you relate to him on this basis even when things go wrong?

The gospel is not a theory. It is really true. God is not just a theory. He is real. When you are diagnosed with something serious, it is a mistake to hide behind your early childhood programming and defense mechanisms. Don't just do what you've always done and behave like you've always behaved—because, as I will suggest below, the chances are that might be part of the problem. God is teaching you to know him and his ways better. That is what he does, in his immense power and kindness.

Our Story (by Lyndsey)

I very much enjoyed reading John Piper's little pamphlet *Don't Waste Your Cancer.*[2] I expected it to have lots in there about the evangelistic opportunities of cancer. Actually, it didn't. It was mostly about my relationship with God. I loved it! To say that cancer is primarily an evangelistic opportunity is to say to the world, *I've got this amazing gospel thing sorted, even though my body is falling apart. Would you like some of what I've got?* Many people would rightly say, *No, thank you.* To think I will inspire other people by my stoicism and serenity as my body crumbles is usually a mistake. This is not what disease is supposed to produce within me. There may be a place for beautiful and serene suffering, but it is absolutely not the *first* place to go with disease. Bible accounts of disease and suffering do not give us room for that reaction.

2. Piper, *Don't Waste Your Cancer.*

More than perhaps any other experience we can have in life, ill health is a God-given opportunity for us to know him better. It is an opportunity to relate to him more closely than we have done until now.

The fact is, he cares. He is deeply and passionately interested in every detail of our lives. He has arranged the details so that we, his children, will not stray, due to our sin, carelessness, or ignorance. He gives joys and sorrows, he gives and he takes away, he gives times of refreshment and times of hardship—all because he cares so much for us.

Bodies: What's the Big Deal?

When you are young, you think you can treat your body carelessly. After all, life is short, live while you can, and—as a Christian—you get a new body after you die anyway.

When you get older, you start to respect your body more. That is partly because you begin to feel the effects of neglect a bit more seriously. The consequences hurt or matter. Neglect limits your usefulness or enjoyment. Partly, also, age brings wisdom, and you learn responsibility. You see that it's worth looking after things—including yourself. Ironically, having a shorter time left on earth increases the value of preserving it. You wish you'd cared more when you were young, perhaps.

Many Christians have latched onto the biblical truth that *life is short.* Eighty years compared to eternity: it's a no-brainer. Imagine your new, perfect resurrection body if you can! It's enough to put a smile on your face; but that is not the whole story.

From another perspective, it is also true to say that *life is long.*

For many years, I had only considered the model of Christian living that thought the body of little importance; flog it while you can, and live for the life to come. It sounds so godly. But our moral reasoning is always distorted, and on the subject of using our bodies we blur godliness with folly, even sin.

On one hand, it's right to risk health for the gospel. Like many Christians, I have travelled to unhealthy climates, risked physical danger, and drunk tea in houses where even the dog has died for lack of hygiene (literally). It all helps you to pray. And because there is a certain amount of carefree, risk-all, gospel passion, we can convince ourselves that in any form the *live fast, die young* attitude is for Christ. But most of the ways we compromise our health are not for the gospel at all: quite the opposite. They are for the sake of laziness, greed, conformity, fear, or pride.

Yes, life is short. But life is long also. We know that. We know it is not wise to live for the moment—because it spoils future moments. Our bodies are to last us as long as we live on earth. Is it really so godly to make yourself more tired, more often ill, less useful? It is a warped way of thinking.

We rightly teach children to value their bodies. We celebrate that God made us just the way we are, and encourage kids to enjoy what they have and look after their health. Yet in many of our church subcultures, the way we act ourselves is quite different. If you visit a nephew or niece and find the toy you gave them last Christmas has been left out to ruin in the rain and mud, you might think twice about spending so much on next year's gift. Our bodies are a precious gift from God. Treating our body as a cheap gift is an insult to the Giver.

Have a think about what the following examples say about our use of (and attitude to) our bodies—and see if any of them fit your church or Christian networks:

- Obesity is seen as acceptable and normal, and young men (especially) celebrate gluttony as an achievement.
- People place such value on output and work, even in church ministry, that the daily need for caffeine (to get started) and alcohol (to wind down) is considered a virtue. (At least, the caffeine part.)
- It is fairly common to hear Christians laugh about ruining their body, because, after all, we will get new ones soon enough in heaven.
- People who cut out additives or eat organic are labelled "heath freaks" and considered ungodly for their obsession and for what they spend on food.
- Cooking from scratch is for weekends or fun, or showing what good hosts we are, not for necessity.
- Old age—even midlife—is expected to be dominated by ill health. It's just the way it is.
- Things that used to take up most of the day, such as walking, manual tasks, and domestic chores, are seen as a frustrating or unnecessary waste of time. It is the same for sleep.
- A significant percentage of people take medicines on long-term prescriptions (especially antidepressants, and maybe more than one), and have no plan to stop doing so.

- Concerns such as pollution, electromagnetic fields, and negative health associations with vaccines are for the over-anxious, the obsessed, and the conspiracy-theorists. The godly do not have time for such concerns.
- Most people do not like their own body, still spend a lot of time thinking about it, but don't do much to change it. The ones that do get carried away.

Do you think perhaps that the same reasoning should apply to both soul and body? We will have a future sinless soul; that is not a reason to sin now without care. We will have a future healthy heavenly body; that is not a reason to neglect our body now.

God has granted us a certain number of years on earth. We don't know how many. Yes, life will be better when we get to glory. But in the meantime, there is life to live for the glory of Christ on earth.

One final thought before moving on: if you could choose now to live to a hundred, would you do it?[3] Think about it—and answer carefully. *If you could choose now to live to a hundred, would you do it?* The reasons you may have said no—are they cultural, or spiritual? "Old age is miserable." "I don't want to be a burden." "Life beyond a certain age is pointless." Interesting, isn't it? We have almost forgotten that God declared life to be *good*. But it is good. It is a beautiful thing, to be cherished.

Our Story

People respond differently to a cancer diagnosis, often depending on levels of tolerance for thinking about it, their amount of fear, and responses to that fear. Lyndsey initially researched and embraced step-by-step diet improvement, reading about things that feed cancer or help the body fight it; she also paid closer attention to other aspects of health maintenance. She immediately and ruthlessly cut out all processed sugar, seed oils, processed food in general (anything that "comes out of a packet and contains five or more ingredients"[4] especially if you're not sure what they are or how to say them), things particularly prone to harmful pesticide treatments,[5] alcohol, caffeine, and refined flour. Her main meal of the day became a lunchtime "giant cancer-beating salad"[6] with as

3. A question used in counselling by Siegel, *Love*, 105.
4. Dr. Aseem Malhotra's rule of thumb; see Greenfield, "Cardiologist," para. 2.
5. Environmental Working Group, "Dirty Dozen."
6. From Wark and Wark, *Beat Cancer Kitchen*.

many different varieties of fresh vegetables as possible. Aside from whatever benefit it had to the cancer, other midlife heath issues that she had accepted as a normal ongoing frustration of life all cleared up in a very short time—a painful knee, digestive issues, and heart palpitations. We didn't think we ate badly before; but all this truly raised the question, *What are we doing to ourselves with our "normal" twenty-first-century Western diet?*

Western Healthcare . . .

Some time ago, I asked a group of Chinese Christian friends what they thought about Chinese medicine, as Christians. Many Western Christians view it with suspicion—sometimes because of particular roots it has in pagan religion. (Tellingly, when pushed, they quite often have no idea why, how, or which religion they are referring to!) What did they, as Chinese Christians living in the West, think? Did they think Chinese medicine spiritually suspect too?

At least one in the group had a doctor (in the Western sense) for a parent, and another worked in healthcare herself. They were reluctant to answer, because they didn't want to offend. But eventually they explained that most Chinese medicine was simply about ordinary common-sense healthy living—eating goji berries with breakfast and such. Acupuncture was not seen as strange spirituality to them, but as helpful therapy based on millennia of understanding of the body's connectivity. In fact, the more they opened up, the clearer they became: sure, there are dark arts in every culture—but most Chinese medicine is a wholesome and logical application of sensible living in God's world. Why should we be suspicious?

By contrast, the typical Western attitude to health is generally, to put it bluntly: *Eat rubbish, and wait till something goes wrong.* (Isn't that the sober truth!) Then you can go to the doctor and have it cut out. Or take prescription drugs. Or live the life of a victim of poor health. These are the ways that an average Western citizen lives—including most Christians among them.

At the heart of it, enlightenment thinking treats the body like a machine. The Usborne lift-the-flap children's book *How Your Body Works*[7] puts it all beautifully: the body consists of a lot of parts and processes, and all the different functions happen as if there were lots of little people inside us, all performing their specific tasks. The digestive system? Stuff goes in, and different workers process different bits of it. Respiration? The guys that

7. Dickins, *How Your Body Works.*

work in the lungs, the heart, the blood vessels—they all have their defined jobs. It's fun to study—and like in high school biology, you can begin to see how detailed and marvelous the processes are. But we are just complicated machines.

In our Western system, bodies are much the same as cars, just with more features. If one goes wrong, a trained mechanic is the person to fix it—a motor mechanic for the car, and a biological mechanic, called a doctor, for the body. The body, being far more complicated than the car, requires a better mechanic, and so doctors are regarded as superior to motor mechanics, sometimes even raised to the level of demigods, and paid accordingly. A car sometimes requires a specialist motor mechanic, for a particular aspect of repair. And since the body is so complicated, specialist doctors abound. Those that deal with the *brain* part of the body, sometimes referred to as the *mind*, are called psychiatrists. They are especially clever. Aspirational Indian friends of ours (jokingly) tell their children, "You have a choice: be a doctor, a dentist . . . or a doctor." Aim for the ultimate.

As ordinary members of society, we are glad to have doctors (and mechanics). But we are wrong to think the body is simply a machine. And yet even Christians easily take as a bedrock assumption the viewpoint that the body is a matter of functions, and therefore find the Bible's teaching on health matters hard to relate to. When the Bible comments on healthcare and medicine, it often seems distant, confusing, or plain ignorant.

Attempts are sometimes made to explain Scripture in sound, scientific terms: "They called it demon-possession, but we understand it as epilepsy"—that sort of thing. There is also sometimes an assumption that people in biblical times were less educated, even less intelligent. Take, for example, these quotes from a leading (and generally excellent) evangelical publication. This is common teaching:

- "Even if the medical knowledge of the day had been advanced, it would not have been understood by the readers."[8] Subtext: we are all smarter now.
- "Sincere and honest men, mostly with no medical knowledge, wrote of what they saw as they understood best."[9] In other words, the Bible writers did their best to talk about health—bless them.

8. Trapnell, "Health," 457.
9. Trapnell, "Health," 457.

- "There was scarcely any element in it [the Bible's teaching on health] which could be dignified with the name of science."[10] Dignified, indeed. The modern West knows best.

Well, maybe we do know more about how the machine functions; but perhaps at the same time we're missing something. Perhaps we're not just a machine. Perhaps we're living beings whose thoughts, actions, emotions, behaviors, choices, and desires are bound up with and affect our health—body, mind, and spirit. That's how the traditional Chinese understand it, and that's how many other healthcare systems in the world understand it, and that's how they understood it in Bible times. But still, we in the West think we know better—after all, we've cured diseases that no one else could. And who would not celebrate healthy scientific discovery? It is just worth bearing in mind, before we get too self-congratulatory, that many diseases are specific to Western lifestyle in the first place. Also, there is a healing that others seem to know that somehow eludes us: deep healing, utter transformation.

But Western medicine thinks stuff like that is backward and silly. We've invented chemotherapy.

Our Story

After reading about the tumor-reducing value of intravenous vitamin C infusions, Lyndsey took a course from a nearby doctor. It was dismissed with a total blank from other medics, who had no interest in discovering what it was about. Undergoing surgery to remove the lump was actually one of Lyndsey's regrets, now thinking the tumor would have shrunk of its own accord in time with the emotional, spiritual, lifestyle, and diet work. But hindsight often gives courage and clarity that is not possible in the moment.

A course of radiotherapy was prescribed (if it was called by its true name, "radiation therapy," it might help more people think twice)—"just as a precaution." Lyndsey declined; but later she discovered that her medical notes recorded that she had taken it anyway, such was the system. She asked questions of it all: *Why would she take poison as a precaution?* "It would just focus on the cells around the tumor." *Why do we need to poison the cells around the tumor? They seem ok.* "We would strongly recommend it—sort of belt and braces." Also, a five—no, now ten—year course of a drug called Tamoxifen. It throws women's hormones into chaos, and a possible side effect is cancer. (*Sorry, what?*) What if we refuse it?

10. Trapnell, "Health," 461.

"Then we'd be looking at a mastectomy." (Euphemism for breast amputation.)

The waiting room in the breast department was full of terrified women, dealing with the dreaded word *cancer*. It is so dreaded that they would do anything to deal with it. *Are there no other things that can help?* "You do have to be careful with what you read on the internet." But there are good things written by doctors who have done huge research. "You do have to be careful."

. . . Versus Biblical Healthcare

One of the biggest criticisms of the Western mind toward medical practice in old biblical times—or, in fact, any other time or culture than our own—is that it is nearly always associated with religion or spirituality. Be it witch-doctors, shamans, or prophet-cum-healers, the fact that healing is bound up with *superstition*, in the eyes of the scientific establishment, by definition renders it suspect. I would like to profoundly question this assumption.

When God breathed life into the nostrils of Adam, the man became a living being (Gen 2:7). It wasn't that a life inhabited a body, within but as a separate entity. The body was alive, filled with the breath of God. We are not a separate mix of physical and spiritual: our bodies *are* spiritual. We are not all the same, just in slightly different models: we are each unique, living persons. Our bodies are a part of our personality. We are told not to judge by appearances; but you can tell a lot about what somebody is like just by looking—for example, at their posture, movement, mannerisms, expressions, even their facial features as shaped by emotions, thoughts, speech[11] . . . and their health. It's not that our health defines us. But it is part of us.

When the psalm rejoices in the same breath that it is the Lord "who forgives all your sins and heals all your diseases" (Ps 103:3), it is not that Scripture has failed to understand that the two things are only (at best) loosely related. No, the lack of understanding is at our end—it is the modern, scientific separation of body and person that fails to see the profound connection between sin and health, between the spiritual, emotional, and physical. Different brands of Western Christianity vary between obsession with physical healing and embarrassment over the subject. But few seem to appreciate how thrilling it is to discover the spiritual nature of healthcare. New Agers, Reiki healers, and mystic crystal ladies all seem to know that health is spiritual. But the average Western Christian only rejects such

11. See Fulfer, *Amazing Face Reading*.

people as nuts or evil, instead of being able to point them to the ultimate reality that these people see dimly. When it comes to healthcare, Western Christians seem to assume that the *atheistic* outlook is neutral—not realizing that it as dangerous a false religion as any that ever existed.

When we even allow ourselves to consider the possibility that we are not just machines, subject to random malfunction, but whole, spiritual beings, it lifts us to a fuller life. Rather than being inevitably processed by the great corporate machine of the healthcare system in times of sickness, passively (and anxiously) waiting to see what happens, we throw ourselves instead into the arms of our heavenly Father. We learn to realign our lives, learn to live his ways, learn the lessons he is teaching us. We have an active part to play in our recovery.

Our Story (by Lyndsey)

However much faith we put in the medical system, it has to be the case that our faith should be much more in the God who made us. And also, it might be good to have some faith in our bodies as God made them. We might have poisoned ourselves in all sorts of ways, we might be brimful of toxic emotions and errors of belief in relation to ourselves and the world, deeply poisoning our blood chemistry and body function,[12] but when we turn and face our Savior, we can put one foot in front of the other and move toward him, letting go of the areas where we have resisted him, where we have denied him access, and fully surrender our broken selves to our Creator.

I have never been so grateful for something challenging in my life. It set me on a new course of self-examination and radical honesty: I am still doing this work on myself and will continue to do so. I am a slow learner but I have definitely started to learn properly now. My faith is not a theory, and neither is my Savior. It's all real, much more real than scan readouts and charts showing blood results, than powerful radiating machinery and poisonous drugs. God is more real than all of it, and we will see that plainly one day.

Let's explore a couple of examples in Scripture to see the connection between spiritual and physical health.

12. Lipton, *Biology of Belief*.

A Tale of Two Kings

King Hezekiah of Judah is one of the good guys of 2 Kings:

> Hezekiah trusted in the LORD, the God of Israel. There was no one like him among all the kings of Judah, either before him or after him. (2 Kgs 18:5)

Nevertheless, he became ill:

> In those days Hezekiah became ill and was at the point of death. The prophet Isaiah son of Amoz went to him and said, "This is what the LORD says: Put your house in order, because you are going to die; you will not recover." (2 Kgs 20:1)

What a pitiful position Hezekiah is in. He's become so ill he's about to die. And then the prophet comes to visit. Surely he'll have a word of comfort! After all, Hezekiah has walked as closely with God as any king so far. But Isaiah says something along the lines of, "Cancel your Sky Sports subscription. You won't be needing the renewal package."

But the man has a zest for life. He doesn't want to just roll over and die. (Few creatures do—all things are made with a desire for life.) So:

> Hezekiah turned his face to the wall and prayed to the LORD, "Remember, Lord, how I have walked before you faithfully and with wholehearted devotion and have done what is good in your eyes." And Hezekiah wept bitterly.
>
> Before Isaiah had left the middle court, the word of the LORD came to him: "Go back and tell Hezekiah, the ruler of my people, 'This is what the LORD, the God of your father David, says: I have heard your prayer and seen your tears; I will heal you. On the third day from now you will go up to the temple of the LORD. I will add fifteen years to your life. And I will deliver you and this city from the hand of the king of Assyria. I will defend this city for my sake and for the sake of my servant David.'"
>
> Then Isaiah said, "Prepare a poultice of figs." They did so and applied it to the boil, and he recovered. (2 Kgs 20:2–7)

Amazing! And is that not the response the Lord was looking for—humility, grief, dependence? Hezekiah's prognosis of days turns into fifteen years as he searches his heart and seeks the Lord. Can you imagine the joyful celebrations and songs of praise among his family—and nation—at this time?

Contrast King Asa. We meet him several generations before Hezekiah, in 1 Kgs 15. He was a pretty good guy too:

> Asa did what was right in the eyes of the Lord, as his father David had done. He expelled the male shrine prostitutes from the land and got rid of all the idols his ancestors had made. He even deposed his grandmother Maakah from her position as queen mother, because she had made a repulsive image for the worship of Asherah. Asa cut it down and burned it in the Kidron Valley. (1 Kgs 15:11–13)

But like many, though his heart was "fully committed to the Lord all his life" (1 Kgs 15:14), he didn't deal with the congenital sin of the nation, and let the pagan worship at hilltop shrines carry on. Still, he's basically good. He's a real follower of the Lord, and faithful leader of God's people—he just didn't deal with everything. A little weak or compromised, perhaps.

It's only in the fuller account of him in 2 Chr 14–16 that we find details about some of his more inglorious moments. He, too, had a visit from a prophet with unpleasant news. Hanani the seer (a little less famous than Isaiah the prophet) rebuked him for relying on the king of Syria rather than the Lord, when he was under threat. The punishment would be ongoing war through Asa's lifetime. His response? No hiding his face to the wall in tearful prayer, like Hezekiah. Instead, he was angry and had the prophet put in the prison stocks.

And then he suffered his own illness:

> In the thirty-ninth year of his reign Asa was afflicted with a disease in his feet. (2 Chr 16:12)

It would be nice at this point to read that he humbly sought the Lord, Hezekiah-style. But no:

> Though his disease was severe, even in his illness he did not seek help from the Lord, but only from the physicians. Then in the forty-first year of his reign Asa died and rested with his ancestors. (2 Chr 16:12–13)

The writer does not view this as a positive, does he? God gave him two years of disease—that's plenty of time to seek help from the giver of life. Eventually the disease took him, and he never found out how much God could have helped him if he'd only asked, and meant it, as Hezekiah was to do years later. Yes, *meant it* is an important point. It's not just a simple "Please heal me" that was needed—he had sins that needed addressing; real repentance was called for. The illness was his wake-up call, his opportunity. But he failed.

The Man Who Wasn't Sure

In John 5, one of the many accounts of Jesus's healing miracles is of a man who'd been disabled for thirty-eight years. He spent his days in a place where there were many disabled people, next to some sort of magic pool called Bethesda. It seems that, when the water was somehow stirred up, the first one in got healed.

> When Jesus saw him lying there and learned that he had been in this condition for a long time, he asked him, "Do you want to get well?" (John 5:6)

Interesting question. *Of course he wants to be healed!* we might think on a first reading. He's lying there among the blind, lame, and paralyzed; he's at the place that offers some rare possibility, a chance to get well. He's been there for *thirty-eight years*!

But perhaps the time scale betrays him. Even if he'd not been actually there for the entirety of his *invalid* status, he'd still been there a *long time*. Why had he not tried something else? How desperate was he? Listen to his answer to Jesus's question:

> "Sir," the invalid replied, "I have no one to help me into the pool when the water is stirred. While I am trying to get in, someone else goes down ahead of me." (John 5:7)

Can you see what's missing? The word *yes*. It's a straightforward question: *Do you want to get well?* Answer: *Yes, sir, I do! More than anything*. But instead he just explains the reason for why it's always hard luck for him. If he missed out last time because he had no one to help him, why does he think he'll have a better chance next time, if he still hasn't got a friend at the ready? What is he even doing there? Has it just become a way of life, for his whole life, to lie there being the victim of circumstances? Has it become his identity?

In case we're being too harsh on a man we've never met, and an unfortunate one at that, the rest of the story seems to confirm something of it: Jesus heals him anyway. It was a Sabbath. The Jewish "fun police," rather than being blown away by the miraculous healing of a man who'd been lying in the street longer than half of them had been alive, start whining because he's carrying the mat he'd been lying on all that time.

You might have expected the man to have a few choice words at the ready for people like that. He might have said, *What's wrong with you? Can't you celebrate for once? I've got my life back!* Or, *It's just a mat on a Sabbath! Why don't you look instead at the legs I'm walking on? Why don't you see me as a person?* But no. Instead, he says, *It's not my fault! The fellow who healed me told me to:*

> So they asked him, "Who is this fellow who told you to pick it up and walk?" The man who was healed had no idea who it was, for Jesus had slipped away into the crowd that was there. Later Jesus found him at the temple and said to him, "See, you are well again. Stop sinning or something worse may happen to you." The man went away and told the Jewish leaders that it was Jesus who had made him well. (John 5:12–15)

I'm not sure if Jesus was suggesting that his original condition was due to his sin. But he is certainly saying that there is worse awaiting him if he does not straighten out his heart and his life.

Do you want to get well? Four chapters later, in John 9, Jesus tells us that misfortune is not always a direct result of sin. But the intricate connection between body, mind, and spirit says that true healing involves more than a joyless series of medical appointments and treatments. There is something deeper needed, a whole-person attitude, a healing of the soul.

~

God's work in the world is to "Restore all things" (as Jesus said of John the Baptist, Matt 17:11). Since the first rebellion of Gen 3, the world has been stuck in rebellion, out of fellowship with its Maker, unable to re-enter the garden and eat from the tree of life, spiraling instead into ever-deeper depths of lostness and depravity, hopeless and sick. But the Lord God is the restorer, reaching down: sometimes to individuals, sometimes to cities or nations (especially Israel), and ultimately through the great Redeemer, his Son Jesus. One day we will see all things made new.

But healing now is not a distraction from the ultimate fulfilment of God's promise of restoration—it is a foretaste. As Neil T Anderson puts it, "Shoot for this world and that's all you'll get, and eventually you will lose even that. But shoot for the next world and God will throw in this one as a bonus."[13] Healing in Scripture is part and parcel of the saving work of God—it's spiritual! Examples through Scripture (usually) show healed people as spiritually restored, refreshed. The question we're being asked is, *Do you want this restoration? Do you want to be healed?*

We can follow our cultural model and remain convinced that any spiritual element is a distraction from the actual work of medicine. We can desire physical healing, without wanting to make it too much of a spiritual

13. Anderson, *Bondage Breaker*, 38.

issue. We can desire to be well, but still pray, *Lord, make me well as I trust in the idols of the age. I want restoration without the deep work you require. I want to be well without thinking about my sin, without deeply searching my soul or your commands, and without repentance.* We could do that. Or we could trust that the living God is perfectly able to communicate timelessly through his word, and that what he's given us in Scripture is the real deal, far superior to any limited cultural understanding of getting well.

Confession and Healing

> Is anyone among you in trouble? Let them pray. Is anyone happy? Let them sing songs of praise. Is anyone among you sick? Let them call the elders of the church to pray over them and anoint them with oil in the name of the Lord. And the prayer offered in faith will make the sick person well; the Lord will raise them up. If they have sinned, they will be forgiven. Therefore confess your sins to each other and pray for each other so that you may be healed. The prayer of a righteous person is powerful and effective.
>
> Elijah was a human being, even as we are. He prayed earnestly that it would not rain, and it did not rain on the land for three and a half years. Again he prayed, and the heavens gave rain, and the earth produced its crops.
>
> My brothers and sisters, if one of you should wander from the truth and someone should bring that person back, remember this: Whoever turns a sinner from the error of their way will save them from death and cover over a multitude of sins. (Jas 5:13–20)

Our Story

We didn't understand James chapter 5. At least, we didn't know how it was supposed to work, or what anointing with oil looked like. I have heard it taught many times almost as euphemisms, with the words *healing* and *salvation* being synonyms so that it really didn't have anything to do with physical healing at all. I think I may have even taught it like that in the past. But when faced with Lyndsey's diagnosis, it seemed overwhelmingly appropriate to stop explaining texts away and take them ever so seriously. Still without understanding it well, we nevertheless decided to simply obey it, and asked the elders of the church to gather in prayer and anoint

Lyndsey—which they did with great care and love. In doing it, something astonishing happened, not apparent at the time to anyone else—and the meaning became clear over time in the weeks and months that followed. Lyndsey, in the quiet presence of these core members of the church, and also afterward, in prayer, was able to utterly expose her inner self before the Lord. Hidden, deep, unacknowledged sins—personal and individual, and also received cultural sins—she asked the Lord to reveal all of them, with a thorough willingness to repent, whatever it cost. What a profoundly refreshing time. As drops of olive oil were poured on her head, she received deep reassurance of cleansing, of her Father's love, of forgiveness, acceptance, and restoration.

There are certainly things that make Jas 5 hard for us to understand. To start with, in what sense are we just like Elijah? He seems in a thoroughly different category, praying for rain to stop and start as he did. And if James's argument is based on that, it's hard to believe that our prayers can make sick people well, unless we take healing in some other sense.

However, a little thought—and putting it into practice—brings it wonderfully to life. Elijah's prayer for rain was about something greater: it was about the turning the idolatrous hearts of God's people back to the Lord again. That was the great miracle at Carmel, in 1 Kgs 18. Sinners turned back to the Lord. People were restored to *life* through his prayer.

But it is deeper still, and more specific. James is not simply saying that we should pray for those who have drifted from the faith, with the expectation that they will be restored as in Elijah's day. If that's all we take, we will find ourselves discouraged, wondering why our prayers are still unanswered. James is writing about a particular, conditional, circumstance in which we will see prayers answered and sinners restored—it is when a Christian, laid low by sickness, seeks prayer and anointing, forgiveness and restoration. That is when the power of righteous people's prayers is seen, and works, to save a sinner's soul from death.

Do you see the point of God's "gift" of sickness? We hold on to many sins. Some are the sins of the culture we live in, and we accept them as readily as the air we breathe. Some are the sins of our family, inherited patterns we might think of as normal, or dreadful things that have shaped our family history. Some are individual: ways of thinking or patterns of behavior we refuse to let go of, bad relationships, resentment, even underlying attitudes we have never considered—or never allowed ourselves to consider. When life goes on as normal, we rarely bother to do anything about our sins, or see that they matter. But there is nothing like sickness—be it physical pain, loss of ability, or threat of imminent death—to wake us out of apathy. That is the time to repent—to seek healing at every level, by coming afresh to the Life Giver, starting again with him.

What if the sickness has nothing to do with sin? James 5 also allows for that possibility. It uses the word *if*. It says, "If they have sinned, they will be forgiven." The point is, there *might* be a connection. "Therefore confess your sins to each other and pray for each other so that you may be healed." Don't assume there is no sin connection. Because even if there isn't, this is the opportunity God has given you to examine your heart and grow. Be open before God, honest and humble before him and others, search deep like the psalmist:

> Search me, God, and know my heart;
> test me and know my anxious thoughts.
> See if there is any offensive way in me,
> and lead me in the way everlasting. (Ps 139:23–24)

That is where healing is found.

Our Story (by Lyndsey)

If we take the James passage seriously then we have to consider the connection between sin and sickness, and we have to consider it personally at a very vulnerable level, most especially when we are sick. I have been angry and frustrated when other believers have said to me, "I think many people have been harmed by being told that their sickness is due to sin." And this while I was telling them that my sickness was connected with my sin. It felt as if these nervous and often social-justice-inclined believers were telling me to leave this rigorous self-examination behind me and just embrace the sympathy they wanted to give me for my totally random and unexplainable disease. I think I made them nervous. This risked being unhelpful to my repentance and learning process.

James 5:14–16 is a problem to many conservative Christians. It also seems to be a problem to many charismatic Christians as well. Conservatives find it difficult because it's scary and threatening to their worldview. Charismatics trip up when it's interpreted like some kind of Jedi trick that the believer can magically summon up. I have known a respected and large conservative evangelical church refuse to do the anointing and prayer when asked, as per Jas 5, by a church member. The pastor's response was, "We don't do that here." Imagine refusing to obey any other passage of Scripture. There would be uproar.

But the wake-up call to repent has been so valuable to us. Together with the anointing and prayer, Lyndsey's radical changes to her diet were part of deep repentance for her. It wasn't just the discovery that "sugar feeds cancer" or "pesticides poison us" or "organic has better vitamins." It was the acknowledgment of cultural sins—the laziness of convenience, the greed of demanding food for far cheaper than it ought to be, the indulgence of "treat food" being the only food. People in the developing world tend not to suffer from cancer—and that's not just because they die of other things first. That's a myth. There are plenty of old people in poor countries too. Western diseases expose Western sins.

The diet opened the way to deeper issues still. Her training in psychotherapy had already steered her toward examining her own heart and life, but now the *emotional* roots of her cancer also became important to identify. Anxieties, griefs (some vicarious and inherited), resentments, over-protection, a need to be in control—all such things are associated with sin, either our own, or someone else's. And even the sin of others requires us to examine our own hearts in how we respond.

Far from being introspective, this soul-searching transformed Lyndsey's prayer life. Her love for the Lord and his word have visibly blossomed; her love for other people has grown too.

In my church circles, there has been lots of talk about "lamenting" in recent years. We're all very sorry for (often other people's) sins. But lamenting must go deeper than being sorry; it involves *repenting*. It's praying sincerely, *Lord, what do I need to change? Search me, O God, and know my heart.*

Sometimes, when our hearts are slow, God graciously forces us to go deeper. In his grace, God gave Lyndsey cancer.

Deep Sins and Cultural Sins

So far, you may think I have sounded rather negative about Western medicine. If you have disliked that, please bear with me—I'm afraid it is about to get a little worse! But first, it is important to say that there is much to be thankful for. When a thing has built itself up to the status of being absolute truth, of being unquestionable, it is right to question it. (The prophets of Scripture even mock such things.) But equally, please don't hear me being absolute in its condemnation.

When something is wrong with the body (or mind), it is often right to go to the doctor. Many medical staff are truly caring people. There are plenty of Christians working in heath care, applying their faith by being compassionate, working hard, even praying for patients. There are doctors who invest their vast pay in the kingdom of heaven; I know a church network that deliberately encourages bright young men into medicine specifically so they can be self-supporting in church leadership through part-time medical work. Perhaps most glorious of all, doctors, nurses, and other health-care professionals have used their abilities in the poorest parts of the world, alleviating huge amounts of suffering and proclaiming the good news of Christ as they do so. Many have trained in medicine for that very purpose. Church, school, and hospital have formed a wonderful triad throughout the world wherever the gospel has spread in the last couple of hundred years from Western nations. Glory be to God.

But even the best of Western medicine generally fails to see its limitation. How could it be otherwise? The peer-reviewed papers that form medical journals, which in turn inform medical opinion and practice, depend on expensive research. Such expense can only be afforded by pharmaceutical companies—or governments, backed by pharmaceutical companies. Who could afford research that would genuinely question pharmaceutical products, to find they are not working, or causing harm? Not many.[14] Multinational companies have power to silence dissenting views. It seems to be a dangerous set-up, one in which well-meaning people can administer treatments in good faith based on scientific evidence—but evidence that is not neutral, not without benefit to those behind the scenes who fund it.

It is important to think this through spiritually. If we would dismiss some other form of "healing" for its dangerous spiritual connections, perhaps we should be alert to the dangers of Western healthcare—especially if it is the one most loudly dismissing God's word, steering us away from it, even patronizing and mocking it. Its sins may include corruption and greed. But is it more sinister still? Think about this:

- While the unbelievably cruel human experimentation by Nazi doctors (such as Josef Mengele) on Jewish concentration camp victims rightly shocked the world at the Nuremberg trials, reputable medical literature still contains use of their research.[15] Why was it kept, and what are the moral and spiritual implications of its use?

14. See Kennedy, *Real Anthony Fauci*, for a thorough exposure of corruption within the public-health industry.

15. See, for example, Cohen, "Nazi Medical Experimentation."

- Flesh from parts of aborted babies is commonly used in the pharmaceutical industry in the development of vaccines.[16] I wonder what God thinks about such medicines? I wonder how many of us give a second thought to the contents of what we allow to be jabbed into our children on government recommendation—or legislation?
- Until very recently, medical students learned anatomy by dissecting the dead bodies of people who had donated them to medical research. Perhaps we would immediately recognize witchcraft in someone casting dry bones on the ground, or collecting a lock of hair or drop of blood from an enemy. But if you discovered for the first time that doctors cut up dead people to find what's inside, would that not seem a little dark to you? Who cuts up dead bodies? What would early Christians think of that? What did it do to young medical students' attitudes to the soul and spirit of their future patients, to have had this brutalizing experience of re-forming their thinking about healing into the cold and butcher-like experience of human dissection?
- Experiments on animals are involved in much medical research. While we can appreciate that doing such tests on people would be far worse, we still have to ask what it says about the spiritual health of our methods. Torturing animals to see if drugs work: is that not a little disturbing?

> Nowadays we don't think much of a man's love for an animal; we laugh at people who are attached to cats. But if we stop loving animals, aren't we bound to stop loving humans too?[17]

If we are quick to dismiss medical practices from other cultures on the grounds of spurious spiritual roots, I wonder why we are so slow to question our own. Perhaps we are too easily like giant searchlights, eager to pick out anything that doesn't sit right on the horizon, but never shining the light to expose our own base camp. We are comfortable to find fault with all other methods but our own.

Where could it possibly lead, if the medical system is not all pure and innocent? What moral decisions could result? Given that spiritual forces are always at play, what could we be giving ourselves to, if we are not alert? Where could it lead our culture and society? What will it do for your cancer?

16. See, for example, McKenna, "Use of Aborted Fetal Tissue."
17. Solzhenitsyn, *Cancer Ward*, 294.

Universal Laws

Meanwhile, there are things that are just true because they are true. God has made them that way. And people who may know little or nothing of God still find health-giving and healing gifts from him in medicinal plants, lifestyle, rituals, behavior, or even special places. Certain things work—even if mainstream Western medicine has not acknowledged it.

If you can get over the idea that remarkable healing happens beyond the Christian realm, it is a fascinating thing to look into, and very helpful in seeing how God has ordered life on earth. Some brief examples:

- Lewis Mehl-Madrona, the Native American healer (and Stanford University School of Medicine graduate), describes the value of community, submission to a spiritual power, and willingness to lay everything on the table for change. Relating it to mainstream American medicine, he writes,

  > I believe rational explanations are destroying medicine today, as well as our society at large. To be healed, we need to believe in the possibility of healing, and in a greater world, and in higher powers than our own. We should not trivialize spiritual experiences, saying "It's just *this*, it's only *that*." It is a grave and sometimes fatal mistake to insist that every experience have an explanation that avoids the spirit. We cannot live without spirit. It is arrogant and in a sense dishonest—dishonest because scientific thinkers are not so much trying to explain as trying to explain *away* the miraculous.[18]

- Kelly Turner draws together nine common threads of people whose cancers spontaneously shrink, in ways that doctors cannot explain. It absolutely always involves a deep *dying to self* and rebirth into a better way of being. Other factors are involved, but there is an overarching theme of dying to self in every single case study and each common thread. It is not a Christian book.[19]

- Bessel van der Kolk writes about the connection of mind, brain, and body, in particular regarding the effects of trauma. Trauma contributes to illness. When it comes to healing, talking and drug therapies are one thing, but (among other things) *relationships* are essential.[20]

18. Mehl-Madrona, *Coyote Medicine*, 119.
19. Turner, *Radical Remission*.
20. Van der Kolk, *Body Keeps the Score*.

- Grace Gawler, writing particularly about recovery from breast cancer, emphasizes the importance of a *desire* to be well, as opposed to a fatalistic submission to the lottery of cancer treatments. The medical prognosis, she says, is a kiss of death:

  > To be given a sentence or prognosis which involves the patient taking on a specific time limit for their life, almost always leads to a punctual appointment with death.[21]

- Paul Leendertse goes so far as to argue that cancer is not even a disease, as such:

  > Cancer may be the result of a survival response that our body uses to give us more time to resolve the main source(s) of unresolved stress in our life.[22]

  Recovery is therefore far more about *emotional* work than medical. Leendertse reports a significant success rate in the reversal of stage 3 and 4 cancer through his Root Cause Institute.[23]

- Gabor Maté's bestseller *When the Body Says No* highlights personality types especially prone to cancer. In particular,

  > the most consistently identified risk factor is the inability to express emotions, particularly the feelings associated with anger.[24]

  As he points out, fair-skinned people are physically at higher risk of malignant melanoma; but persuasive research finds emotional factors are every bit as important, and, sadly, "repression is not as easily remediable a problem as sunscreen."[25] I had a skin graft for a small basal cell carcinoma a few years ago. I was given clear advice about avoiding sunshine, but never introduced to the world of learning to understand and express emotions in a healthier way.

- Adding to all this, Simonton, Matthews-Simonton, and Creighton have researched specific timescales relating to stress and cancer:

21. Gawler, *Women of Silence*, 144.

22. Leendertse, *Root Cause*, 57. This assertion is based on the extensive research of Andreas Moritz, unpacked in his publication *Cancer Is Not a Disease*.

23. https://www.rootcauseinstitute.com.

24. Maté, *When the Body*, 99.

25. Maté, *When the Body*, 120.

> We believe that cancer is often an indication of problems elsewhere in an individual's life, problems aggravated or compounded by a series of stresses six to eighteen months prior to the onset of cancer.[26]

It may just be that God is bigger that we thought. (You think?) The reality of Jas 5 is not just a magic trick that sometimes works for Christians; it is built in to the universal laws of God, various aspects of which others have noticed, such as community, humility, and repentance. It adds up; it works in the real world, in people's real experiences. It does not need reinterpreting to fit our material understanding; our material understanding must give way to Scripture, to accept it in a way that other people would more readily do. Community, humility, repentance.

What does the process of repentance look like in a Christian, and why does a form of spiritual healing seem to be open to nonbelievers as well? If God is reaching into the life of a believer sometimes to effect miraculous healing, why doesn't he do this for every believer, and why do nonbelievers sometimes totally reframe their lives and find that their cancers have shrunk or even disappeared? The fact is that repentance and confession are things that many Christians take lightly—or at least their small-minded and nervous worldview leads to an unambitious perception of what is possible.

Meanwhile, others, not even knowing God, are willing to give up everything that may have caused their condition.

Our Story (some reflections by Lyndsey)

Very sadly, when somebody has a serious diagnosis and somebody close to them, or even their doctor, suggests cleaning up their life in terms of diet and exercise, that is often too difficult to entertain by the sick person. Seriously. It seems impossible for some people to do something like cutting out sugar or processed food. These things seem beyond us in our convenience-laden Western existence. If we can't do something about our diet and lifestyle, then there's absolutely no way we can do the "dying to self" that Jas 5 is talking about. It's basic. How much are you willing to change? How much are you able to change? What are you enslaved to that means you can't change? What are your idols? I am not dismissing the genuine addictions we live under. But I want us to recognize that they are addictions and are absolutely not acceptable for those who follow Christ. And if nonbelievers can ditch their idols in a similar

26. Simonton et al., *Getting Well Again*, 10.

process, then if we have the Holy Spirit of God, we can too, even if it takes time and therapeutic work.

If God has put a serious diagnosis in your life then he's calling you to change. And by change, I mean change everything. Become a new person. What is God teaching you with this diagnosis? Why do you have this disease? If you think it's totally random then you haven't understood God and you also haven't understood the way the world works. (God and the way the world works are very closely connected.)

If healing is possible by confession and repentance, then we should confess and repent. James says, if he has sinned, he will be forgiven. Amazing. You will be forgiven. Therefore confess your sins to one another, so that you may be healed. Let's not hide from this passage any more, let's sit and allow it to penetrate our thinking and our emotions, and let's admit: I'm all wrong. Jesus, help me to change even the things I have refused to change before.

Many cultures and belief systems have healing rituals, they genuinely engage with the spiritual world and they see real and lasting healing of all sorts of sickness. This is undeniably evidenced, and Christians are often unwilling to look at this reality because it might undermine their faith in Jesus. But it doesn't have to—and ought not to. The reason such healing rituals work is because the process of surrender is the same as the Christian should be aiming for. It's just the way the world works. This is one of God's universal laws.

If the Christian believer's internal narrative is threatened by this, then not only is their understanding of God way too small, but also they will not be healed. It is too easy to imagine our worldview is the definition of true faith—that anything undermining it is a threat to our salvation. But if a Christian thinks that way, their belief is operating at the level of uncertainty. It's a tentative hope and belief, not a knowing trust. Such an attitude is afraid to risk complete and total change; the person doesn't have a knowledge of the God who will catch them when they are willing to fall backward into the unknown. It is ok to have a weak and unsure faith. But weak and unsure faith can grow, and sickness and a healing anointing is the opportunity to grow. Don't refuse it.

Your Cancer Diagnosis

We never know what's round the corner. We just have to face the thing God has given us now. A cancer diagnosis? Ok, so that's the next stage of life God has given us—cancer. Let's trust and obey him in this.

It may all be well and good when churches set a five- or ten-year plan, with mission strategies spelled out, and even particular outcomes. Ambitions and forward thinking are ok. But really, we have no idea what will happen; and (have you noticed?) such strategies never include dealing with a serious diagnosis in the church. Yet that is where God brings real growth. That is where God does his deep work. Our primary task is not to plan the unknown future; it is to obey him now, in what he gives us now. That is all we are as his creatures.

People can imagine that God sometimes acts, but usually doesn't. Psalms can even use this language; it feels that way in our experience. But God always acts. As well as guiding our every move, such that even the hairs on our head are all numbered (as Jesus says in Matt 10:30), he has also set laws of cause and effect. State of mind affects health. Sin has consequences. Seeking God's face has consequences.

James 5, like all of Scripture, might raise questions it doesn't answer. Why me? Why now? What about people who don't have the capacity to search their souls in humble repentance to seek forgiveness, such as young children, or those who've never heard of James 5?

We don't understand God's ways, why he treats people in different ways, gives different trials, or gives different outcomes. Sometimes we can have a vague idea, or guess. But we don't know. What we do know is that cancer (or any diagnosis) is an opportunity to do the soul-searching and repentance: "*If* they have sinned . . . " That's the response. Pray; seek forgiveness and healing.

James 5 is not to condemn those who haven't responded as it says. Sometimes an illness is so advanced, or "treatment" has taken such a toll, that someone can no longer bear to face the past or no longer has the strength to think. We will all die.

But for those who are able to hear it: Do you want to get well? The question ought not to embarrass us. *Yes* is not the wrong answer. Our hope in death is not the opposite of a zest for life. Death simply brings focus to life. Do you want to get well?

Our forefathers seemed to be quite comfortable to pour out their hearts, publicly and passionately. In the Anglican Book of Common Prayer, the welcome to the morning gathering does not include notices about where to find the toilets, a joke or anecdote from the week, or who has a birthday. It is a serious call to repentance and prayer:

> Dearly beloved brethren, the Scripture moveth us in sundry places to acknowledge and confess our manifold sins and wickedness . . . ask those things which are requisite and necessary, as well for the body as the soul.[27]

Did you notice the last bit? Confession of sin and heartfelt prayer are not just about the soul but the body. Pray for life now. If you have cancer—and if you haven't done so already—ask the elders of the church to pray over you, to anoint you with oil in the name of the Lord. Because the prayer of faith will save the one who is sick.

27. Church of England, *Book of Common Prayer*, 2.

5

Governments Are Against Us

The kings of the earth rise up
and the rulers band together
against the LORD and against his anointed, saying,
"Let us break their chains
and throw off their shackles."

Ps 2:2–3

Government secrecy is not for security reasons, overwhelmingly—it's just to prevent the population here from knowing what's going on.

Noam Chomsky, *Understanding Power*

IN THE TOWN WHERE I live, there is a man with a sandwich board—one of those old-fashioned, home-made walking placards. He is seen most often outside the local council offices or at the busiest traffic-lights in town, turning to face the oncoming traffic as the lights change. He is part of the town furniture; he has been displaying his simple message for at least as long as I have lived here—over twenty years. Occasionally a word on his front and back white rectangle is changed—crossed out and replaced with different color marker-pen—as different local government councils take charge. But the basic message reads, *Tory Council Corrupt!* or *Labor Council Corrupt!* or *Police Corrupt!*

There was presumably something particularly painful and frustrating that got him started on his mission. I don't know what it was—I have never engaged him in conversation. (I am afraid of the commitment, of not being able to escape.) I don't know how much he is achieving, and I do think there are better things he could do with his life. But one thing I have little doubt about: he's right. There is corruption in the council, and the police, and, in fact, all forms of human government. He knows it; many people know it. It is a fact of life.

It's the sort of thing you might hear on any building site or in any men's locker room when talk of politics comes up: "They're all liars!" "Can't trust any of them!" "Bunch of hypocrites!" "They hate us!" My observation is, you don't hear much of that sort of talk among Christians. Churches might be divided along political lines, or upset about particular issues. But wholesale mistrust—not so much.

Perhaps that's a good thing. Perhaps it's because Christians like to show proper respect to people in charge. Maybe they don't like to slander, especially without knowing all the facts. It could be that Christians like to notice the good things and appreciate the hard work governments do and always look on the bright side. But I am convinced that there is something else going on. The refusal of many Christians to view their government as a threat does not come from a generous heart or a biblical conviction—though it may be dressed up that way. The real reason is that the church has got confused.

There are telltale signs. For one, most churches are quite slow to spot when government moves are anti-Christ and anti-human. Other people ask the obvious questions: "If it's true, why do they have to keep saying it? Why do they keep shouting at us? What's even the point of these new laws?" Less so among Christians.

For another, Christians aren't even that clear about what the Bible says about governments, on the whole. They have their go-to passages about governments; but most have never thought about the Bible's overall picture on the subject.

And third, many Christians tend to be a little uneasy around politics, unsure whether to engage or not, whether to love or hate, whether to appreciate or fear. When Martin Luther began to see clearly that the authorities were fundamentally anti-Christian, it gave him a freedom and clarity in relating to them:

> Luther's certainty and confidence and faith and courage in speaking to no less than the pope are at least impressive, but he would speak just as openly with the emperor himself.[1]

Christians elsewhere in the world seem to engage with government with a similar clear voice, freedom, and confidence. Some *unbelievers* in our own society do the same, as they realize what they're dealing with. I would like more Western Christians to enjoy a right relationship with their government too. I want to help repair the blind spot.

But why is there a blind spot in the first place?

The Background to the Blind Spot

The apostle Paul was tearing his hair out as he wrote his first letter to the church in Corinth. The issue in chapter 6 was about lawsuits. Arguments and wrongs got out of hand; church members were heard saying to one another, "I'll see you in court!" So Paul began addressing the issue with two basic facts:

> If any of you has a dispute with another, do you dare to take it before the ungodly for judgment instead of before the Lord's people? Or do you not know that the Lord's people will judge the world? (1 Cor 6:1–2)

One fact is about who *they* are: *the Lord's people*. They are God's holy people, his precious children, who will judge the world. "Remember who you are!" he appeals; "have some dignity and take some responsibility."

The other fact is about who runs the law courts. These are the secular authorities. Paul describes them with one word: *ungodly*.

There are plenty of caveats for another discussion, about times to go to court and generally getting involved with the state authorities. But Paul sums up those authorities with a word: *ungodly*. It's very clear.

Yet I suspect some will have flinched even at the statement that titles this chapter: *governments are against us*. Why is it not black and white for us, when the apostle Paul is so matter-of-fact? At least part of the answer lies in a combination of the following three things.

1. Metaxas, *Luther*, 190.

The Lack of Spiritual Clarity

Do you remember Eph 6? "For our struggle is not against flesh and blood, but against the rulers, against the authorities, against the powers of this dark world and against the spiritual forces of evil in the heavenly realms" (Eph 6:12). If we saw the world through those eyes, we would have a far greater alertness to the state of things, especially with regard to people of influence. We ought to be asking ourselves, "What is the spiritual significance of this law, that debate, that decision?" Of course, our lack of thinking about spiritual significance is made worse by the lazy-headedness that comes with receiving screen-based information. It is too easy to receive news passively without thinking, "What is really going on? What is it really saying? What are the implications? Are there hidden agendas?"

If ordinary men in the locker room see evil when they look at government, how much more should Christians spot spiritual forces at play? Especially because, as children of their heavenly Father, they are the prime targets of evil forces.

The Legacy of Christendom

Christendom—that's the name given to the spread of countries that are effectively run as Christian countries. Western nations have been hugely shaped by the gospel and Christian culture. We are so used to people being nice that it undoes our own doctrine of sin! Political leaders have been influenced by the gospel, or even converted—it seems wrong for us to see them as an enemy most of the time. Much of what our governments do is good; so how can it be helpful to make a sweeping statement about them being bad?

Well, let's try and think that one through biblically.

The Love of Comfort

It's painful to mention this as a problem. But sometimes Christians even go against their own conscience to go along with government agendas or decisions. It is easier to comply than to complain. Sure, our governments get things wrong from time to time, and we are shocked when they do—sometimes even shocked enough to sign an online petition. But it all settles down, and we get on with life. We like not to think too hard, not to bother, not to need to take action, not to change our lifestyle. So long as I've got my job, my car, and my Wi-Fi I won't bother thinking about what the significance of it all is.

The result of this combination of factors is threefold—and actually quite ugly. First, it *distorts* God's word. It leads to half-baked Bible study, reshaping Scripture according to assumptions into convenient proof-texts on the subject of governments, rather than being transformed by the living word that instills courage in the church.

Second, the assumed mindset *divides*. Christians who sound the alarm relating to government actions and policies are dismissed, labelled *conspiracy theorists* or other such dismissive terms, and generally considered a bit of a pain. The majority avoid such people, pity them, or worry about their salvation. Christians should not get too involved in politics.

Third, the dominant Western church mindset *destroys*. It is *self*-destructive. When you live in peacetime, you get soft and flabby. As people say in my neck of the woods, "Some people are built for comfort, not speed!" But it's a dangerous thing when the church is not fighting fit. Well, the church may have forgotten it is at war. But the enemy has not forgotten its own reality, or that the war is real. And it becomes an easy job for it to bully the church out of existence. Governments play a significant part in that.

The aim of this chapter is not to uncover the deep faults of current Western governments. (There is much written to expose shocking details, for those willing to find out.) It is also not my aim to create fear. That is the work of our enemy. What I would like you to see from this chapter is the reality of where governments fit into God's great plan. And what that will mean for us, to put it in a nutshell, is: *obey them; but don't trust them*. See if you think that is reasonable, by the end.

To say that *governments are against us* is not to suggest that they are only evil all the time. Some may be pretty good; all may do some good things. Christ, on his great throne, has appointed them to theirs; it does not follow that they honor his. The hearts of kings and governors are in God's hands; but that doesn't make them the friends of God's children. Western Christians may have a much nicer experience of our governments than many of our fellow Christians—most of whom have a very clear understanding of what their governments represent. Some of us have even enjoyed overtly Christian national leadership from time to time. Yet texts like the one from Ps 2, quoted at the start of this chapter, should make us a little wary even at the best of times.

And we are not at the best of times now.

Romans 13 Is Not the Whole Story

The Nazis are everyone's favorite enemy. They are our go-to bad guys. I'm told that if you put *Hitler* in the title of your book, it doubles the sales. (I couldn't quite force it into this book's title.) I guess the reason we're so fascinated by them is that they are the worst people we can think of, and they existed in fairly recent history—and not so far away either. When it comes to politics, it is amazing how often people compare their opponents to Nazis—whatever side of the political spectrum one happens to be coming from. And that says something interesting about ourselves too: we love to place ourselves on the good side—we're always the good guys. Perhaps that's another reason we like talk about Nazis—we're on the side that did good. Some of us.

The Nazis liked to quote Scripture to church leaders, to persuade them to fall in line. Their favorite text was from Rom 13:

> Let everyone be subject to the governing authorities, for there is no authority except that which God has established. The authorities that exist have been established by God.
>
> Consequently, whoever rebels against the authority is rebelling against what God has instituted, and those who do so will bring judgment on themselves. For rulers hold no terror for those who do right, but for those who do wrong. Do you want to be free from fear of the one in authority? Then do what is right and you will be commended. For the one in authority is God's servant for your good. But if you do wrong, be afraid, for rulers do not bear the sword for no reason. They are God's servants, agents of wrath to bring punishment on the wrongdoer. Therefore, it is necessary to submit to the authorities, not only because of possible punishment but also as a matter of conscience.
>
> This is also why you pay taxes, for the authorities are God's servants, who give their full time to governing. Give to everyone what you owe them: If you owe taxes, pay taxes; if revenue, then revenue; if respect, then respect; if honor, then honor. (Rom 13:1–7)

It is hard when opponents quote Scripture to prove their point. So it is worth our asking, what is actually wrong with the Nazis' use of this passage? Because we would want to be careful not to make the same mistake when we use it as our proof-text for relating to governments. After all, it does seem pretty persuasive in its clarity. You might not agree with the regime, but the commands are clear: *submit*, *do good*, and *pay what you owe them*.

What makes their use of it wrong is both the *context* and the *flavor*.

The context is multilayered, including the whole Bible, the historical regime of Rome, and the letter itself. The Bible as a whole encourages a certain wariness toward earthly governments. The context of Rome is not one of happy partnership with the church. And the context of the letter ought to make Christians pretty uncomfortable to have it quoted by the governing authorities to tell the church to fall in line regardless of the government's actions. Just the previous verse (and bear in mind, chapter divisions are a later addition to our Scriptures) states, "Do not be overcome by evil, but overcome evil with good" (Rom 12:21). By following immediately with the paragraph about governments, there is an underlying assumption that we are dealing with something evil here.

That changes the flavor of the commands in Rom 13. It is about being a good citizen—not living under a good government. Yes, the institution of government is God's, and rulers punish evil and reward good. Government is better than anarchy; it is God's kind means to maintain law and order on earth. So fall in line with that: submit (that's always hard, when it comes down to detail); do what's right (the thing we always want from everyone else); pay the taxes you owe (grrr!); pay the respect and honor you owe. But what is quite meant by that last one? How much respect and honor *do* we owe? Some, by virtue of the government's authority and title; but also some by virtue of their character?

Perhaps the flavor is best illustrated by comparing it to marriage. There are certain parallels between the two sets of relationships. (Sorry if I've just spoiled your marriage by saying that.) Both are instituted by God to be a blessing to society. Both have a given order. Wives are commanded in Scripture to submit to their husbands (Eph 5:22).

But it doesn't follow that every marriage is a happy one, or that every woman must *trust* her husband. Some simply can't. In 1 Peter, wives are told to submit to husbands who don't believe the gospel in order to win them over (1 Pet 3:1). The command doesn't assume a Song of Songs paradise; in fact, the women are told, "Do what is right and do not give way to fear" (1 Pet 3:5). The marriages in mind are not ideal; but the instructions are because there are still right ways to behave within them, which make the best of the opportunity to glorify God.

It is the same in relation to government. The commands of Rom 13 do not assume a happy relationship. They don't assume we are on the same side.

So let's explore the wider subject of government. Let's see where the governments of the West fit in with God's plan for the world. And let's see what this really means in relating to them.

What Is a "Nation"?

This is a good question to get us thinking about the bigger picture. I wonder how you would answer it. The direction of our cultural teaching makes *nation* a vague concept these days, and borders so fluid that nations are unimportant. With multinational companies and global production lines, you could find yourself in the shopping center of any major city and barely know what country you are in, such is the familiarity of brands and styles. There is often very little to identify something as specifically *Dutch* or *French* or *German* any more.

Such identity is often seen as a definite negative too. People who value their nation too highly should be given a label: they are *nationalistic*, even *racist* or *xenophobic*. But the notion of nations is a real thing. And whenever culture strives against reality, it finds it is inconsistent. On my own island, for example, the English are supposed to despise all love of country, but the Welsh and the Scots are encouraged to relish theirs. (No, I'm not bitter. But thank you for your concern: I'm ok.)

The concept of a nation is a biblical one. Genesis 10 is where they are first defined and an important place to start. After the flood, people multiplied and spread out across the earth. They formed clans around their patriarchal heads and grew into distinct peoples that identified as nations. It is part of the positive growth of the human race. Genesis 10 lists seventy nations that sprung from Noah's sons, and carries the sense that this symbolic number[2] goes on multiplying. The different directions of travel as people groups spread hint at the development of varying ethnic distinctions; and the names, origins, relationships, and places give each a sense of unique identity. So, from this point on, there are nations on earth. Each one has its own:

- *Language*—thanks to the attempt of some of them (at least) to build a great city with a skyscraper on the plains of Babylonia, in Gen 11. God was not having it that people would unite together to reach heaven and glorify themselves. Where would it end? So he confused their languages to stop their cooperation. And, under his judgment, they dispersed to the ends of the earth in disunity. (And then they formed the United Nations to try again.)

  Languages change over time, for convenience or political reasons. They can be imposed or banned from use. But language is still

2. The number seven always carries the sense of totality or completion in Scripture, and multiplying by ten (or a thousand) often expands the completion to a sense of vastness.

a powerful part of identity for many people. (Visit Wales to see for yourself.)

- *Territory.* That is one of the refrains of Gen 10—each nation has a territory in which it lives, a land it calls its own, with boundaries. As history goes on, boundaries are moved by one means or another, so our present-day political world map marks territories that often do not correspond completely with national identity. But a land is an important aspect to being a people, such that a displaced people are generally an unhappy people—literally "unsettled."
- *King.* (Or sometimes queen.) In recent history, many nations have been experimenting with other forms of governing authority, such as democratically elected presidents or parliaments. While democracy has been promoted as an absolute good, it clearly hasn't solved the world's political problems, and, in the final analysis, is not all that different to the old idea of king—they, too, could be elected or deposed by popular opinion, and made decisions that affected the lives of people under their rule. However we try to reorganize it, nations are defined by having leaders. Deuteronomy 17:14 tells us Israel's experience: "When you enter the land the Lord your God is giving you and have taken possession of it and settled in it, and you say, 'Let us set a king over us like all the nations around us' . . . " See the assumption, the norm and expectation? Nations have kings. They have a figurehead, a leader who rules.
- *God.* That's right—each nation has its own god. It was the Lord God, the true and living God, who handed out the nations to the various gods. Yes, God is the Lord of all the earth; but he effectively leased nations out to lesser spiritual beings. According to Deut 32:8, the seventy nations were divided because of the number of the sons of God:

> When the Most High gave to the nations their inheritance,
> when he divided mankind,
> he fixed the borders of the peoples
> according to the number of the sons of God. (ESV)

Michael Heiser[3] helpfully unpacks this idea: these *gods* are in no way equal to God, but are nonetheless real spiritual beings. Many Old Testament nations had their particular idols made of wood and stone, but behind them were living spirits. These spirits are not regarded as good ones by Scripture. Some are positively nasty, and as a result,

3. Heiser, "Deuteronomy 32:8."

the nations that lived under them performed "abominable practices" (Deut 18:9).

Still today some nations clearly identify with particular religious allegiances, such as India, Japan, or Bhutan. As such, they are under the influence of certain spiritual beings. I'm not sure how the ongoing spread and evolution of nations relates to the specific gods linked to the original seventy. But nations today still have identifiable belief systems and values. These are spiritual values, and therefore under the influence of spiritual forces. Your nation, to some degree and in some sense, is ruled by a spiritual power. This power is ultimately under the power of the true God; but at the same time, it has a force and nature of its own.

Israel was unique—in a category of its own. It was not numbered among the seventy nations, but instead the promised offspring of Abraham, Isaac, and Jacob were to be a blessing *to* the nations, bringing them hope and life. Israel is set apart. In the words of Balaam, they are "a people who live apart and do not consider themselves one of the nations" (Num 23:9).

For four hundred years of its early history, Israel, as a nation, was slave to another nation, living in Egypt. Later on, Judah (the remaining part of Israel) lived exiled in Babylon for seventy years. These episodes of Israel's history, the exile to Babylon in particular, become a helpful parallel in the Bible of the New Testament church: they are God's people, set aside as his—yet they live among the nations, not in the land of their own.

So, that is you, if you are a Christian. You live in one of these nations of the earth. You are resident in a particular nation, that has its own identity, set of beliefs and values, and place on the map. Even the United States of America, with its amazingly gospel-based constitution, or the Afrikaners, with their Bible-based ethos, are not the definition of God's country. In various respects they will be utterly at odds with God's kingdom. Even if you live in modern-day Israel, it is now no different in this respect.[4]

Christians, therefore, are in the slightly unstable position of belonging to two nations: the kingdom of God and the kingdom or republic they happen to live in. They have citizenship of a nation on earth and are also citizens of heaven. As the second-century *Epistle to Diognetus* puts it, "They dwell in their own countries, but simply as sojourners. As citizens, they share in all things with others, and yet endure all things as if foreigners."[5] Christians

4. I appreciate that readers will have varying views on the status of modern-day Israel. But to live there as a Christian is not to live somewhere that has all the values of heaven, our true home. Its national values are not synonymous with God's values.

5. Mathetes, *Epistle to Diognetus*, ch. 5.

living in the most defiled nations (like the ones Israel was to drive out of Canaan, Lev 18:24) must still play their part as citizens. Christians living in the most gospel-shaped nations will still find themselves as aliens—if they are true to their faith.

The Kings of the Earth

All nations have governments in some form or another. For shorthand, we will call the leaders of nations, as the book of Revelation does, "the kings of the earth."

Revelation might be the playground of religious eccentrics, but at one level it is pretty straightforward to understand. As a work of art in its own right, it can be helpful to liken it to an impressionist painting. If you get too obsessed with one detail, the colored blobs of oil paint make no sense. It's when you step back and see their place in the whole thing that it comes to life. It is the same with Revelation: rather than getting stuck on particular details, step back and see how those details make up the glorious whole.

Looking at the theme of governments in Revelation, the message is clear. "The kings of the earth" are almost like a character in the play. As the sky recedes like a scroll in chapter 6, the kings of the earth lead a long list of people who flee (6:15). Why? Because they are against God, and his day of wrath has come.

By chapter 17, we have met Babylon, the seductive driving force behind the nations of the world. That is what Babylon represents in Revelation: the whole anti-Christ culture, the thing that lures nations and their leaders to oppose God by the offer of indulgence, a sense of power, of freedom. With her, "the kings of the earth committed adultery" (17:2). She is not the wife they ought to have, but the prostitute they are in bed with, "intoxicated with the wine of her adulteries" (17:2).

Stepping back to view the picture, that says something chilling—and realistic—about national leaders as we experience them. They ought to rule knowing there is a greater King over them. But they are seduced by the power that their position in the world offers them, and have cause to be ashamed before God.

It gets deeper. The prostitute, Babylon (the seductive culture), has a pimp—a dark, sinister figure in the shadows. He doesn't care for the woman; he only uses her as bait for his business. In Rev 17 he is called "the beast." He and his agents (pictured as his ten horns) are in absolute opposition to God. Yes, God uses even the beast to fulfil his ultimate purposes. But the demonic beast seeks only to undermine God. And where do the kings of the earth fit in? "The woman you saw is the great city that rules over the kings of the earth" (17:18). That's right: leaders of nations are under the dominion of the woman. They can't resist her. And the woman is controlled by the devil.

That is a picture worth dwelling on. Revelation is not suggesting that the kings of the earth are the source of evil, or possessed by the devil. But the devil mightily uses them as his tools, manipulating them by the seductive power of the woman he controls. Perhaps that is why we see so many enter politics with the best intentions but end up crooked: Babylon seduces them with promises of power, fame, reputation, wealth, indulgence, success, popularity, or influence. They can't resist her any more than the Greek sailors could resist the Sirens.

At Babylon's destruction in chapter 18, it is the kings who are the first to mourn over her—because she gave them their status and luxury. They have grown to love her so much they need her. They lived for her. Losing her is devastating. So in chapter 19, "the beast and the kings of the earth and their armies gathered together to wage war against the rider on the horse and his army" (19:19). Who is this on the horse? He is the "Word of God" (v. 13), the "King of kings and Lord of lords" (v. 16). When the battle lines are drawn, the kings of the earth fight against Christ. The beast cares nothing for Babylon or the people under her: "The beast and the ten horns you saw will hate the prostitute. They will bring her to ruin and leave her naked; they will eat her flesh and burn her with fire" (Rev 17:16). But the kings of the earth do love her and don't see that they are being totally played by Satan.

It is not normal that the kings of the earth should be united, is it? Yet here they are, united against Christ Jesus, when all is stripped bare for the final showdown. They lose, by the way—because God's authority and sovereign plan always remain unthreatened. In the end, birds gorge on their flesh (19:21). The warning to the church is to avoid being on their side. The encouragement to the church is that even the greatest and worst of them will be unceremoniously wiped out.

It is only in the new creation, in the new, sinless, everlasting order reserved for those loyal to the Lamb, that the nations walk by the light of the Lamb and the kings of the earth bring their glory to him (21:24). Again stepping back to see the big picture, instead of getting bogged down with questions of how the new world order will be governed, just imagine nations living completely in worship of Jesus! Imagine what it would look like for kings to be utterly and uncompromisingly committed to Christ! If we will only take the time for that thought to soak in, we will realize how different it is now. We will realize that this is not a Christian country that we live in now; that living in *relative* peace and safety is not good enough; that merely having leaders who allow us to carry on being Christians is not the end goal.

Chewing over the teaching of Revelation does not only show us how our nations and governments fall short. It tells us there is more behind the scenes too—dark powers lurking. This accounts for the strange Orwellian[6] political alliances that we see, the *madness of crowds*,[7] and the strange (sometimes imperceptibly slow, sometimes astonishingly quick) turns of events and new ideas that are adopted. I am not sure exactly of the role of such entities as the United Nations, the World Economic Forum, or the World Health Organization, who really controls them, or how they operate. Their existence, at least, illustrates that there are powers greater than governments: they speak, and governments jump to attention. But, however they operate, there are deeper and darker powers still behind them: human, demonic—or some strange combination of both. Occasional glimpses come to light of the most shocking demonic practices by some of the great and mighty of the earth (think Epstein Island, Diddy parties, and dark rituals unearthed within secret societies). But why should we be surprised? It is only the picture that Revelation paints for us: there are very dark forces at play.

The conspiracy theorists, whoever they are, are right. All Christians should be absolutely clear that there is conspiracy at every level. Scripture tells us "the nations conspire" (Ps 2:1). Revelation exposes the conspiracy of people, governments, cultures, and spiritual beings against God. It is not a cause for panic—although when you first take it in, it can feel very troubling. It is the way the world is.

As a child, you ought to be sheltered from the worst horrors of life. But as you grow, it is right to face reality more fully, as appropriate to each stage of life. Christians should not remain in the blissful naïveté of ignorance like a small child. They should face reality, as much as is reasonable for them to take in.

Where are you up to in seeing the spiritual realities? When you notice examples of things that indicate that there are dark powers at play in the ruling of nations in the world of today, you simply start noticing more and more, such that people talk of *going down a rabbit hole*. After a while, you can reach the point where nothing surprises you any more: evil is worse than you thought, more prevalent, more ingrained in every part of society. You could also quickly reach the point of being overwhelmed with details of information and inner workings that we simply don't all need to know. (It

6. It is one of the many profound observations of George Orwell's *Nineteen Eighty-Four* that sworn enemies can suddenly unite against a common enemy, leaving everyone bewildered, but accepting it as the new "normal."

7. . . . to quote the title of Douglas Murray's 2019 book. He explores the absurdity of what people will believe under ever-new waves of ideology.

could easily drive you to madness.) What is important to know is that God knows all about it. This is the world God has reached into to rescue. It is the world over which God is in complete control, using even the worst to fulfil his purposes.

Revelation does not tell us to gain a morbid fascination over every dark conspiracy. But it does help us to know the enemy; we at least shouldn't bury our heads in the sand and pretend all is well. With it in view, we will notice things—such as when governments sanction death-loving projects like abortion and euthanasia, or rob life by promoting isolation, or impose oppressive control, or undermine family life and marriage. Such things should be seen for what they are. Evil is evil: even—or perhaps worst of all—when delivered with a charming smile or earnest brow.

Life on the Ground

So how does it look to relate to *the kings of the earth*, to put Rom 13 into practice, knowing what we know about governments?

The Bible has plenty to say on this. First, it acknowledges what we see in our experience: that there is a wide range of governments, and God's children have different experiences of living under them. Some are hideously hostile—like Pharaoh, the demonic king of Egypt, killing Hebrew babies and despising the living God, or Herod and his determination to annihilate the Messiah. They are the extreme bad guys, the Hitlers of the Bible age. There are governments in the world today that openly and passionately oppose the church of God.

But opposite examples are also found in Scripture, like the mysterious, Christ-like Melchizedek, king of Salem, of Gen 14:18, or the queen of Sheba in 1 Kgs 10. They are very friendly to God's people. And there are national leaders in some places today that seek to strengthen Christ's church.

Some kings in the Bible are even led to worship the true God, such as in the mind-blowing story of the Babylonian King Nebuchadnezzar in Dan 4—a chapter he wrote himself as a testimony to God's grace. The story is especially amazing, because the Babylonians are the true bad guys of the Old Testament. They are the ones who carried out God's judgment on his people and had no respect for them or their God—think of Belshazzar's guests desecrating the sacred goblets taken from God's temple, in Dan 5. There are several monarchs or presidents through history who have stood out for their serious devotion to Christ. Some have lost their lives for it.

Each category obviously involves a different way of relating to the government, in many respects. But if we want the Bible's clearest teaching on how, in practice, to relate, we need to go to the book of Esther.

There are four things that make Esther such a great guide for us. The first is its place in history. Israel's time in Egypt and Judah's in Babylon certainly show what it's like for God's people to live in hostile nations. But even Babylon is not typical because the nature of the relationship is one of victors and slaves from the start. But following the exile, when the Jews were allowed home in the days of Ezra and Nehemiah, not all went. Many remained as a scattered people across the empire of the new superpower, the Persians. So here were God's people, like Christians today, having to navigate their dual citizenship.

Second, Esther is grouped in the Hebrew Bible among the *wisdom* literature. That means that it's not primarily an account of history—it's more than that. It's about how to navigate life in this world. And Esther herself has to relate to the king and his officials as one of God's people living among the nations. This is God's direct wisdom about relating to one of the kings of the earth.

The third way that Esther serves as guidance in relating to governments is that King Xerxes is portrayed as a typical king. Actually, *typical* is not the right word—he is more of a caricature of everything a king stands for. The book reads a little like a Shakespeare play in terms of the almost comedy characters. Xerxes kindly left many of his belongings and records to the British Museum in London, which only confirm what we know of him through Esther: he is the extreme of everything about a king—his power, wealth, and influence border on the ridiculous. And yet (in keeping with Revelation), in spite of the overwhelming appearance to the contrary, he actually has no power at all: he is subject to his advisors, his passions, and, ultimately, the unstoppable hand of God.

Which leads to the fourth way Esther shows us how to live under the kings of the earth: Xerxes is not the main character at all. Although it *feels* as if he is. To be his ally is to enjoy his protection and wealth, and even parties at his palace. But to cross him, even walk toward him uninvited—even if you're his wife!—is to face likely impalement within the hour. (I think Xerxes had been studying Rom 13 ahead of time.) Yet all this, and the tremendous tension involved in living under it, is merely a sideshow to the work that the unseen (and unmentioned) God is doing. It is just a means to God achieving his purposes to rescue his people and defeat their enemies.

As for living under the kings of the earth, the book makes it clear: the king might even be your husband, but he's not a friend you trust unguardedly. You tread very carefully. He might like you—but you are to be wary.

The king is a looming, oppressive (but sometimes nice) figure of dread and power. But *God's* guiding of politics is the thing to watch and trust. The king just needs to be carefully navigated as the people of God bravely obey their God and see his purposes come to pass. In the final analysis, the king himself is something of a joke: with all his power, he can't control his own affairs.

Which all sounds strangely familiar—a national leader who makes decisions that affect your life (and death), but who can't even keep his private life in order. Esther paints the picture of any government leader who ever lived.

There is more too. Mordecai is Esther's adopted father and a Christ-like figure in the book. He is a model citizen, informing Xerxes of a plot against his life, even when Mordecai had every reason to detest the king. (I'm not sure I would have acted with such loyalty if the king had taken my daughter by force into his harem.) Yet there's a limit. Haman is second-in-command to Xerxes and a devil-figure in the book. When everyone dutifully takes the knee before Haman, as commanded, Mordecai refuses. He alone stays standing, conspicuous among the other players. He disobeyed the government when their rule meant honoring the enemies of God. It was the same principle as Peter and the apostles before the Jewish council in Acts 5:29: "We must obey God rather than men" (ESV). You might also be reminded of Daniel, boldly and courageously disobeying the edict of King Darius against Christian prayer (Dan 6:10). There is a limit to the Rom 13 command to submit to governing authorities: that command is never an excuse to disobey God.

In the New Testament, the Xerxes flavor of government—frightening, yet somewhat ridiculous—continues: the backdrop of Rome through the Gospels has just the same feel. The Romans are a threat, a force of evil against God's people, hostile overlords. On occasion, that comes shockingly to the surface, such as the time when Pilate had slaughtered some Galileans together with their sacrifices in Luke 13:1. Yet Pontius Pilate, the local governor, even when brutally executing the Lord of Glory, is a tragic figure, unable to execute obvious justice, unable to control the mob, unable even to heed his own wife's warnings. He is left pathetically washing his hands while committing the greatest crime in history—all under God's sovereign and glorious plan.

And so, through the rest of history, governments have followed suit. They have at times been awful toward Christians and at other times quite favorable. Yet always lurking beneath, even at times when the church has seen greatest favor, there is a threat: the threat of mighty hostility.

Government at Its Best: The Blessed West

No, I haven't turned into a rapper. But it's important to understand something of the heritage of the West, to help us put together two seemingly opposite ideas: the government being hostile (the claim of this chapter), on one hand, and the relatively positive experience of government enjoyed by Western Christians, on the other. Relationships are rarely two-dimensional. We can appreciate what is good—and see God's gracious hand over it—while still bearing the pictures of Revelation and Esther in mind.

Jesus told his disciples to go and "make disciples of all nations" (Matt 28:19)—not just *from* all nations, but *of* all nations. Therefore Christians down the ages have obediently sought to win nations by winning governors of nations—or, at least, getting them onside—so there is the possibility of evangelizing the people.

One only needs to read accounts from the great Victorian missionary era, as British and other Western Christians went forth into newly discovered, unevangelized lands, to see this approach. They sought an audience with chiefs, governors, and kings, seeking to win both their hearts and their permission to live and evangelize in their territory. It would have been foolish to do otherwise. Take, for example, this matter-of-fact account of the arrival of Christianity in Uganda by Bishop Alfred Tucker:

> On Monday, December 29 [1890], accompanied by the whole Mission party, I paid my first visit to the king. . . . We passed through a number of enclosures the entrances to which were guarded by gatekeepers and their friends. . . . The impression the king gives one is that of being a self-indulgent man. When he knits his brows, as he does not infrequently, his aspect is very forbidding.[8]

While many in the West (including, strangely, some Christians) have turned to lament such imperialism, Christians in Uganda celebrate the costly efforts of Western missionaries. Their church history is relatively young, yet the gospel has already shaped much of civil life, as it has in many such countries. But the gospel has had a much longer effect on Western nations.

Within the Roman empire, under which the New Testament church was born, the church largely spread under the radar—especially in times of particular persecution. Yet even by the early fourth century AD, such was its influence that even Emperor Constantine converted to Christianity, and made it the official religion of the empire.

8. Tucker, *Eighteen Years*, 1:103–4.

While the decline of Roman influence was followed by the decline of the church in many places (such as in North Africa), missionaries from the established centers continued to spread the gospel, sometimes re-evangelizing places where it had been lost. For example, in the seventh century AD, a handful of Italian missionaries saw the church established in four of the seven Saxon kingdoms of Britain in just a little over a quarter of a century. Conversations were held in royal courts between the Christian missionaries and the king, with his advisors and priests. For example, the Christian Paulinus taught the gospel to King Edwin of Northumberland. According to the early Christian historian Bede,

> King Edwin, with all the nobility of the nation, and a large number of the common people, received the faith and the washing of regeneration in the year 627.[9]

Paulinus is said to have baptized ten thousand in a day. Typical of the ups and downs of gospel spread, the amazing revival of that particular part of history was short lived; all but one of the kingdoms which had received the gospel returned to the old paganism with the succession of new monarchs. But future attempts from various sources kept the word spreading.

The Western world is called *the West*, not because it is further west than some other places, but because it is influenced by the Western church, as opposed to the Eastern, following the split of Catholic and Orthodox in AD 1054. Centered in Rome, the Western church held such sway over nations that kings answered to the pope, the church educated the nations through its priests, lawyers, and monks (universities and schools were entirely established by the church), and even the Holy Roman emperor, who governed most of Europe from the early middle ages, was called *holy* because he was seen to rule under the authority of God—and was appointed by the pope. The nations were so immersed in Christianity that it was hard to distinguish between church and state. When Western nations went to war against aggressors (the Crusades),[10] so bound were church and state that campaigns were undertaken in the name of God, for righteous causes. It would be unthinkable to do otherwise.

Through the Reformation, Luther and others pressed their governments, not just ordinary people, to break ties with corrupt Rome. All Western nations considered themselves *Christian*, and had to choose whether to stand on the principles of the Reformation—Scripture, grace, and salvation

9. Quoted in Cutts, *Turning Points*, 43.

10. For a fresh understanding of the Crusades, see Stark, *God's Battalions*, or Ibrahim, *Defenders of the West*.

by faith, not works. By prayer and immense courage, Christians in positions of influence persuaded their monarchs to embrace the Protestant faith.

The monarchs themselves might not have been converted in the truest sense (think Henry VIII). But they were nevertheless figureheads of the church in their nation. Countries were shaped according to the flavor of the beliefs accepted and embraced by their leaders.

Over the centuries, the gospel has influenced leaders of Western nations, both in terms of what they are like and how they operate. They themselves might not even be aware of the roots of their values; but even today, Western governments still largely assume certain principles that are uniquely Christian—such as the idea that leaders are servants (we still speak of *civil servants* and people in *public service*), the rule of law, and the assumption by leaders that the people are not simply *mine* to do with as I please.

But the influence of the gospel goes far beyond a few practical or moral observations. God's blessing can be seen upon nations that honor him and call on him. In fact, with the eye of faith, it is hard *not* to see the hand of God at work in critical moments of history in favor of the nations that most honor him at those times.

With all the faults of my own country, there are so many examples of when otherwise inexplicable freaks of weather have turned battles in Britain's favor and sealed the outcomes. For example, in the Battle of Plassey, on the Hooghli River in India in 1757, Robert Clive and a force of three thousand (three-quarters of whom were sepoys) were confronted by a fifty-thousand-strong Bengali army backed by French artillery. Sudden heavy rain caught the Bengalis by surprise; they didn't keep their gunpowder dry and were effectively disarmed.[11] Or again, the extraordinary combination of calm seas and a gentle breeze to cover the beaches with smoke and cloud cover between May 28 and 30, 1940, enabled Operation Dynamo to rescue 338,000 British soldiers from Dunkirk. John Scriven and Tim Dieppe have written a whole book of such examples from the twentieth century alone.[12]

There are many areas of life that give us foretastes of the new, heavenly order of things. But to a greater or lesser extent such shadows are always hazy. God is kind, not only in giving us foretastes, but in always showing us that those foretastes are not substitutes for the real thing. Politically speaking, the best of the West is still marred by evil, even at times when there is much to celebrate. Even back in the heyday of Christendom, the relationship with governments was actually extremely fragile for Christians, as they sought to hold their national leaders to the standards of the faith. Now that

11. Wilkinson and Szudek, *Battles*, 130.

12. Scriven and Dieppe, *Beyond the Odds*.

Christendom is being thrown off with fanatic zeal, we should be in no doubt of government shortcomings. Whatever the future holds, we need to keep our wits about us.

Keeping Our Wits About Us

The tour of Bible and church history is over. We return to Rom 13, but now with a clear picture of the spiritual backdrop shaping governments and of the real danger they pose. Those basic commands from Rom 13—to be subject, to do what's right, and to pay what's owed—are not simplistic. The relatively comfortable experience of government has given Western society as a whole a certain naïveté, an assumption that the horrors of elsewhere "wouldn't happen here." The church should know better—and should even have a degree of wariness when things seem well. Relating as godly, honorable subjects means being involved in national life to some degree, remembering who we are, and watching carefully.

Be Involved

There is a generally accepted (usually unspoken) mantra about keeping religion out of politics. There is, of course, a legitimate argument for the separation of church and state. That reminds the church of its purpose, and limits the state's interference in the life of the church. (At least, it ought to help.) But separation doesn't mean the church has no role as the conscience of the state, or that the gospel should have no bearing on the political life of the nation. Christians should be involved.

But if you mention your Christian faith at a meeting run by your local politician, you can normally expect a rolling of eyes or a groan from the room. The days of hurling rotten fruit might be gone, but there are likely to be some people who get very angry. You should keep your religion out of it, to their mind.

That mantra is actually quite demonic when you think about it: politics *is* religious, if by "religious" you mean spiritual. The very idea that Christianity should be kept out of it should sound some alarm bells: who is trying to silence the truth? Who decided politics should be a gospel-free zone? Why should secular atheism be the only accepted viewpoint, as if *its* political and moral record is so pure? I would have thought that the more you are told to be silent, the more you should consider whether there is reason to speak. There is no realm of life that is beyond God's business—including leadership of nations.

Some people—like Esther in the Bible—find themselves placed uniquely by God for dramatic involvement. Mordecai's famous words to Esther gave sharp focus to her position:

> For if you remain silent at this time, relief and deliverance for the Jews will arise from another place, but you and your father's family will perish. And who knows but that you have come to your royal position for such a time as this? (Esth 4:14)

Most of us have not been thrust by God into a particularly public setting. We are simply placed as God's people in the societies in which we live, our voices heard by few. Nevertheless, God has made you *you*, and placed you where you are in the time you live.

We have the words of truth and the opportunity to speak, act, or refuse to act in the realm God has given us. You might not be in the senate or parliament; but you might have contact with the local school or have to confront political agendas in the workplace or socially. Political issues are thrown your way. They are all opportunities to stand for truth; failing to get involved is, sooner or later, a denial of the gospel.

Remember Who We Are

We need to remember that kings and governors answer to our heavenly Father. We can be gracious and submissive as we do engage—but Christians must not be squeezed out of the public square. It is our Father's square. As his children, we have insight: we know that it is bad, for example, to allow a parallel Islamic justice system in the country; we know that all lives are precious, from conception to natural death; we know that marriage is the stabilizing foundation of family and society—and whatever other issues confuse unbelievers. We don't speak because we ourselves know better and would do a better job of running things—but because we are representatives of the living God on earth. Of course, politicians are unlikely to listen to us; but they will have to answer for that on the day of judgment.

We mustn't believe the lie that the church is irrelevant. Nations rise and fall; wars rage and cease; but only the church will survive into the new creation.

Watch Carefully

There are two political scenarios in which the church needs to be on careful lookout. The first is when everything seems to be well—that feeling of life going on as normal.

What is the devil doing at times like that? Is he just busy elsewhere, persecuting other parts of the church, creating carnage elsewhere in the world, and leaving us alone for the time being? Or is it a time of equal spiritual danger? I don't have access to his game plan, but I suggest the devil is just as happy with comfortable disbelief as he is with carnage and distress. When he hides in the background behind clean-cut politicians and lures the church into a deadly state of apathy and comfort, perhaps we should train our eyes to recognize him then too.

I wonder, was it harder to be a Christian under Nero or Constantine? I know which I would prefer: Nero threw Christians to the lions; Constantine honored them. It is true that persecution sometimes drives the church out of existence in places. But even today, the stories of church growth, courage, joyful perseverance, and conversion that escape from places like North Korea and Afghanistan are astonishing. Perhaps apathy kills more churches than heavy-handed violence.

Like the poor fools of Aldous Huxley's *Brave New World*, Christians, along with everyone else, can be swept into blissful oblivion, simply by failing to see the dangers of a government that seems pretty ok.

The other dangerous scenario is when the tide turns, when the screw tightens, and the government becomes more obviously anti-Christian.

The New Testament tells us to pray for governing authorities:

> I urge, then, first of all, that petitions, prayers, intercession and thanksgiving be made for all people—for kings and all those in authority, that we may live peaceful and quiet lives in all godliness and holiness. (1 Tim 2:1–2)

The purpose of prayers is so that we can live *a peaceful and quiet life*. We want our government to rule and protect—not to interfere in every detail of our lives. The more laws there are, the less dignified our lives become: law enforcers become oppressive and controlling. It seems impossible for the number of laws to ever decrease, so that once they go on increasing they ever will—until our very thoughts become a matter of government interest. That is the meaning of *totalitarianism*.

The big question for German people after the Nazi disaster was, "How could it have happened *here*? In Germany of all places, birthplace of the Reformation, center of Europe's great Christian heritage." That is a lesson for us, if we think *it couldn't happen here*. It can. And perhaps there could even be something *worse* than the Nazis.

I have often wondered how German people and their allies cope with the grief of their national memory and all the dreadful loss. We, in Britain, have our Remembrance Sunday and other sober celebrations, when we are thankful for those who gave their lives to gain our freedom. (Small comfort still, for many.) But what do Germans have to hang on to, apart from simply learning lessons of the past? And then I came across a direct answer to that in an interview with a German survivor from the dreadful Monte Cassino campaign in Italy. It stopped me in my tracks. Was there anything to be thankful for in the whole mess, from a German point of view? Was there anything positive? To that question, the soldier insisted, "I want to say it was a fortunate thing." He explained, "Because of Hitler, Europe did not become communist."[13]

Pause there, and take it in. It's quite a chilling thought. Whether you agree or not, he believed communism would have been a worse fate for Europe than the fallout of Hitler's regime.

Rod Dreher's book *Live not by Lies* makes the point that a form of communism is fast creeping across the whole Western world by the back door. It's not the hard-line version that has oppressed so many countries from the mid-twentieth century until now; Dreher calls it *soft totalitarianism*—and our version, he argues, is more pleasant, but no less dangerous:

> The old, hard totalitarianism had a vision for the world that required the eradication of Christianity. The new, soft totalitarianism does too, and we are not equipped to resist its sneakier attack.[14]

Are we really in such danger? Surely it can never happen here! Solzhenitsyn said otherwise:

> It can happen. It is possible. As a Russian proverb says, "When it happens to you, you'll know it's true."[15]

There are great moves in the West to eradicate Christianity. Subtle policies and clever tricks make the gospel unacceptable, squeeze it into the private lives of a few backward—no, *dangerous*—people, and then outlaw its doctrines, bit by bit. But can you see? The two scenarios—of feeling that all is well and of the screw tightening against Christian belief—they are going

13. Parker, *Monte Cassino*, 370.
14. Dreher, *Lies*, xiii.
15. Solzhenitsyn, *Warning*, 48.

on hand in hand. Like Kipling's Mowgli in the clutches of the snake Kaa,[16] the church can enjoy a blissful trance while being squeezed to death by Satan.

Come Out of Her, My People!

That is the heavenly cry of Rev 18:4, as Babylon receives her judgment. When you recognize who the kings of the earth are in bed with—then be sure not to take part in her sins!

So what does that mean? Join a revolution? Take up arms against the establishment? Maybe there would be a time for that. Maybe there are times to share Dietrich Bonhoeffer's conviction—that when we see a madman driving into innocent people we share the responsibility of stopping him. But we're not there. Not yet, at least.

Solzhenitsyn, speaking of life in communist Russia, says the option of fighting back was simply not there anyway. "We, the dissidents of the U.S.S.R., have no tanks, no weapons, no organization. We have nothing. Our hands are empty."[17] What clear conviction looked like for those under such a totalitarian regime was simply saying *No*. That is what is within the reach of all of us: we always have the option to refuse to join in with evil—even when imposed by culture or law.

It is culturally unfashionable to speak in terms of *good* and *evil*. These days, we should just see that there are different viewpoints. It's a bit rude to tell someone their worldview is wrong. But unless you see clearly that the church is engaged in a war between good and evil, God and Satan, you will not decisively stand. You will kind of know you should. But what will happen is that the crucial issue will always be just round the corner. It will always be *nearly* a matter of right and wrong. It will always be ok just to go along with this thing, this present compromise. Unless you recognize that the nation, the government and its policies are anti-Christ, you won't say *no*.

We have reached this perverse situation whereby we think our governments are good because the gospel has influenced them in the past—even as they embrace godless ideologies in the present. Instead of saying *no* to going along with new language, ways of life, and national values, the church just tries to be friends with the world. It gives so many caveats to its teaching that by the end you're not clear what it's actually saying. It's as if Paul's method of "becoming as a Jew, in order to win Jews" (1 Cor 9:20) applies to embracing godless agendas. It becomes so confusing, as one small compromise leads to another. Where will it lead? I now worry about which of my friends (so

16. Kipling, *Jungle Book*.

17. Solzhenitsyn, *Warning*, 38.

principled at Bible college) will be the first to conduct a gay wedding. I wonder what their justification will be. I wonder how soon.

Clarity leads to confidence. Where Christians believe what the Bible says about the kings of the earth (and where they end up), you see what the courage to say *no* looks like. Let your imagine run wild for a moment, and picture a church like this:

- A national church figurehead gives a bold public statement: but this time it is not to agree with whatever the government is saying—about recycling, driving less, or loving black people too. (How bland!) Instead, he challenges the government about abortion, assisted suicide, greed, deceit, gender nonsense, and the dangers of Islam—just as national church figureheads are doing in other parts of the world.
- Other leaders follow suit. Instead of cowering to power, they speak truth to power. The nation is shaken up. People actually start paying attention to the church.
- Ordinary church leaders work hard to study the Scriptures and watch the world. Without telling us what to think about each detail, they equip the rest of us to see things for ourselves, to watch the news with our eyes open and not be deceived. The whole church is emboldened to say *no* at certain times in their schools, workplaces, and neighborhoods.
- The youngsters in church no longer live in crippling fear of the future induced by their "education." They *live*, enjoy good things, marry and reproduce, and proclaim fullness of life in Christ to the terrified, confused, and mentally battered people of their generation. They love the Bible's teaching about boys and girls, and confidently see through whatever madness is next imposed on their peers.

It's a nice dream. But it's not a hopeless one. When Christians recognize the nature of government, they are emboldened to take their stand, like Daniel, Mordecai, or Esther. The more they do, however quietly, the less the sincere people of the world will be drawn to Islam or the media personalities. Yes, media personalities might insightfully, helpfully, and bravely point out something of the truth. But that's all they can do. Christians can offer more.

When you know what you're dealing with—that governments are against us—it clears the mind. The Scripture speaks into our world more straightforwardly. You realize what a joyful, engaging, and enormous message the church has.

6

Brains Are Blind

I praise you, Father, Lord of heaven and earth, because you have hidden these things from the wise and learned and revealed them to little children. Yes, Father, for this is what you were pleased to do.

Luke 10:21

Here's a good rule of thumb:
Too clever is dumb.

Ogden Nash, *Many Long Years Ago*

We have all met the egg-head buffoon. He (or she) is so smart he can't tie his own shoelaces. He can calculate great equations, but his own shirt buttons are all off by one. He can navigate all knowledge, but gets lost in his own living room. Poor thing: he's never cracked a funny joke, but is the brunt of many. There is normally one of him in any school year-group, or church, or somewhere in the neighborhood. (Some neighborhoods are strangely full of them.) And if you can't picture him at all . . . I hate to break it this way—but there's a chance it could be you!

Actually, in a way it is you—and all of us. Our clever friend is a very helpful picture of human nature: so smart, but so stupid; so bright, but so blind.

Mankind was created to study, invent, and understand. Down the ages, people have conceived and achieved so many things. Forget space rockets and microchips—I sometimes stare at my own ballpoint pen in wonder or marvel at Sellotape. The genius of man! But there's that other side to us that brings us down to earth, and those moments that make us doubt whether we have a brain at all—moments we hope nobody else sees. There was the time my dad spent an evening trying to phone me with the TV remote control. Or when my dear mother phoned my auntie to tell her she'd left her phone behind—and then answered the phone when it rang. Ok; maybe our family's special. But don't mock; we all do such things from time to time. I bet even Einstein at least once searched the house for his glasses only to find them on top of his head.

And yet here we are, in awe of expertise. Preachers are valued for their profound insight more than their personal godliness. Christian maturity is measured by Bible knowledge, not by bearing the fruit of the Spirit. The expert speaks, and we all comply. Scripture loves to talk about the foolishness of man's wisdom; but many readers of Scripture, shaped by Western culture, simply can't compute. Brains are blind? It's as if the concept is simply outside our box; but it's right there in the Bible.

What's Wrong with Knowledge?

The short answer is: nothing. Knowledge is a gift of God celebrated throughout the Bible. In the beginning, it was God's delight to make Adam the first scientist: he named all the animals.

You may have seen collections of bugs in a natural history museum—beetles, flies, or butterflies, each impaled and individually labelled within great glass frames. There are sometimes thousands of species and varieties, each according to their kind and quite beautiful when you look at them. Every collection says somebody had spent a long time hunting for creepy-crawlies and playing "spot the difference." You are unlikely to find mention of his name in a natural history museum; but that study of the world started with Adam.

Scripture celebrates discovery, wisdom, and knowledge. But from that first generation, it went wrong. Adam and Eve's original sin was a twisted grasping for knowledge. God's one prohibition was that they should "not eat from the tree of the knowledge of good and evil" (Gen 2:16). But they were tempted to eat, to make the fruit their own, that they would define good and evil, right and wrong. The terrible moment in Gen 3 is generally called the fall, and from that moment onward mankind is marred by a grasping to know best—to know better than God.

Something good became twisted. That is the foolishness of the sinful human condition—people are so bright, so full of insight and life, and yet so blinded to the basic fundamental of life: knowing their place under God. Adam had it all going for him; but every time I read the story, I find it agonizing: "Come on, Adam! Think about it! This is not a difficult issue!" But he fails every time.

It has been the same for all humanity ever since. But there is something particular about *now*. Never before have people been bombarded with so much information and knowledge, clever ideas and facts at our fingertips, as we are today. Even in the church, endless resources, often good in themselves, feed the *we-know-best* syndrome. Christians follow current trends and opinions and fool themselves into thinking that by them they are wise and godly. Information overload! Yet one prayer of Jesus can get lost in the noise of it all:

> I praise you, Father, Lord of heaven and earth, because you have hidden these things from the wise and learned and revealed them to little children. Yes, Father, for this is what you were pleased to do. (Luke 10:21)

God has revealed the things of the gospel to *little children*. Christians, by definition, are the little children in Jesus's prayer. But, as we shall explore, the *wise and learned* outlook can powerfully attract and damage those who start out as little children. Products of our culture that we are, Western Christians today easily drift in that direction. If first-century Greeks loved spending their time "doing nothing but talking about and listening to the latest ideas" (Acts 17:21), then imagine them with the internet. That's our world and our struggle. At root, my own greatest failings are all about replacing my *little child* status before Christ with *wise and learned* pretensions. So are yours. And it's not hard to see that the church as a whole is the same: obsessed with the impressive, and confident in its own knowledge.

There is nothing wrong with knowledge. But when you put your trust in braininess, then that is almost the definition of sin. Rebellion against God is about respecting your own intelligence too highly. The more you have of education, expertise, and information, the harder it is to see the danger of it. God hides the things of the gospel from the wise and learned; because they think they already know.

It is a shame to see in the West so many Christians, churches, even denominations that are so clever that they lose the plot.

This is a fairly simple issue. But it is worth giving it some thought. I want to explore it in four parts. First, let's understand how the whole process works—the process of being blinded in our wisdom and understanding (And yes, let's be careful not to blind ourselves further by trying). Second, let's see how and why being suckers for the false value of braininess has especially invaded our culture—and church. Then, third, let's listen to Jesus's teaching and learn to take it seriously. Fourth, and finally, let's rediscover the freedom of being little children. Because it really is good to see worldly wisdom for what it is. You can enjoy without being intimidated by nonsense—or dragged into it.

At heart, this is an appeal to common sense. But, of course, common sense isn't actually that common, given the damaged nature of the human heart, shaped by a warped grasping of knowledge. That's something that is seen most brutally when it comes to brainy people—the *wise and learned*.

Part 1: Why Are Clever People Dumb?

They are. As George Orwell once commented, "One has to belong to the intelligentsia to believe things like that: no ordinary man could be such a fool."[1] Without even knowing the context, most of us can imagine exactly what he meant.

The awkward individual at the start of the chapter is only a picture, not an example. There are many people who are delightfully clumsy with their larger-than-average intelligence, socially or physically. That can just be the slight downside to being super gifted.

But in Luke 10:21, Jesus is talking *spiritually*, not mentally or physically. People may be intelligent—but miss what is of spiritual importance. My friend Doug was from a particularly bright family. One day he found them looking up Proverbs in the Bible for amusement: "Like the useless legs of one who is lame is a proverb in the mouth of a fool" (Prov 26:7). They read that and laughed their heads off. Such irony! Proving it true by quoting it for a giggle. Very smart people can miss what's staring them in the face.

Why is it that brainy people can be so resistant to spiritual truth? More generally, how is it that cleverness can blind people to what others can see? How are they so sure they're right when the average Joe can see they're wrong?

Psychologists talk about two related processes that explain why people often get stuck in their own tunnel vision, struggling to see a different point of view to their own. These processes also help us see why greater intelligence

1. Orwell, *As I Please*, 429.

or learning tends to make someone more susceptible to backing their own delusional views—even to the point of madness, in the eyes of others.

The first of these processes is called *confirmation bias*. It's what Kendra Cherry calls "Cherrypicking the facts to support an existing belief."[2] We all do it to some extent, whenever our eyes light up at things that confirm our own viewpoint, but switch off to things that don't, or when we interpret things to confirm what we want to believe. Classically it's when the sports fan yells at the referee for the terrible decisions he makes against our team, but thinks he's got it spot on when he penalizes the other. More pertinently, we select news outlets according to the slant we want to hear—opinion trumps truth, sometimes. That's why society (and the church) becomes divided on issues such as politics, without empathy for the opposing point of view. We listen to what we want, and dig our trenches deeper so we'll never budge.

Many political preferences are split roughly 50/50 within a nation or society—most votes are reasonably close to even. But people still easily assume that everyone around them must surely think the same as themselves. Why? It is because the algorithm of preferences is not just on their newsfeed, but in their own mind. Confirmation bias leads people to assume there must be only one way of looking at things. Those strange people, out there somewhere, who think differently—they may as well be from another planet. They surely can't be anybody I know! But in reality, many people see things differently.

The second process is similar, but goes a little further: actively looking for ways to interpret information to support the conclusion you've already reached. It is called *motivated reasoning*. It's the thing that lawyers are paid to do: a prosecuting attorney will take the evidence and produce as reasonable an argument as possible in order to reach a guilty verdict. The desired outcome, as far as the lawyer is concerned, is settled; the job is to show that the evidence supports it. Back to the sports fan, it's the argument with workmates on Monday morning as to why his team was better—even though they lost.

Science experiments in school often followed this pattern. (And don't tell me I was the only one!) If you knew what the outcome ought to be, you ignored any evidence that didn't fit. It was obviously wrong, and the report would be easier to write up if the experiment all went according to plan. The *motivation* was to find a certain set of data (and draw up an easy report); the *reasoning* made sure the data were found.

2. Cherry, "What Is Confirmation Bias? Cherrypicking the Facts to Support an Existing Belief."

Confirmation bias reinforces existing beliefs by selective information gathering; but motivated reasoning further forms beliefs by arguing them out until they are more certain. Clever people are better at that. In fact, even *well-educated* people (if not necessarily clever) may be well equipped to do that: debating skills are precisely along these lines—can you argue a case so that it is actually believable? Or so that you actually believe it?

People who are smart, articulate, or quick-thinking are very good at finding evidence for their conclusions. They are good at arguing their points—and they are good at convincing themselves. But if such people convince themselves of something that is not actually right . . . then being clever is not really very clever.

"All a person's ways seem pure to them, but motives are weighed by the Lord" (Prov 16:2). We do love to convince ourselves we are right. But it is a dangerous way to exist. Religious views are formed by these processes; there are vast and powerful religions based on falsehood. Even entire churches, no doubt, are built on falsehood, even (or especially?) some very big ones, bolstered by the echo-chamber of their own voices, arguing themselves to a point of absolute certainty—looking like a true church in many ways, but false. Jesus warns over and over against the danger of kidding yourself. And the brighter you are, the better you can do it.

Real, and good, intelligence is about being willing to change your mind. It is very rare to hear a debate on a news program where the expert guest says, "That's a good point. I'll need to think about that. Maybe I'm wrong." And wouldn't you just love to hear someone say that?

But this is more than a nice quality—it ought to be the bread and butter of Christian living:

> Do not be conformed to the pattern of this world, but be transformed by the renewing of your mind. (Rom 12:2)

That is a basic definition of the life of a Christian. So it is a bit strange how little our churches change their views at all. Sure, the gospel doesn't change. But *we* should! There are all sorts of things to keep learning, and relearning, things that will change the way we live and operate. But then what do we see? Churches *do* make changes—but changes that are in keeping with the world, not in contrast to it! Churches can be just like any other group of people—they can find all sorts of reasons to confirm what they know, or justify what they do. Churches can even be selective on which parts of Scripture to focus on—the ones that support their preferences or beliefs. To all this, Jesus's prayer in Luke 10:21 ought to make us take stock; maybe we're not all as smart—and right about everything—as we thought.

Part 2: Why Is Today's Church So Entranced by Intelligence?

Perhaps, to you, that question seems like the wrong one. Perhaps in your experience the church is not into clever ideas. Maybe you'd even say the opposite—that, if anything, your church culture is totally *unimpressed* by intellectuals. Anyone who sounded a bit full of their own ideas wouldn't last a single Sunday in your setting. Sure, you might say, your kind of church has its own issues; but intellectual arrogance isn't one of them.

But there are different versions of the same thing. Different styles and flavors of church are influenced by different aspects of cultural thought. Broadly speaking, more *conservative* or *liberal* types of church today owe some of their assumptions to the cultural influence of *modernism*. By contrast, churches defined as more *charismatic* have sometimes taken on board aspects of *postmodernism*. In both cases, the culture encourages us to think we're right (when we're not) and to think we know (when we don't).

Modernism and the Church

The term *modernism* refers to the era of our history shaped by the Enlightenment. Back in the heyday of modernism, everyone was into absolutes, rational thinking, and clear distinctions. People could debate true and false, and truth tended to be certain. It was the age of science, and the Enlightenment excelled in logic.

As a movement, modernism became a threat to the church. Scientific discovery shifted more and more things from the category of *mystery* into the category of *nailed it*. God became less and less necessary for explaining things that were beyond us; he became the "God of the gaps,"[3] but the gaps in knowledge were becoming narrower. In a short time, we wouldn't need him at all.

Atheism became an accepted viewpoint. Eventually, the philosophers declared "God is dead,"[4] the naturalists worked out the *Origin of Species*,[5] and the first spaceman, the pinnacle of scientific advance, announced, "I

3. The coining of the phrase is sometimes accredited to Coulson, *Science and Christian Belief* (first published in 1955), but it summarizes a much older concept.

4. At least, that's how people have summarized Nietzsche's observations about the implications of atheism becoming the acceptable norm.

5. Darwin, *On the Origin of Species.*

didn't encounter God."[6] Modernism was not just a Western thing; its atheistic logic spawned *communism*, which served as one of modernism's greatest logical outworkings through the twentieth century.

Modernism was an age of clever people, who discovered some very clever things, thought some very clever thoughts, and made some very clever inventions. But something was missing. The age of intellectual advance lost the meaning of knowledge.

What the age of modernism did was to elevate one narrow definition of knowledge to the status of absolute. It's sometimes called *empirical* knowledge—something that can be proved by deduction or demonstration. You can demonstrate that two apples plus two apples makes four apples. But you can't prove that apples are nice. That's just opinion. And the modernist mindset assumes that anything not scientifically verifiable is mere opinion, or faith.

Apart from simply leading to a miserable, communist-like outlook on existence, it is just wrong—demonstrably wrong, ironically. Because nobody actually lives their life as if the only real knowledge were empirical. Much of what we do in life is based on "faith" (to use the modernists' derogatory term)—or overlapping words like *trust*, *intuition*, *experience*. Every time you drive a car you exercise faith in all sorts of things—if you didn't, you would have to check every mechanism every time, the tensile strength of every part, and so on. No one does that. To ultimate modernist logic, driving a car is an act of faith. Being a passenger needs even greater faith. Sharing the road with other users verges on lunacy.

But knowledge is far broader than *data*, as all cultures through all of history have understood. The Bible, too, uses many words in its original languages to express a range of aspects of knowing that include relational and historical senses, as well as what we think of as wisdom and prudence. Most things do not present themselves to us in terms of mathematical information. Courtrooms do not rely only on demonstrable fact, but testimony and other evidence. Television's homicide detective Adrian Monk says at some point in every episode, "Here's what happened!" He can't replicate the events that led to a murder, but he can discover what happened in the past.[7] When we say we "know" someone, that does not imply that we view them like the Terminator,[8] with a load of computer code about their dimensions and

6. The words attributed to Yuri Gagarin are almost certainly communist propaganda and false. But they sum up the direction of atheistic scientific advance.

7. Breckman, *Monk*.

8. Cameron, *Terminator*.

skills; *knowing* goes far beyond that sort of thing. But modernism has inclined our thinking to assume all of that is a lesser sort of knowing.

As for the church, the first great direct influence of modernism was the explosion of *liberalism*. Nineteenth- and early twentieth-century German academic theologians led much of the Western church into trying to engage with modernism on its own terms. The Bible was approached with a materialistic and basically atheistic outlook, re-explaining miracles and the like in scientifically acceptable terms. As archeologists invented wild theories of past civilizations to impress one another, so biblical scholars sought to impress with source theories and novel reinterpretation. It was the epitome of Enlightenment arrogance, with ever-more-clever new insights in Babel-like self-glorification. There is little to be said in praise or defense of this sort of thing. Yet liberalism continues to this day as Scripture is weighed according to human understanding. Parts of the Bible that don't sit with reasonable ideas are effectively ripped out—the whole Old Testament is generally dismissed for a start, in spite of its description as "the embodiment of knowledge and truth" in Rom 2:20.

There is a better side to those still broadly influenced by modernism. Following a tradition far older than the Enlightenment, more *conservative*-leaning churches sit under the authority of Scripture, dissecting it not to peer in curiosity but to feed on its deep riches. Without realizing it, however, these Bible-based churches have sometimes taken on modernist attitudes to knowledge and logic.

Maybe you've heard preachers say things like this: "Obviously the hills don't literally melt away—it would make mountaineering very dangerous!" Or, "The sudden furious squall on the lake, probably caused by an underwater earthquake . . ." Why would preachers feel the need to offer scientific plausibility to Bible stories? More fundamentally, why do people assess the value of churches according to how "deep" the teaching is—rather than godliness or prayerfulness? Answer: the church is shaped by modernist thinking.

Clever arguments, great knowledge, and quick thinking can sometimes wow listeners. Certain favorite authors, preachers, or "systematic theologies" can almost became a lens through which the Bible must be understood. Fervor for Christ and the wonder of salvation can sometimes give way to competition for recognition of status or a show of being wise and understanding. That is really not ideal, in terms of Luke 10:21.

Postmodernism and the Church

Conservative-leaning churches, being generally about a half century behind the culture in most ways, often still operate with a modernist frame of mind. But Western society has largely moved on from modernism.

Western culture began to get tired of cold logic through the second half of the twentieth century. But rather than a move back to pre-Enlightenment premodernism, with its acceptance of wondrous depths of mystery, it moved forward to a whole new outlook: *postmodernism*.[9]

Throwing the baby out with the bathwater, postmodernism took modernism's reduced view of knowledge and reduced it even further. While modernism made great claims of absolutes, postmodernism became disillusioned with grand narratives and questioned the very notions of truth and reality. If science doesn't actually explain everything after all, and viewpoints about meaning and morality around the world vary so enormously, then who's to say what's right and wrong? Modernism hamstrung belief in Almighty God, but left nothing of substance to replace him.

In the postmodern world, *truth* became a matter of personal opinion. Nothing is absolute. "Do what you want, just don't bother me." With postmodernism, feeling carries more weight than fact, and things are much more emotionally driven than argument driven. Arguing over facts is all *so last century*.

In the church, telltale signs of the influence of postmodernism tend to be seen in more *charismatic* types. Across the divide from the conservatives, the more theologically charismatic churches are well up to speed with the broader culture. They understand the limitations of sitting under cerebral, authoritarian teaching week by week. The gospel is something to feel and experience. The outworking of the Christian life is a little more subjective, and church meetings focus far more on emotions than truths. After all, the gospel is about a relationship, not a set of facts.

These are somewhat wild generalizations,[10] and caricatures are always a little unfair, but let us imagine, if we can, the most postmodern-shaped church out there. This is a church where blatant anti-intellectualism reigns supreme. Historical opinions and traditions are dismissed as irrelevant;

9. Cultural observers suggest that things are moving beyond postmodernism already. That makes sense; postmodernism is a reaction against modernism, and has little defined substance in itself. The replacement is sometimes called "post-postmodernism." Perhaps somebody will give a clear definition of it before too long.

10. There are a number of charismatic churches that recognize the limitations and errors of the postmodern outlook, and many have discovered (or are returning to) more serious exposition of Scripture. But, by and large, charismatics are likely to feel they are miles from being blinded by academic pride.

direction is determined by personalities with the right vibe; teaching does not unpack Scripture, but is only the vague (or forceful) apparently Spirit-given imaginings of the person at the front. Members are largely conditioned to be skeptical about authoritarian truth-claims, especially if those claims have roots in the world of Western-culture academic thought.

If we assumed that this church is not vulnerable to the danger of intellectual pride, we'd be wrong. The very anti-intellectualism itself is itself a position of extreme intellectual arrogance. The whole postmodern movement assumes it knows better than great minds of the past or present. It tends to brush off points of view it doesn't like without weighing them. It can assume anything that doesn't conform to a personal or fashionable viewpoint is worthless—at least, of no greater worth than any other.

Whether in society or church, a dislike of learning or understanding means our beliefs become shaped by persuasive personalities or popular opinions. Even education itself in the postmodern world can become as much an echo chamber as the nineteenth-century liberals, dismissing historical points of view as worthless compared to the current trend. And in a world where strongly held viewpoints are reached with little real thinking or debate, it becomes easy to hold beliefs that are wrong. The *I-know-best* attitude, which is the heart of sin, is rife in an anti-intellectual culture.

Put all this together—confirmation bias, motivated reasoning, intelligent people's ability in both, and a culture that has shaped us to think we know everything and then assume everyone else knows nothing—and we find a church that is blinded by its own wisdom and understanding, even if it does, at heart, love its Lord. It's a church that doesn't understand as it ought to. It's a church that is doing its best to put itself in danger of finding, before long, that the things of God are hidden from it, and revealed to others—to little children.

Are you ready to hear Jesus's teaching afresh?

Part 3: Learning to Take Jesus Seriously

Here, again, is our verse, but in full:

> At that time Jesus, full of joy through the Holy Spirit, said, "I praise you, Father, Lord of heaven and earth, because you have hidden these things from the wise and learned and revealed them to little children. Yes, Father, for this is what you were pleased to do." (Luke 10:21)

This is the only time in the four Gospel accounts that Jesus is said to be full of joy.[11] There are many times we read of Jesus's sorrow, sadness, anguish, tears; but here alone Luke tells us he rejoiced. The cause? A combination of two things. While the educated experts—the religious insiders—rejected the Christ, those like little children were given eyes to see. By the Father's grace, truths were revealed to them.

Those people are called Christians. Christians are not the *wise and learned*, who are blind. The *things* he speaks of—the wonders of the gospel, the gift of salvation—are revealed so that those who believe, *believe*. If you do believe, it is not because you heard a clever argument, but because God has chosen to bypass clever arguments and ideas and open your eyes to see the truth of who Jesus is.

Can you appreciate Jesus rejoicing in what he saw? It really is an incredible thing. The scribes and teachers of the law and the Pharisees have not been mentioned in Luke for a while, at this point in chapter 10. So it's not just they who have failed to follow Jesus. There are the *crowds*, like those who "laughed at him" (Luke 8:53), assuming he was deluded, and Samaritan villagers (Luke 9:53) who were prejudiced, and would-be followers who had other priorities or agendas (Luke 9:57–62), and the hometown citizens for whom familiarity bred contempt (Luke 10:13–15). Who would have thought all these people would reject the Messiah when he came? The majority—could they not see? The average person with a brain in his head—could he not put the evidence together? The well-educated and learned, the wise and understanding—could they not work it out? Could they not observe what was before their very eyes? No, they were blinded to who Jesus was and to the life he came to bring. Instead, Jesus was surrounded by other people: the poor and uneducated, the simple and the ordinary—people like the twelve disciples themselves, people for whom God had revealed Jesus's identity. What's more, people who had never seen Jesus had been set free from the clutches of Satan by the preaching of the disciples. But the focus of Jesus's joy, and what he has just told the disciples to rejoice over in the immediate context, is that *their* names are written in heaven (Luke 10:20).

Yes, those disciples were saved! Thanks to God's grace, they *saw* Jesus and were given all the benefits of the gospel: new life, forgiveness of sins, a restored relationship with God, and eventual access back into paradise, the surpassing paradise of God's new creation. They had all that. But that wasn't the end of the story.

Learning to take Jesus seriously was to be an ongoing process. The disciples still had much to learn. And—much like us and our situation

11. A point observed by Ryle, *Luke*, 363.

today—one of the disciples' greatest blind spots was around this very issue at the heart of their salvation. They were saved as *little children*; but their nature inclined them to a *wise and learned* outlook. They needed to be taught about it—and it was pretty painful to watch.

Take, for example, Jesus's interaction with his disciples in Mark 9:

> They left that place and passed through Galilee. Jesus did not want anyone to know where they were, because he was teaching his disciples. He said to them, "The Son of Man is going to be delivered into the hands of men. They will kill him, and after three days he will rise." But they did not understand what he meant and were afraid to ask him about it.
>
> They came to Capernaum. When he was in the house, he asked them, "What were you arguing about on the road?" But they kept quiet because on the way they had argued about who was the greatest. (Mark 9:30–34)

It's one of those slightly excruciating conversations between Jesus and the disciples. Twice, in quick succession, they are silent. First off, Jesus speaks to them again about the central event in the history of all God's plans—his death and resurrection. But they don't get it, and don't want to ask. They're scared to.

There can be all sorts of overlapping reasons to be scared to ask at a time like that. Maybe their fear is that they will get into a conversation that's going to hurt their heads. They kind of get how the world works, enough to get along day by day; and now Jesus is going to do that thing where he challenges *everything*. And they don't want what he's saying to go anywhere, because it's unsettling, and they'd rather think about things the way they do. It's quite a common response for most of us: *I know I'm wrong about stuff, and I know I don't understand everything; but it's too difficult to learn much more.* Plus that other fear that goes with the brain-ache of being taught: *I don't want to look stupid when I don't get it.*

Jesus is talking about something that's central to their life and eternity, and so it will mean living differently. But these disciples: they've got a sort of inability to understand that the Christ must die before rising. It's a moral, willful incapability that makes them follow in the footsteps of their ancestor Adam. They are wired to think they already know best in some way. It's a *wise and learned* mentality.

And it gets worse. They arrive where they're staying—good old Capernaum. And as they sort their stuff out or whatever they're up to, Jesus asks a devastatingly awkward question: *So—what were you guys chatting about on the way?*

Of course, there's silence—again. They didn't want to ask about the being killed thing, and they definitely don't want to answer this simple question—because they were chatting about who's the greatest. How awkward. What are they going to say? I imagine if the disciples did finally answer, it was done with a point of the finger: "*Those guys* were saying they were the greatest, because they went up the mountain and saw things they're not allowed to speak about!" "Well *that lot* were saying they were doing the real work down in the valley, like real disciples!"

Silence about the cross, and silence about their ego-trip conversation. And actually, the two issues are connected. They don't get their need for Jesus's whole different view of what has to happen *because* they're still playing their let's-pretend game of thinking they're something. They're ok; they know best. It's a *wise and learned* outlook.

It took a long time for the disciples to learn the lesson of giving up their *I-know-best* attitude, and it was a painful lesson. Peter finally began to learn it as the rooster crowed. Remember those words of Luke 22:62: "He went outside and wept bitterly." Peter needed to experience that to become the much humbler apostle we know through Acts and his New Testament letters.

But the letters of the New Testament show us that, even after the coming of the Holy Spirit, the teaching point was still needed in church after church. To the Corinthians (who had it bad), the basic principle of Luke 10:21 is spelled out:

> "What no eye has seen, what no ear has heard, and what no human mind has conceived"—the things God has prepared for those who love him—these are the things God has revealed to us by his Spirit. (1 Cor 2:9–10)

And,

> The person without the Spirit does not accept the things that come from the Spirit of God but considers them foolishness, and cannot understand them because they are discerned only through the Spirit. (1 Cor 2:14)

Those glorious truths meant the salvation of believers from within the intellectually arrogant culture of Greece. But, to a great extent, the church was "still worldly" (1 Cor 3:3). Perhaps they sincerely sang their equivalent of *Rock of Ages*: "Nothing in my hand I bring. Simply to thy cross I cling."[12] Yet they clung also to their own wisdom, their own understanding of order,

12. Toplady, "Rock of Ages," v. 3.

existence, and life. Just as we do. It is in our worldly nature. And overcoming that is the struggle of the Christian life.

That is why Paul very deliberately avoided any hint of coming across as *wise and learned* when he came to Corinth:

> When I came to you, I did not come with eloquence or human wisdom as I proclaimed to you the testimony about God. For I resolved to know nothing while I was with you except Jesus Christ and him crucified. I came to you in weakness with great fear and trembling. My message and my preaching were not with wise and persuasive words, but with a demonstration of the Spirit's power, so that your faith might not rest on human wisdom, but on God's power. (1 Cor 2:1–5)

Every church and every Christian is faced with the choice, daily: *Will we receive God and his word like little children? Or will we think we know best?* Many churches lose their way, and the church can even be lost from regions and nations. For the sake of ourselves and our children, Christians in the West need to stay alert to the danger: *brains are blind.* God has hidden the things of the gospel from the *wise and understanding*. We need to keep learning to be little children.

Part 4: The Freedom to Thrive

The *little-children* view of life is deeply liberating. In today's world we are bombarded with expert opinions that can confuse or terrify. It's a lovely thing to be able to step out of the frenzy of facts and fads and see it all for what it is: *These people are totally blinded to things of God. They don't know what really matters.* In fact, without knowing the things of God, they're often wrong about lots of other things too. Experts can reach stupid conclusions. It's good to realize that.

Our Enlightenment view can lead us to draw the Venn diagram of "all knowledge" like this:

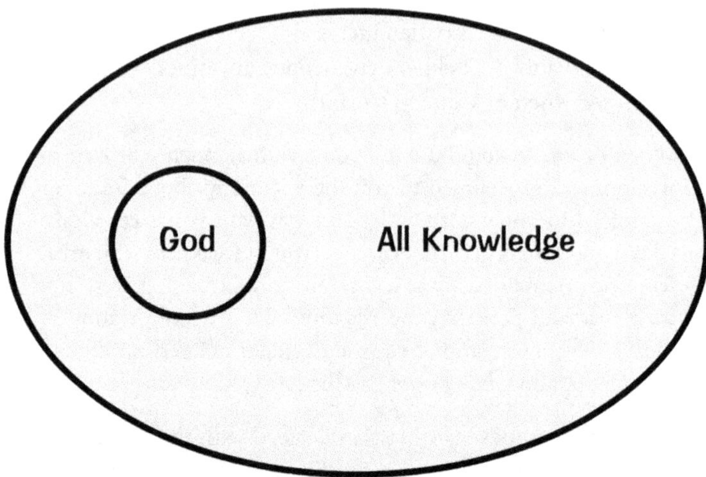

. . . as if God were just a part of all there is to know. With this false view, experts in all sorts of fields can speak with great authority. God (the ever-diminishing area according to a modernist worldview and ever-more-vague according to a postmodernist worldview) is something Christians may have opinions on. But don't let that affect what we know out here, in real life. There is a mantra that becomes a settled conclusion: *Having a Bible doesn't make you an expert in everything; submit to those who are experts in their given field.*

True, the Bible doesn't give you the details of a medical or engineering textbook. There are things people can know that the Bible doesn't explain. But there is a problem with assuming there is knowledge to which God has no relevance. In any given field, the Bible will have loads to say on how to understand it—and why, and what for.

Here's a more helpful Venn diagram to fix in our heads:

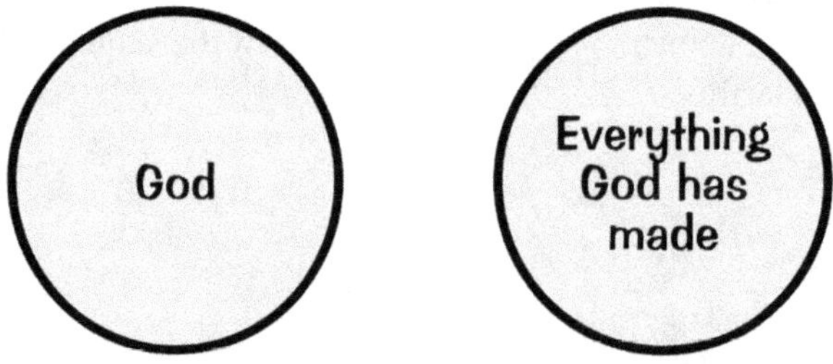

There are two distinct categories: God, and everything else. To the second group belongs all matter, all people, all knowledge—it is defined by the fact that God made it all, according to his own purposes.

If you try to understand anything in the right-hand category without reference to the left-hand, you're going to get it wrong. That's not to say atheists don't make great discoveries or understand things in great depth. It is just to say that, for all their genuine intelligence and ingenuity, their fundamental worldview is wrong.

There is "intelligence"; there is also such a thing as "moral intelligence." It is really helpful to spot the difference. People can have brains. But their lack of moral intelligence renders their great brainpower stupid. Sometimes that will show in obvious and important ways, in our politicians or other great influencers of our age. If you have the courage to see that, you are free from being compelled to believe someone—even if they are qualified, and even if the majority of others seem to be swept along by an idea or course of action.

Scientists and politicians can get lost in their urgency to save the world. With the diminished God of the first diagram—or taking God out the picture altogether—people in charge have to invent the moral framework as well as find the solutions to our problems. Some of the strategies to fight epidemic diseases in either animals or people in recent decades have seemed like madness to the people on the ground. Computer modelling repeatedly predicts wild scenarios that never come to pass: British farming devastated in 2001 and billions of pounds spent on foot-and-mouth disease by slaughtering healthy herds and flocks.[13] "Up to 50,000 people might die from mad cow disease," in 2002.[14] (Less than two hundred did.)[15] Two hundred million might die from bird flu in 2005, we were told.[16] A local funeral director told me he had been issued with piles of body bags, ready for that apocalypse. There were less than three hundred deaths worldwide in any way associated with that one.[17] And so it goes on.

If I were to even mention COVID-19 at this point, half my readers would switch off. Because it is so unthinkable that the "experts" might have been wrong, that measures were allowed to be so enormous, that the moral state of those in charge might have allowed for corruption, that vaccines might have caused harm, that we might have been mugs to have gone along with it all and been taken in.

But . . . don't you think God's *little children* ought to see through some of this stuff? There's madness out there! It's a worldview without God, without

13. Highfield, "Has the A-Team."
14. Ferguson et al., "Estimating Human Health Risk," 420.
15. Fund, "Professor Lockdown."
16. Sturcke, "Bird Flu Pandemic."
17. Fund, "Professor Lockdown."

prayer, and without a godly purpose. It leaves people in the hands of expert scientists, statisticians, and pharmaceutical companies. Well, I know whose hands I'd rather be in, thank you: God's are much bigger and safer. And yet what happens? Another threat to world survival comes along (fortnightly, it seems, these days), and even Christians get swept along with the crisis. How about enjoying freedom from the fearmongers, the freedom to thrive?

The world is full of horror stories of suffering from experimental medicines. Or attempts to adapt weather patterns for political or environmental reasons: what could possibly go wrong with that one?! Wooed by the possibilities of technology, there is a tendency to "do it because we can" rather than stopping to think about whether we ought. But questions of "ought" are hard to answer without God in the center of all things.

The world of human braininess is a frightening world, because people are not God. At high school in the 1980s I vividly remember the emotions associated with being taught about global warming, caused by overuse of the earth's resources. The article we studied in geography[18] outlined a United Nations report stating that even conservative estimates spelled disaster for countries like the Maldives, which would more than likely be underwater by the year 2000. The world needed to stop its use of fossil fuels very soon, or there would be no turning back. It was very frightening. We had to change the world! And it was very hard to know what to do from the geography classroom in B-block.

Similar statements have been made before and ever since, by government leaders or scientific authorities. The forecasts of disaster are beginning to sound similar to the Jehovah's Witness predictions of the end of the world that never come to pass. It seems sensible to ask, sooner or later, whether there might be something flawed with the whole modelling methodology. It seems sensible also to think about how a modernist and postmodernist worldview might affect the studies, the conclusions, and the whole discussion.

Things like the "climate crisis"[19] require drastic action. They involve a serious change of lifestyle for everyone. Some of these things aim for human depopulation. The climate issue is used more and more openly as justification for abortion, euthanasia, destruction of farmland, veganism, intense surveillance, restrictions in travel, heavy taxation, and one-world government. You don't need a huge sense of intuition to wonder if some of these

18. United Nations, "Senior U.N. environmental official."

19. It's hard to keep up with ever-changing terminology. I think it's now the "climate emergency," which is one step up in scariness. By the time you read this, perhaps newsreaders will have found a stronger word still.

things are a little dark. But the most passionate advocates of these things are articulate, well-educated people—Christians among them.

I thoroughly understand the importance of preserving the world for future generations. But what has happened when Christians are persuaded it's wrong to eat meat, or to keep warm, or to have children, for the sake of the climate? I have known Christian students at top universities who are convinced that it is irresponsible to procreate. They will miss out on family life (which is something commended, commanded, and promoted by God) because of expert predictions that never come to pass.

What a dreadfully oppressive belief to live under! Will you live under its spell? What if you discover it is based on falsehood? What if those basic Bible teachings about food, family, and God's provision are true in a straightforward sense after all?

Yes, this is sensitive ground. Maybe you are offended. Maybe you will see that I have written with my own confirmation bias and motivated reasoning. What's quite useful, therefore, is to find some of those rare people who have changed their mind on some of these polarizing issues. For what it's worth, I am one of those people. But if you need an expert (in addition to Greenpeace's Patrick Moore, mentioned in chapter 1), read Steve Koonin's book *Unsettled*.[20] Koonin was the former under secretary for science for the US Department of Energy under the Obama administration, and was chief scientist for BP, researching renewable energy options to move the company "beyond petroleum." His book mostly just unpacks the reasons why the bold assertions about climate change ought not to be so certain.

What a relief to know experts might be wrong, to even allow yourself to question governing narratives! Jesus's reply to one clever argument applies to many: "You are in error because you do not know the Scriptures or the power of God" (Matt 22:29).

Richard Adams's *Watership Down* follows the adventures of a bunch of rabbits. I always wondered why such a book was so popular—until I discovered it is an allegory of human nature, and that Adams was a civil servant who knew something of human social nature. Realize that, and the story about the *snares* really chills the blood. It's about a warren of fine rabbits who enjoyed the luxury of vegetables being left by a farmer. Life was good for them—except occasionally a rabbit disappeared:

> They knew well enough what was happening. But even to themselves they pretended that all was well, for the food was

20. Koonin, *Unsettled*.

> good, they were protected, they had nothing to fear but the one fear . . .[21]

These are smart rabbits, who think they know what's good for them. They seem reasonable. But in order to enjoy the life they lead, they must deny the data that doesn't fit—the snares. By clever reasoning, they blind themselves to a horror so that they can't see what is blindingly obvious to other rabbits: that their worldview leads them to a terrible death. Brains are blind. Even fictional rabbits teach us to question our own judgments and assumptions.

Psalm 104 gives a thoroughly different picture to the experts on pandemics, technology, climate, and anything else:

> LORD my God, you are very great;
>   you are clothed with splendor and majesty . . .
> He set the earth on its foundations;
>   it can never be moved . . .
> You set a boundary [the waters] cannot cross;
>   never again will they cover the earth . . .
> He makes grass grow for the cattle,
>   and plants for people to cultivate—
>   bringing forth food from the earth:
> wine that gladdens human hearts,
>   oil to make their faces shine,
>   and bread that sustains their hearts . . .
> Praise the LORD. (Ps 104:1, 5, 9, 14–15, 35)

Does that feel refreshing? With God, the tide will never advance against its given limits; the CO_2 cycle continues happily; the land produces food; his people receive life. The psalm leads us to a deep sense of assurance: whatever happens in the world, God's got it all safe in his hands. It frees us to enjoy the good things the world provides—bread, meat, wine.

But belief in the things of this psalm is increasingly viewed as dangerous to our atheist world. The experts have decided that the opposite is true: no one has the world in his hands, so we'd better step up into the empty chair where God isn't sat. They ought to see that it's a bit of a tall order to take on that role. At some point they might see it doesn't make life good. All false teaching and ideology robs life—even with the best intentions. Why? Because brains are blind. The wise and understanding people do not comprehend the things of God.

Since the experts are often in charge, you might get a hard time for questioning them. Phrases or words such as *religious extremists* or *skeptics*

21. Adams, *Watership Down*, 152.

or *deniers* threaten to bite us sooner or later. But there is great freedom in that still. With the confidence to question the true expertise of experts, we are no longer trapped by threats or afraid to be dissidents. It's a freedom that has great benefits—in relation to other people and the world around, to church life, and to our relationship with the Lord.

I lived for a few years in the city of Cambridge. It can be an intimidating place, surrounded by world leaders in every field imaginable, and teenage students with IQs off the scale. I admit that I spent my first few months there feeling utterly out of my depth, both intellectually and socially.

However, a turning point came when I realized that some were not super-clever, but just well-schooled, and even those who were very clever did not know everything. Most never claimed to know everything, and people are people with the same needs whoever they are. Brains get in the way of the gospel just like every sort of pride. But bright Christians could be models of humility, saved by grace as they were, and the gospel did not need presenting in a clever way to reach and serve clever people. Being in awe of intelligence was a barrier; seeing the flaws of intelligence allowed friendship to flourish. Seeing that *brains are blind* turned cowering into confidence, trepidation into more openness.

And that is a very attractive thing to see. Many people around us, perhaps especially the more down-to-earth working class communities, have a deep unease with the "experts" of this world—for good reason. It is a shame when people see the church as one more institution that goes along with their foolishness. Be slow to jump on bandwagons; be willing to question (and publicly question) what the "wise and learned" voice so confidently. You might find people are very ready to receive clear sense, the message that God is in charge and without him we haven't got a clue.

As for church life, when you recognize that the agendas set by the world are probably wrong, it frees you from trying to please public opinion. You don't need anxious meetings about heat pumps or anxious sermon applications confirming that we, too, care about the latest imaginary crisis. When you stop taking experts quite so seriously, you can get on and live the life of the gospel more directly. That sounds like a breath of fresh air, wouldn't you say?

And finally, our relationship with the Lord grows richer when we grasp that brains are blind. Living under the spell of "experts" can be intimidating; but the Lord is never intimidated. He's bigger than them—and besides, they're don't know the important things anyway. Instead of being fixated on the latest (predicted) crisis, or thrown by the latest theory of existence, we are freed to live for greater—and better—realities. Read Ps 104 again, and remember whose world we are in. Remember who's running it, and to where it's being run. What brings joy to Jesus is that *little children* have graciously been shown the great things of God. The *wise and learned* people—they don't get it at all.

7

Salvation Involves Sacrifice

In fact, everyone who wants to live a godly life in Christ Jesus will be persecuted.

2 Tim 3:12

Jesus promised His disciples three things—that they would be completely fearless, absurdly happy and in constant trouble.

William Barclay, *Gospel of Luke*

As a *bit of the Bible we barely believe*, this is different to some of the other chapters. We know the fact of it very well: the life of salvation involves sacrifice. The problem is we are generally strangers to the practical outworking of it. It is a familiar idea in our heads, but a foreign idea in our lives.

Self-sacrifice is central to the life of following Christ. Disciples must "take up their cross and follow" (Matt 16:24). Christians are to offer their bodies "as a living sacrifice" (Rom 12:1). The blind spot for today's Western Christians is that, in practice, they don't really expect any of that to hurt, or to cost very much at all. They know it to be true; but they don't really believe it.

No one is suggesting that Christians of the past *enjoyed* sacrifice, suffering, and pain. But in other eras or places they have *embraced* it as the way of life for disciples of Jesus. For example, contrast today's church to the first century Christians:

> Caesar of Rome was the Lord. As a matter of fact, when public employees and soldiers met in the street, they had to say as a greeting, "Caesar is the Lord!" And the standard response was, "Yes, the Lord is Caesar!"
> So the Christians had a problem. When they were greeted with "Caesar is the Lord!" they answered, "No, Jesus Christ is the Lord." That immediately got them into trouble.[1]

That does not feel like the experience of the average early twenty-first-century church. Perhaps our setting is not unique in recoiling from the cost of discipleship, but its aversion to suffering is fairly extreme. Do you not think it should surprise us when an archbishop of Canterbury is bullied by parliament into imposing same-sex blessings on the church, as Archbishop Justin Welby was in 2023?[2] But such things don't surprise us—we have grown to expect such characters to have no backbone. It follows that ordinary Christians are often just as reluctant to risk any cost for the sake of Christ, be it their job, their relationships, or their reputation.

But two things make sacrifice especially hard to grasp for Christians in the West. The first is that the church is used to the Christian life being acceptable within society. To say we are in a "post-Christian" society does not mean that in the past everyone was a Christian, but that Christianity has shaped the Western world over many centuries. Whether or not people lived by them, the Christian standards were generally agreed upon as the right ones. We are conditioned to expect that by living God's ways we will, on the whole, receive broad approval from the world around rather than their fury. The church is just beginning to get used to the idea that people may now take against us for living for Christ. But it is a new idea for many of us.

The second thing that makes it hard for us to embrace the life of sacrifice is the vilification of masculinity. The Great Feminization is a much-attested-to cultural phenomenon, described as "prioritizing the feminine over the masculine: empathy over rationality, safety over risk, cohesion over competition."[3] We have been conditioned by our culture to be anything but masculine. Even my gritty northern English town is becoming filled with gyms and men's grooming salons, because men are more interested in their beauty than their duty.

1. Ortiz, *Disciple*, 12.
2. Lee and Andersson, "Same-Sex Marriage."
3. Andrews, "Great Feminization," para. 10.

The church, in its own particular way, has followed suit. We have tended to emphasise the passive, receiving aspects of the gospel ("For it is by grace you have been saved, through faith" [Eph 2:8]) over the active demands on the Christian's life:

> Therefore, my dear friends, as you have always obeyed—not only in my presence, but now much more in my absence—continue to work out your salvation with fear and trembling. (Phil 2:12)

That is a powerful verse: gentle affection combined with great force, a call to urgent responsibility to be sure of being found among the saved at the final reckoning. That is what I mean by *masculine*. The rigors and risk of a sacrificial Christian life have been de-emphasized in favour of a safer, more passive gospel.

To be clear, this is not an attack on femininity. It is simply to warn against feminine-coded theology. It is an appeal to rebalance the gospel message. Neither am I talking about a macho Christianity. Real and wholesome masculinity, as historically understood, does not involve being macho, toxic, testosterone charged, or aggressive. It is about giving, protecting, and self-sacrifice. But the fact that it needs spelling out, and even that the language of masculinity may be uncomfortable to us, is an indication of how far we've drifted from the mentality of Christian soldiers of less than a century ago. What follows is a list of ways to *work out our salvation with fear and trembling*. It is a toolkit for a driven, deliberate—and sacrificial—Christian life.

Would you like to do that? Would you like to "take hold of the life that is truly life" (1 Tim 6:19), the life that "demands my soul, my life, my all,"[4] that sees Jesus's power and provision through all the adventures, the challenges, the ups and downs? This is the life of salvation. It involves sacrifice.

But before launching into the list, four more brief words are needed by way of explanation.

First, this life of sacrifice is *simple*. This forgotten aspect of the gospel, that *salvation involves sacrifice*, is straightforward to put into practice. We don't have to go looking for martyrdom, or finding an opportunity to make a great splash for the gospel. Most of the instructions in the New Testament are about our character; those are the sort of things I am going to list below. They are about day-to-day, ordinary choices and attitudes. Those are the things that change the world—and always have done.

And that is a second important point: these things are *nothing new*. The things that follow are old-fashioned ideas; you might even find them

4. Watts, "When I Survey," v. 4.

quaint. But they are timeless Christian qualities and to be valued all the more in a society that has abandoned them and forgotten them. As Jeremiah wrote,

> Stand at the crossroads and look;
> ask for the ancient paths,
> ask where the good way is, and walk in it,
> and you will find rest for your souls. (Jer 6:16)

Please don't suppose, as you read on, that I am taking Jeremiah's *ancient paths* to refer to the 1950s, or the good old days of Charles Dickens in some nostalgic, rose-tinted dream world. It might be easy for some to dismiss all this as a simple pining for the old. But remember, this is about a specific aspect of the gospel that today's church has largely lost. Jeremiah's appeal is to get back on track: not with the past, for the sake of it; but with the life that is right and has stood the test. It is a call to escape the traps of our time, and to get back to walking in the *good way*. Do you want to find *rest for your souls*? Here it is.

There may be nothing new about the life of self-sacrifice. But—and here's the third point of explanation—it is *vital*. Churches can die in a generation, simply because they are taking it easy, being passive and not active in their day-to-day decisions about what it means to live a godly life. We need to avoid repeating the errors of the ancient Israelites, who refused to walk in the old ways when their culture drifted from them. It is so simple to go with the flow and never take stock, even to justify living by our cultural norms. We mustn't do that. It is the paths of the gospel that are good and pleasing, wholesome and healthy. They are life-giving, reviving the church—and they show the world what real living is, all over again. That is what the Christian life involves. And now that our culture is shifting fast from its Christian heritage, we have an opportunity: it is to have the sort of impact had by the first-century church simply by their new way of life that accompanied their gospel. We have the opportunity to stand out like Christians in the pagan cultures of our world.

But it *costs*. And that is the final thing to say before spelling out some of the specifics. Second Timothy 3:12 ("In fact, everyone who wants to live a godly life in Christ Jesus will be persecuted") is an easy verse to slip past. We can read it soberly, and believe it, but all the time leave it only in its future tense—*will be* persecuted. One day. As for now, we may think, I don't need to put myself in the line of fire. It's not *wrong* to have the things I have, or live the life I lead. I'm not living an *ungodly life* by fitting in with people around me in the ways that I do. There seems nothing wrong with deciding these battles are not the ones to fight; I should spare myself for another day. But actually, the opportunity is for now. The battle of the Christian life is not coming—it's happening. The simple choices of today are what it means to live for Christ, are how the kingdom of God advances, how we are transformed, and how the world sees the truth and power of God. But it all comes with a promise: a promise of persecution. This is a call to live a life that is right, that is good and pleasing, that is responsible and works—but one that costs.

You can find various lists in the New Testament of what the life of self-sacrifice involves. Rather than taking just one of those lists, here is a compilation, a rewording, for our generation. Salvation involves sacrifice, and here are the ways we've forgotten how; here are some basic old paths to tread, principles of what sacrifice needs to look like for us.

Courage

> The brave man dashes into danger without any hesitation, when a less brave man is inclined to hang back. It is very like bathing. A lot of boys will come to a river to bathe, and will cower shivering on the bank, wondering how deep the water is, and whether it is very cold—but the brave one will run through them and take his header into the water, and will be swimming about happily a few seconds later.[5]

As Baden-Powell points out to his boy scouts, few men are born brave—though anyone can learn to be brave. But how hard in today's world. There are health and safety directives for every step we take; we end up with a mentality where caution is always king. Kids' playgrounds today are very different to those in the 1970s and 1980s. Some readers may be old enough to remember the slide that seemed fifty feet tall, with wooden edges that gave you splinters and metal that burned your legs as you squeaked down. Kids would come flying off the roundabout onto the tarmac or gravel, and run home to get smothered in Germolene. But now the ground is made of recycled rubber tires and a council official complete with hi-viz and clipboard has decided it's far too dangerous for the see-saw to go more than a foot in the air. Someone could get hurt. I'm not saying I enjoyed skinning knees on tarmac—but certainly we are conditioned now to be very cautious. And great caution creates a culture of cowards, who are unable to withstand invading cultures or even to gain any of the basic prizes of life: "Faint heart never won fair lady."

5. Baden-Powell, *Scouting for Boys*, 233.

Alongside health-and-safety directives, the world of safeguarding has added to our nervous disposition. Again, it's there for good reason; but fear of accusation inclines us to be cautious in all sorts of relationships. I have heard of a teenager being left in pain while the responsible adults waited for an ambulance, worried that touching her might come back to bite them.

And on top of all this, what really saps us of any attempt at courage is the current hyper-sensitivity about offending people. You could lose your job for a joke that someone deems inappropriate, or face a disciplinary for voicing the wrong opinion. What has become of the *days of old when knights were bold*?

Into this, a command throughout Scripture is speaking firmly to us: "Be strong and courageous" (e.g., Josh 1:7). That charge from God could almost be the title of the whole book of Joshua. The leader of God's people must not fear the battle or the enemy, but act on God's promises. As Christians, we are not stepping into the unknown, nor are we at the mercy of the pathetic powers of our age that don't know what they are fighting for so forcefully or why they are fighting for it. We obey the living God, who knows the end from the beginning, whose promises stand through all the changing fashions of human thought.

Paul's command to the morally lazy Corinthians to "be courageous" (1 Cor 16:13) is more accurately translated "act like men" (ESV). Courage means doing the right thing, even when you've failed before. It means doing the right thing even though there is risk to yourself of reputation, rejection, failure, pain, injury, even death.

And *risk* is an important word when it comes to courage. It is better to get some things wrong and to fail than to freeze in fear. With God, well-intentioned mistakes and flawed plans are used for his glory. Cowardice is not.

Let's be aware of our cultural conditioning to be over-careful, to assume it is not worth getting hurt for. Remind yourself instead that quite often the fear of pain is worse than the actual event. Trust God and do the right thing—and when you do, it normally becomes easier to show courage the next time.

Fortitude

Fortitude is the quality of sticking something out. It is the soldier fighting a righteous cause who won't give up till he's dead. Our convenience culture has become one of instant gratification, and that has made fortitude a foreign concept. Many children I know cannot whistle, click their fingers, or shuffle a pack of cards—because scrolling a phone screen requires no effort or practice. So, too, the lack of sticking power is true for adults—even in church life. If a church does not seem to be going well, people leave to find something with more obvious success. If the work is slow, the pastor leaves to find something more fulfilling.

But experiencing disappointments and setbacks in any task is normal, and part of the normal process of learning, training, and improving. Any athlete or musician knows the importance of pushing through pain barriers. And for Christians, it is often through obstacles that the Lord works most powerfully to change us into his likeness.

Paul, in 2 Cor 12:7, wrote of his *thorn in his flesh*. He doesn't invite us to speculate as to exactly what it was, but tells us the lesson God taught him: "My grace is sufficient for you, for my power is made perfect in weakness" (2 Cor 12:9). Setbacks and frustrations are training in trusting the Lord—not a sign that you should quit.

There are few tales to match those of Special Forces like the SAS when it comes to illustrating fortitude. Chris was behind enemy lines in Iraq, in 1991. After a first night's hike of eighty-five kilometers in pitch darkness and temperatures low enough to freeze diesel, Chris was separated from his patrol. His countless trials included constant risk from the enemy, an almost complete lack of food, and severe dehydration. He found water only twice, once from waist-deep, foul riverside mud, and the other from a stream that burned his mouth, later found to be outflow from a uranium-processing plant. He lost all his toenails on his frozen and blistered feet. But eight nights and over three hundred kilometers later, he made it out alive, to Syria and safety.[6]

Fortitude develops every time you pick up and carry on following a difficulty. Joshua's charge for courage was repeated after the devastating disaster of Ai (Josh 8:1). Fortitude is an embracing of the life of sacrifice—and an outworking of courage. Put beautifully by Harper Lee's character Atticus, teaching his son about the difficult life of an old lady who lived down the road:

> I wanted you to see what real courage is, instead of getting the idea that courage is a man with a gun in his hand. It's when you know you're licked before you begin but you begin anyway and you see it through no matter what. You rarely win, but sometimes you do.[7]

6. McNabb, *Bravo Two Zero*, 348–57.

7. Lee, *Mockingbird*, 124.

So don't give up when life is hard: God is at work. A great step to living the Christian life of sacrifice, working out our salvation with fear and trembling, is to be able to stand disappointments. Keep going when the chips are down—because God is never defeated, and his *power is made perfect in weakness.*

Principle

The life of self-sacrifice involves *acting on principle*. The opposite is to compromise your conscience on an issue. You might do so because you do not share the majority opinion—others think differently, and you go along with them out of fear or respect. You might even talk your conscience around, because to obey it would be inconvenient. But that is to be *weak-willed.*

In his lengthy discussion on disputable issues in the church, Paul says to Christians on both sides of a given debate that each "should be fully convinced in their own mind" (Rom 14:5). It is ok to change your mind on things through Scripture and discussion: Paul himself did. But while you hold a conviction, don't go against it. Your understanding may be wrong; but the important thing is that, under God, you do what seems to be right.

A current example is about our churches' relationships with the wider institutional historic structures. Some have broken ties with the old structures as a point of principle; a life of godliness involves official distancing from those who promote falsehood and ungodliness. Others have set themselves stoically to stay and oppose errors in their structures—also a decision of principle. But the majority, dressing it in finer words, argue: "But there are opportunities for the gospel if we stay in this compromised position." I can't see that that can ever be an acceptable way to operate. Do what's right, and trust God for the opportunities.

Acting on principle means accepting loss. And accepting loss is something you have to experience to understand the blessings of it. My own church left the historic Church of England, no longer wanting to associate with the compromised doctrine and behavior it has adopted. The most common response from friends and associates in church leadership was along the lines of: "It's easy for you—you owned your own buildings, you organized your own finances." In the event, it's true: it cost us very little. But that's largely because we had made decisions years before in preparation for this possible eventuality. They were costly.

It is also true that we don't meet in a building that has stood in God's name for a thousand years or more, as many in my country have. I sincerely appreciate the worth of beautiful, prominent church buildings, their heritage, significance, and the opportunities they bring. But I do wonder if more of those congregations made the sacrificial decision to leave it all behind, even to kit out an ugly warehouse and rehouse their staff, whether they would find the joy of acting on principle. For all the loss—financially, sentimentally, and probably half the congregation—they might find money appearing from nowhere, outreach like they've not known before, and the joy of having done *the right thing*—even if there is some blur of the line between right and wrong. Act on principle, whatever that means specifically. Accept loss. And it will be a blessing.

Imagining the first Christians, in Jerusalem, Peter Leithart wrote,

> When Christians started meeting to break bread from house to house, they could look up the hill and see the impressive temple complex, gleaming on the Temple Mount, apparently immovable for all eternity. It took an act of faith to say that the temple was childish and the little gatherings of disciples were mature. It took an act of spiritual bravado to say that the little gatherings of disciples were the thing of which the temple was only a shadowy figure.[8]

Granted, that is not an exact equivalent of the situation today. But, still, acting on principle can mean leaving behind the security of the large, the seemingly immovable—yet the spiritually corrupt.

The biggest difficulty with acting on principle is when compromise is presented in a series of small increments over time. The latest change is never quite the one to demand a huge reaction. But stepping back to see the big picture, what would Christians of our grandparents' generation say about cultural compromises we've already made because we were scared of loss of finance or face? What would they say when they heard that some of the things being discussed are even points of discussion for the church?

In big decisions, such as breaking ties with a denomination, there is often a window of opportunity to act. But it is just a window, because in time the small compromises mount up; they blur the mind and dull the spirit. Take a costly stand—on something, in some way.

Honor

Have you heard of Edward Ferrars? His engagement to Lucy Steele is a major storyline in Jane Austen's *Sense and Sensibility*.[9] He proposed when he

8. Leithart, *Delivered*, 227.
9. Austen, *Sense and Sensibility*.

was young and foolish. But even though he soon realized she's a conniving and manipulative little wench (my language, not Jane Austen's), he sticks with her. Why? Because he is honorable. He is set in contrast to another character: the flighty John Willoughby—fun and romantic, but self-serving and untrustworthy. Willoughby is a heartbreaker; Ferrars is noble—to the point of sacrificing his own happiness simply because it is unthinkable to a character like him to abandon a pledge he has made.

There are not many like Edward Ferrars in today's world. In fact, I suspect most people who read or watch *Sense and Sensibility* today will be willing him to give her up, cut his losses, move on. To be sure, the story is written to create the tension between honor and desire, duty and happiness. Honor and duty are not simply about doing what's *right*—they are about standing by a responsibility, being reliable at whatever cost to self, sticking to your post so that you don't let others down. Jesus taught his disciples to have an attitude that says, "We are unworthy servants; we have only done our duty" (Luke 17:10).

Being honorable as a general quality is something expected of Jesus's followers, in the Bible. Jesus said, "Let your 'Yes' be 'Yes,' and your 'No,' 'No.'" (Matt 5:37 NKJV). First Thessalonians 4:4 says, "Each of you should learn to control your own body in a way that is holy and honorable." Hebrews 13:18 asserts, "We . . . desire to live honorably in every way." And 1 Cor 7:36 is concerned about a man "acting honorably toward the virgin he is engaged to."

An attitude of honor can be cultivated in early life by learning to play nicely. Play to win, but accept loss with a smile and genuine congratulations for the winners. Children who play games competitively and imaginatively but according to the rules have a good chance of growing into honorable adults. Unfortunately, the culture of sports is commonly one of ego promotion, excuses, and complaint against officials. As Christians *work out their salvation* they need to buck that trend.

More generally in life, honor involves honesty in business, truthfulness in speech, and reliability with responsibilities. Being honorable means being the person that people trust to be discreet with sensitive issues, knows when seriousness is called for, and can be relied on to keep others safe at the cost of self-safety.

As it is, in today's church (as well as society) it has become commonplace for people not to show for appointments, or to text shortly before to cry off. If people do bother to actually cancel, it's normally not even with a straight and honest reason. I'd almost be happier to be told by someone, "A better option came up," "I can't be bothered," or even, "I don't want to see you any more." At least I'd know where I stood. As it is, it's normally with a euphemism or a vague excuse: "About coming over tonight: could be tricky . . ." or "Something's come up."

But being honorable is about sacrificing the better option for doing the thing you said you would do.

Discipline

A couple of generations ago, discipline was sometimes pretty harsh in the way it was imposed on others, especially children. Now, as the pendulum has swung in reaction, people are very reluctant to engage in much discipline at all. Disciplining children in particular, in any meaningful way, is frowned upon. In many countries across the world (including Scotland, Wales, and Ireland) spanking your own children is even forbidden by law.

Nobody wants to see children abused or hurt in anger or frustration. But when Scripture says, "Whoever spares the rod hates their children, but the one who loves their children is careful to discipline them" (Prov 13:24), it is not promoting cruelty, it is not outdated, it is not ignorant, and it is not an overstatement to be translated in practice as *tell them off sometimes*. It is about real love and real care. But it flies in the face of the current sensitivity around imposing discipline.

Since many people now recoil at the idea of chastisement—whether of children, self, or within church—a generation is growing up with very little sense of the importance of discipline. For many children, some of the basic concepts of self-control or self-restraint are utterly foreign ideas, having had no consistent and clear guidance in early years. Parents increasingly expect the school to do the job of parenting. The state, in turn, steps into the role of parent more and more. But it is not working well: schoolteachers are unable to teach lessons to a classroom of kids who run wild, often feeling powerless to impose order, and then sometimes confronted by parents when children are unhappy at the existence of rules and punishment.

As a way of life, ill-discipline is self-perpetuating. Undisciplined children grow into adolescents and adults with a sense of entitlement; they assume they can have what they want. They have a low capacity to cope with disappointment, and little idea of the value of delayed gratification. Left to run wild, this all results in the social carnage we see all around us: where sex is not reserved for marriage, but with anyone, any time; where the world is expected to dance around someone's made-up pronouns.

Finding themselves in this world, or turning to Christ from it, Christians have to learn some very basic principles. If we have not been taught discipline as children, we have to work harder at learning it ourselves. And if we are not learning to discipline ourselves, we will be of little help to others—including our own children.

Paul taught Timothy that all Scripture "is useful for teaching, rebuking, correcting and training in righteousness" (2 Tim 3:16). The practical application of Scripture is to point out wrong paths, to show us right ones, to equip us to live rightly. Paul didn't just instruct others; he said of himself, "I beat my body and make it my slave so that after I have preached to others, I myself will not be disqualified for the prize" (1 Cor 9:27 NIV, 1984).

Learning to be disciplined is about applying your "thinking brain" over your "feeling brain." It is about talking to yourself and asking, *What would be the good thing to do here?* The thing that's good for you, as well as for others. It applies to what you look at, what you eat and drink, how you exercise, what you spend or earn, what you do to relax, who you spend time with and how. The more used you become to thinking about such things, the more you develop good habits—habits that are healthy physically, spiritually, and socially. Sometimes you have to beat your body into submission, because its will to do its own thing is particularly stubborn. Alarm clocks, fasting, cold showers, prayer apps, set bedtimes, mealtimes, diaries, prearranged social events, cut-off times, and cooking or cleaning rotas are all examples of tools that can be very helpful with this.

It is important to know that self-discipline is not an optional extra for the Christian. "Train yourself to be godly," writes Paul (1 Tim 4:7). To be a *disciple* is to be under the *discipline* of God our Father—and if we don't practice self-discipline, we will be disciplined by him. It's always best not to have to learn the hard way.

Hebrews 12 talks about the discipline by which God shapes us. It says, "No discipline seems pleasant at the time, but painful. Later on, however, it produces a harvest of righteousness and peace for those who have been trained by it" (Heb 12:11). That's the fact; so what's the application? "Therefore, strengthen your feeble arms and weak knees. Make level paths for your feet, so that the lame may not be disabled, but rather healed" (Heb 12:12–13). Learn to fall in line—otherwise our loving Father, if we are truly his, will knock us in line. And that hurts more.

Soldiers suffer drill so that basic actions are taken without the need to stop and think. Musicians practice scales and arpeggios so that basic movements are second nature. In the same way, self-discipline shapes our lives so that we form patterns of living that we are no longer aware of. Most of what we do in a day we don't even think about. But it's the things we're not overtly conscious of that make the biggest difference between a good life and a bad, a life that functions well and one that doesn't.

Chivalry

King Arthur bravely led the ancient Britons in battle against the invading Anglo-Saxons. Over fifteen centuries later, he is still a national hero, with his "sword in the stone," his round table, and, most of all, his knights. (Made up legend or real historical figure? Experts argue either way. I guess we'll never know. But Excalibur is not still in the stone. Just saying.)

The knights were like private law-enforcers—but not in a bad way. They galloped round the country on great big horses, with young sidekicks called squires and a gang of men-at-arms. They were strong protectors who in times of peace busied themselves with good deeds and in war led men to stand against aggressors.

Their legacy is *chivalry*: a way of life that is always mindful to protect and respect those who are weakest—notably (for the regular man) women, and children. But chivalry has become an awkward idea in recent times, because men have been taught to be uneasy about treating women as weaker (having believed the absurd idea that we are all the same), and also because in our age of sexual confusion they are afraid that any act of kindness could be perceived as romantic interest.

Some women may misunderstand, wittingly or unwittingly. But most will be glad of Christian men who walk them home or to their car after an evening out, or rise to offer them a seat on the bus. However it is perceived, it is proper for a man to respect a woman "as the weaker partner" (1 Pet 3:7), not just in marriage but in any relationship. When walking with her, he should instinctively walk on the side nearest the traffic. He should spring to her defense if harassed in any way, without hesitation. He should open the door and allow her to pass through first, with a smile but without it being a grand gesture. If a woman has an indiscretion with her clothing, a man should look away, so as to be a gentleman, not a predator. In an accident or emergency, men should be sure that women and children are helped to safety first before thinking of themselves.

If this sounds quaint and old-fashioned, it is an indictment on today's generation. A female friend of ours was recently assaulted when she bravely accosted two shoplifters outside the supermarket. She suffered significant trauma and concussion, as well as other injuries sustained as she tried to defend herself. There were men and boys around, watching at a safe distance; none came to her aid in spite of her shouting for help. What a sorry lot—along with all who sneer at chivalry.

You are unlikely to find *chivalry* in any Bible dictionary or thematic index of Scripture. It is not generally considered by those who compile such things. But though it was exemplified by King Arthur and the orders of knights that followed, the concept was not invented by them. It is simply the application of basic standards God has set, for both gods and men:

> Defend the weak and the fatherless;
> uphold the cause of the poor and the oppressed.
> Rescue the weak and the needy;
> deliver them from the hand of the wicked. (Ps 82:3–4)

> Be devoted to one another in love. Honor one another above yourselves. (Rom 12:10)

> In everything I did, I showed you that by this kind of hard work we must help the weak, remembering the words the Lord Jesus himself said: "It is more blessed to give than to receive." (Acts 20:35)

There is a broader underlying principle—a heraldic attitude of "looking after" that pervades all of life. It is expressed in someone's manner, relationships, and care for the world around them. It is sometimes most clearly seen in the way they treat animals. Not everyone likes having pets around the house; but a person's contact with animals is a good reflection of their attitude to other people. Poetically put by G. K. Chesterton,

> Wyndham once told me that he had seen one of the first aeroplanes rise for the first time, and it was very wonderful; but not so wonderful as a horse allowing a man to ride on him. Somebody else has said that a fine man on a fine horse is the noblest bodily object in the world. Now, so long as people feel this in the right way, all is well. The first and best way of appreciating it is to come of people with a tradition of treating animals properly; of men in the right relation to horses. A boy who remembers his father who rode a horse, who rode it well and treated it well, will know that the relation can be satisfactory and will be satisfied. He will be all the more indignant at the ill-treatment of horses because he knows how they ought to be treated; but he will see nothing but what is normal in a man riding on a horse. He will not listen to the great modern philosopher who explains to him that the horse ought to be riding on the man. He will not pursue the pessimist fancy of Swift and say that men must be despised as monkeys, and horses worshipped as gods. And horse and man together making an image that is to him human and civilised, it will be easy, as it were, to lift horse and man together into something heroic or symbolical; like a vision of St. George in the clouds.[10]

10. Chesterton, *Everlasting Man*, 16.

What a contrast to the modern veganism that squirms at animals, the callous cruelty of many farming practices or wayward children, or the relational ignorance of people incapable of training their own dog. Fans of Laura Ingalls Wilder's *Little House* books will remember the contrast between young Almanzo, who trained his ox calves Star and Bright, and his cousin Frank from the town:

> "You get down off there!" Almanzo said, and he took hold of Frank's leg. "Don't you scare that colt!"
> "I'll scare him if I want to," Frank said, kicking.[11]

Whether in relation to animals or other people, you can be sure that an attitude of chivalry will be despised with ever-increasing passion as society moves more boldly against anything resembling Christ. Christians ought to be alert so as not to go along with the scorning of *old paths*—when those old paths are the way of the gospel.

Some may be offended by being offered a seat or a helping hand. But it's better to be reviled for doing what's right than blend in with what isn't. Better to be confident in doing good than fail for fear that others may sneer.

Purity[12]

> But among you there must not be even a hint of sexual immorality, or of any kind of impurity, or of greed, because these are improper for God's holy people. (Eph 5:3)

Sometimes the Bible gives scope for wriggle room with its moral rules. For example, it's clear that lying is wrong—but there are times in Scripture when it seems to be ok, for a greater good. At least, it's a point Christians can discuss, and wisdom is needed to work out the details.

We love to do the same with any rules, so we can find the exceptions for why it doesn't quite apply to us and the situation right now. "Sure, stealing is wrong," we say, "but does *this* qualify as stealing?" Or, "Of course I honor my parents; but it doesn't mean I have to do *that*."

The nature of sexual desire is that a little leads to more. Sex is designed that way. And so the scope for wriggle room when it comes to sexual sin is given as zero: *not even a hint*. Sexual desire is also one of the deepest and most powerful emotions within us, and therefore the temptation most

11. Wilder, *Farmer Boy*, 321.

12. I wholeheartedly recommend Arterburn and Stoeker, *Every Man's Battle*, for a serious, practical, no-holds-barred guide to sexual purity.

readily justified. The clarity of Eph 5:3 (and plenty of other parts of Scripture) is therefore very helpful: we can know the clear limits, the acceptable boundaries of how much impurity is allowed to us. It's *none*.

That is a tall order in any age of history; in today's impurity-soaked world it seems impossible. But the good thing is, wherever our thoughts, eyes, or bodies have wandered, we know where we need to get back to. *Not even a hint*. Cold turkey. Zero tolerance. Sexual activity belongs only within marriage. Anything beyond that is not fitting for *God's holy people*.

That should be clear. But there are four things that get in the way:

- *Secrecy* with sexual sins makes people isolated, compounding the temptations.
- *Shame* makes it harder to be honest, to know the love of God, and robs people of confident Christian living.
- *Shyness* creates an awkwardness in teaching and guiding the next generation in wholehearted purity.
- And *the shrug*—the shrug that says, "What can you do? Youngsters have to make their own mistakes. It's not for us to interfere with their lives." That's a big problem, because youngsters desperately need guidance from the older generation, especially their own parents, even if those parents haven't got it all ironed out perfectly themselves.

And yes, this is an area where the world can be particularly hostile—not just belittling and mocking, but cruelly targeting those who, by the contrast of their own behavior, expose the sordid nature of others. Yet through all that, there are a growing number of people who see the utter sense and goodness of Christian sexual morality. Misconduct can have such painful consequences for people; seeing Christians make the sacrifice of self-control can give a powerful testimony to the goodness of God.

Marriage

There seems to be a wide gap opening between church and world when it comes to marriage. Outside the church, very few people are marrying now. In Britain and Europe at least, even many of our national political leaders have boyfriends/girlfriends/"partners," as if we are being led by a lot of adolescents. But many Christians are marrying, and marrying young—to the bewilderment of the world around. Marriage is not for all. But when the Christian community honors and celebrates marriage,[13] it is a wonderful

13. Heb 13:4: "Marriage should be honored by all."

testimony to God's pattern for society. It is upholding the glorious principle of commitment for life—for better or worse, for richer or poorer.

Who, a century ago, would have thought that such a basic and beautiful thing would become something detested by society to the point of persecution? Yet to uphold marriage (as in *real* marriage, between a man and a woman) is to risk suffering the wrath of many. Christians don't need to apologize to a society that's lost its way. We don't need to keep trying to accommodate people who are forever wandering into new ideas. We simply need to keep enjoying that which is good.

I have known several Christian men who are eager to marry but baffled by the choices apparently available and wary of commitment. Both of these things—the right choice and the level of commitment—are reasonable concerns. On the first, there is teaching in some church circles that says, "So long as a girl is single, above the age of consent, and not a close relative, she'll be fine." The point about being too choosy is helpful enough; but I have seen that applied too literally, resulting in some deeply unhappy and dysfunctional marriages. Even arranged marriages are generally the result of serious discussion between families—they are *arranged* according to all sorts of criteria. It's important to know you can see eye to eye on some basic things, such as gender roles, raising children, or expected standard of living. Christians are free to marry cross-culturally, interracially, or across social strata, but marriage is challenging enough by crossing the gender divide; a couple should be clear about the extra challenges involved by introducing additional divides.

So: choose carefully. But don't be overwhelmed by choice, if you have options. Our world of endless choices, when it comes to shopping or movies, can become ugly in its greedy desires and self-defeating: when the rabbits all bolt in different directions, the dog can be left standing like a fool. It's much easier if there is just one choice. If a girl seems a good option, pursue her, get to know her and, if she is willing, marry her.

Which leads us on to the second concern that can hold people back from marriage: commitment. It is a legitimate concern that single people should be well aware of—once married, there is no way out until death. If there is one thing worse than being single wishing you were married, it is being married wishing you were single. That is why marriage should not be entered into "lightly or selfishly but reverently and responsibly in the sight of almighty God."[14] However, it still *should* be entered into, by most people. It's normal and good. Society may try to condition us to play the field, to

14. Church of England, preface to the Marriage Service, para. 4.

not get tied down, and certainly not too early. But this is the witness of character: honor marriage.

Raising Children

As with marriage, having children is not possible for all. But where it is, it is perhaps the greatest opportunity for *living a godly life* (2 Tim 3:12) in contrast to the world around. Raising children takes everything, every resource a parent has. It is not an aside to a person's career or ministry; it is an all-consuming commitment—and doubly hard for single parents.

Today's parents need to be alert to the onslaught against everything they will want to achieve for their children. If Dr. James Dobson, decades ago, could compare having a TV in a kid's bedroom to welcoming a greasy stranger in to entertain your son or daughter in private,[15] how much more today with the world of phones and internet. It is very difficult to navigate appropriate boundaries when everyone else has a smartphone (younger and younger at that), and where the bedroom is also the child's workstation and homework is internet based. But boundaries there most certainly must be, with the serious and rampant threats of cyber-bullies, pornography, addictive gaming, grooming, and even advertising. If it's hard for adults to steer clear of internet dangers, why do parents expect children and teenagers to handle something so explosive? And explosive it is, both in terms of its quickness to light up and its devastating power.

In the recent past, parents could (to some extent) rely on school to back up the moral values of home, even to do the lion's share of guiding children through right and wrong. No longer. School has become a battleground where Christian parents must be on full alert against the onslaught of sinister indoctrination. Our own children were, for a few years, in a lovely little rural primary school. One day, an innocent-looking mailing from the school included a passing reference to a forthcoming survey from the National Health Service: the children were to partake in it, if we were willing. Following the link, and after bland questions about diet and mealtimes and such things, the survey took a dark turn into whether the child would prefer to explore being a different gender. Raising it with the school, it turned out that not a single member of staff or school governor had even glanced at the survey before agreeing to impose it on our precious children.

Since then, our (British) national government, relishing the role of parent as it does, has decreed, "There is no right to withdraw from Relationship Education at primary or secondary as we believe the contents of

15. Dobson, *Bringing up Boys*, 208.

these subjects . . . are important for all children to be taught."[16] No wonder more and more families are opting for home schooling or Christian cooperatives—although government regulations will doubtless make these options harder, just as recent taxation is crippling private Christian schools.[17] But the government is not the ultimate enemy. Members of government are prisoners of society as much as any, and have simply become advocates for a deep move against family, the foundation of civilization. Dr. James Dobson, with his Focus on the Family, was a prophet in seeing the battlefront on which to fight hardest.

But what of our legacy? For most of us, our greatest and abiding effect on the world will be in the form of perhaps two or three people—people who were born into and grew up in our home, and went on to repeat the process in another. I have heard many old people cooing over prams, telling the bewildered parents, "Ooh, make the most of them while they're small; they soon grow up!" Making the most of them as infants *is* preparing them to grow up. The aim for parents is to produce, as far as they are able, future adults who will serve the Lord faithfully in their decisions and character.

That means being fully involved through the steps of childhood. While many mothers have to work to make ends meet, I am still not convinced that the "need for two incomes" has really understood the differences between luxuries and necessities. Palming preschoolers off to day care at the hands of people who don't care about all the things you care about, and certainly don't love your child as you do, should certainly be a last resort for desperate circumstances. Christian parents should know better than to wish away school holidays, or join the joke with other parents about how good it is to get the little tykes off your hands back into school again, especially in the child's hearing. Time with children is precious. There is no such thing as "quality time"; *quantity* time is the only thing that counts. Sure, watch their TV programs with them. But for little kids, relationships are built by pottering in the back yard, kicking leaves in the park, reading favorite books over and over, building train tracks or feeding baby dolls in the kitchen while Mom does her chores. As they get older, games, regular mealtimes, family devotions, talking through homework and friendships, holidays, outings, sport, and movies—such things keep the relationships growing. Children learn principles of danger, boundaries, kindness, and healthy fun not through rules and instructions but through *time spent* in normal relationship with parents and other caring people. Once you and the kids are barely talking to each other, decisive remedial action needs taking.

16. Department for Education, "Relationships Education," para. 20.

17. For example, see Warburton, "King Alfred School."

One of the first homeschooling families I ever met was in a church I used to belong to. They were not wealthy or highly educated themselves: Dad was a London cab driver. The decision to home-educate started when their oldest boy would not talk about what had happened at school. At that point they realized what danger they were in, and withdrew their children from the tough world of a London school. They taught me the importance of parents making decisive decisions to care for their children. It is not ok to allow them to drift, to distance, to get swallowed up by the cruel machine of the general public—and hope for the best.

Cheerfulness

Cheerfulness is becoming a lost art. The Western mood drifts between three points of a triangle: stress, grumpiness, and hilarity. These are the acceptable moods to portray. Acting stressed is to say you're busy, which is seen as good because you're doing something important. Similarly, a grumpiness says you're focused, therefore obviously doing something important too—or it says you're hard done by for some reason, which is also viewed as customary, because we're all hard done by and as a fellow-sufferer you're one of the gang. And then, perhaps on a Saturday night or at those lighter moments at work, hilarity can run riot for a while. If you're funny, you're popular—because it helps everyone complete the triangle of their existence.

But somewhere lurking in the middle, forgotten, is cheerfulness. It is not always easy to be cheerful, because in the eyes of others, cheerful people think they are better than everyone else, oblivious to the struggles of life that the rest of us are feeling. There is something suspicious about someone who can be cheerful when under pressure, or happy without being entertained. Yet cheerfulness is something that every Christian can and should have:

> Rejoice in the Lord always. I will say it again: rejoice! Let your gentleness be evident to all. The Lord is near. Do not be anxious about anything, but in every situation, by prayer and petition, with thanksgiving, present your requests to God. (Phil 4:4–6)

The fact that social conformity prevents people from showing it makes steady cheerfulness a quality of leadership. And it is contagious. It lifts the spirits of those around. And for Christians, ultimately it points people to the hope we have in Christ.

During the siege of Mafeking in the Boer War, the small British garrison and civilian population held off the besieging army of some ten thousand Boers for an astonishing 217 days. They suffered great shortage of food, ammunition, and military relief, yet fought with ingenuity and energy, and finally beat the enemy altogether. A large part of the success was down to the young colonel in charge of the defense, Robert Baden-Powell. Together with his attentive laboring day and night, he went about the town and defenses with the "light, almost running gait of his and the customary whistle on his lips."[18] And "to the best of their ability the troops copied his neatness of dress, especially on Sundays. Smartness and cleanliness heightened morale, and bewildered the enemy . . . for the unwashed Boers could never quite understand how it was that, from the battered defenses of the ruined *dorp*, men could come forth freshly shaven, with clean shirts and polished boots."[19]

Two older Christian men have made a particular impression on me. They both grew up in colonial Kenya and, perhaps partly for that reason, have a similar air of contagious cheerfulness. One led the team of leaders on a summer camp for teenagers of which I was a part for many years. His bright "Good morning!" alone created an atmosphere that disinclined anyone else to complain of lack of sleep or poor weather. The other man led a nearby local church that had very little by way of visible encouragement. But from his demeanor one would think he had nothing but steady good news week by week. I believe his own prayerfulness reminded him that, in view of God's kingdom, he did.

Christians even under extreme suffering have spurred on the church by their cheerfulness. When the English martyrs, bishops Hugh Latimer and Nicholas Ridley, were burned at the stake in Oxford city center in 1555, Latimer said, "Be of good comfort, Master Ridley, and play the man; we shall this day, by God's grace, light such a candle in England as I trust shall never be put out."[20] He wasn't asking Ridley to grin through the pain, but to have a confident, optimistic outlook—because he had every reason to do so despite the situation at the moment.

Eric Liddell was an Olympic gold medalist. He ended his life aged forty-three in Weihsien, a Japanese prisoner-of-war camp. Even under the appalling conditions suffered, Liddell stood out for morale-building cheerfulness that flowed from his deep Christian convictions. Fellow internee Norman Cliff wrote, "Liddell seemed to be ubiquitous—he was all over the camp, holding friendly conversations with all kinds of people."[21] Another

18. Grinnell-Milne, *Mafeking*, 125.

19. Grinnell-Milne, *Mafeking*, 126.

20. As reported by Ryle, *Five English Reformers*, 18.

21. Cliff, "Eric Liddell," para. 11.

biographer wrote, "In camp he was in his middle forties, lithe and springy of step and, above all, overflowing with good humour and love of life."[22]

So don't see cheerfulness as something dependent on circumstances. When you're stuck around the edge of the stress-grumpiness-hilarity triangle, pray a prayer of thankfulness, walk with a spring in your step, whistle a cheerful tune, and warmly wish people a *good morning*.

Work

The New Testament has a lot to say about work. For example, it says that laziness is a sin that shouldn't be tolerated in the church: "The one who is unwilling to work shall not eat" (2 Thess 3:10). It says even slaves should "obey your earthly masters in everything; and do it, not only when their eye is on you and to curry their favor, but with sincerity of heart and reverence for the Lord. Whatever you do, work at it with all your heart, as working for the Lord, not for human masters" (Col 3:22–23). Christians are urged to "mind your own business and work with your hands . . . so that your daily life may win the respect of outsiders and so that you will not be dependent on anybody" (1 Thess 4:11–12).

We are created to work with our hands, just as Adam was placed in the garden "to work it and take care of it" (Gen 2:15). To not work is to make us less than we are supposed to be; it is dehumanizing. Patterns of rest are important, too, of course; but to rest when you should be working is to buck against the way we are designed, and therefore is an unhappy thing. Days when I procrastinate, putting off the things I should be doing for things I want to do, are unsatisfying. Days when I do what I should do in time to enjoy the things I want to do are much happier days. Productivity is pleasing.

One of our cultural challenges is the great advancement of labor-saving devices. These are very helpful, saving us from spending a day a week at the washhouse, from planting acres of potatoes by hand, or from writing actual letters to people with a pen. New technology can multiply our output and productivity. But the danger is every new luxury becomes a necessity as we lose the skills or time to do it the old way. Producers of technology are very happy for everyone to become dependent on their products. We need to be aware of shortcuts in work that have short-term gains but long-term losses, by handing over all skills. Becoming entirely dependent on the developers of *artificial intelligence* is not a very pleasant thought. But once you get in the habit of using such tools, it's hard to go back. These are dangers for our society.

22. Magnusson, *Flying Scotsman*, 159.

However, the world of the modern workplace brings other challenges that involve real sacrifice for Christians. Equality, Diversity, and Inclusivity (EDI) training, climate change and racial justice policies, LGBTQ celebration months, Halal food in the canteen, and the like can make workplaces pretty hostile to Christians. When confronted with ideological agendas, two things are called for in the Christian: *resilience* and *principle.* Both are difficult; together they require much wisdom.

Resilience means refusing to cave in at the first challenge. Especially when not battle-hardened from years of dealing with such things, it can be quite shocking to be told to conform to thoughts and beliefs that are alien to the Christian way of life. That is to say, the young Christian in her first job, or the boy from a Christian home at his apprenticeship induction, can find the forcefulness of company agendas particularly threatening. The temptation is to quit at once. That might even feel noble—and is principled. But becoming jobless, and thereafter less employable, is often not the right thing. Christians need to survive and thrive within workplace environments, not just to retreat into Christian companies and Christian ghettos. To be *salt* and *light* (Matt 5:13–16), we need to be *shrewd as snakes* (Matt 10:16).

In practice, that means you don't necessarily need to make a dramatic stand during an unpleasant training session. You don't necessarily need to speak out at all, or even aim to be subversive as you talk to colleagues afterward. You might even find, on reflection, that some things you assumed would be terrible were not so bad after all. In any case, you are an employee among some very powerful people, who themselves are under more powerful authorities still. Christians under communism are worth learning from: you don't need to rush into martyrdom to subvert a godless system; you simply need to *live not by lies.*[23]

Three phrases might be helpful to keep in your own mind:

- *Two can play at that game.* At times, workplace agendas can feel like a bit of a game. But if I respect your viewpoints, you need to respect mine too. There are things my religion does not permit. I am not allowed to celebrate this thing with you.
- *I'm a child of the Living God.* You may try and bully me with this nonsense, but my dad is bigger than yours. I don't need to panic here. Truth will be seen.

23. The title of an essay by Aleksandr Solzhenitsyn, taken as the title for Rod Dreher's book.

- *I don't need you to like me.* If I suddenly feel as though I don't belong here, it's ok: I don't. I'm a stranger on earth. My happiness is not based on what the boss at work thinks of me.

That last point is helpful when it comes to being *principled* too. We like to be liked. But being principled means you are not just going to go along with all the agendas or practices you are told to. The attitude must be: I won't be rude or careless; but I won't walk on eggshells around the ever-changing sensitivities. I won't say things to deliberately aggravate those who oppose God; but I won't wear a rainbow badge or the latest colored bow. I'll be warm and pleasant, unthreatened and friendly to all; but I won't agree with everything that's said, or be bullied into saying things I don't believe, and I'm happy to speak the truth when asked. I don't want to make trouble, or get into trouble; but if I do, it's ok. Christians know there is always a higher court of appeal.

Gratitude

For some kids, Christmas is followed by the duty of writing thank-you letters. For some kids, it can be so tedious they wish they'd never gotten the presents in the first place. But they understand the lesson they're being taught: the habit of thankfulness—and expressing thankfulness—is a good one.

For Christians, gratitude should be second nature. Jesus's story of the ten lepers in Luke 17:11–19 is more than a just a lesson in manners for the sake of it—it shows that manners are about relationship. The story goes that ten lepers come begging Jesus for healing. They receive it. Only one, a foreigner, bothers with a *thank you*. Jesus is disappointed with the rest, but says to the one, "Rise and go; your faith has made you well." The one ends up *well* in a way the others don't. The healing is not complete until thanks is given. Any gift is not really yours until you have thanked the giver and thanked God.

Everybody appreciates someone with good manners. But you will find that expressing thanks to God is also met with resentment. Put a comment thanking God on a social media post, and there will likely be someone who can't help themselves from replying, "Don't bring your god into it." Well, that shouldn't put us off. Prayers of thankfulness should be our constant habit. They should overspill into being thankful to other people. And thankful people are happier, less anxious people too. They tend to be more generous to others in all sorts of ways.

~

"In fact, everyone who wants to live a godly life in Christ Jesus will be persecuted" (2 Tim 3:12). It is not just those who speaks boldly for Christ Jesus who will be persecuted. Nor is it just those who are at the forefront of public debate. It is those who want to live a godly life. Do these things, live these ways—in fact, even just *aspire* to live these ways—and people will oppose you. It is a sacrifice to follow Christ.

Pain is not pleasant. But it is an exciting thought that my simple Christian life might be noticed. Few of us are ever given a large platform for proclaiming the gospel. Even fewer of us would be equipped to use it well if we were. But this simple life of walking in the old paths, being of noble character—that is noticed too. We can't help it being noticed.

Growing in character and good habits of life is a very powerful thing. After dictating six long volumes chronicling the details of the Second World War, with all the twists and turns, ups and downs, atrocities and righteous acts, acts of Providence and acres of pain, Winston Churchill produced a four-line summary of the moral lessons learned:

> In war: Resolution
> In defeat: Defiance
> In victory: Magnanimity
> In peace: Goodwill"[24]

In war: Resolution. Keep focused on the purpose and end goal. *In defeat: Defiance.* Never, never, never give up. Don't let the setbacks define you; don't let discouragement stop you. *In victory: Magnanimity.* Don't gloat; after all, you know your own heart and the fragility of any victory you ever have the good fortune to experience. *In peace: Goodwill.* You don't need to go looking for a fight, provoking and proving points. Disagreements come again soon enough without looking for them.

Meanwhile, the war for our souls wages daily. With Paul, we need to take hold of ourselves so that we "will not be disqualified for the prize" (1 Cor 9:27). Our salvation depends on self-discipline. And the mentality is contagious. Sometimes church leaders don't want to be too insistent, too pastorally firm. Perhaps they are conscious of their own slightly wishy-washy attitude to godliness, and squirm from hypocrisy. But if there was a time in the past when, as an individual or as a church or as a whole church culture, there was more seriousness about *working out salvation with fear and trembling*—then let's get back to those days, shall we? The basic habits of learning Bible verses, praying together, saying "'No' to ungodliness and

24. Churchill, *Gathering Storm*, epigraph.

worldly passions" and living "self-controlled, upright and godly lives" (Titus 2:12)—these are the embracing of the gospel: the gospel in which *salvation involves sacrifice.*

The hymn "Jesus, I My Cross Have Taken" seems to have made a comeback in recent years. Have a look particularly at verse 3 in this version.

Jesus, I my cross have taken,
All to leave and follow thee;
Destitute, despised, forsaken,
Thou from hence my all shalt be.
Perish, every fond ambition,
All I've sought, and hoped, and known;
Yet how rich is my condition;
God and Heaven are still my own!

Let the world despise and leave me;
They have left my Savior, too;
Human hearts and looks deceive me;
Thou art not, like them, untrue;
And while thou shalt smile upon me,
God of wisdom, love, and might,
Foes may hate, and friends may shun me;
Show thy face, and all is bright!

Go then, earthly fame and treasure!
Come, disaster, scorn, and pain!
In thy service, pain is pleasure;
With thy favor, loss is gain.
I have called thee Abba, Father;
I have stayed my heart on thee;
Storms may howl, and clouds may gather;
All must work for good to me.

Haste then on from grace to glory,
Armed by faith, and winged by prayer;
Heaven's eternal day before thee;
God's own hand shall guide me there.
Soon shall close thy earthly mission;
Swift shall pass thy pilgrim days;
Hope soon change to glad fruition,
Faith to sight, and prayer to praise.[25]

25. Lyte, "Jesus."

Conclusion

What Now?

The others who thought she was telling a lie, and a silly lie too, made her very unhappy.

C. S. Lewis, *The Lion, the Witch and the Wardrobe*

Come out of her, my people,
so that you will not share in her sins,
so that you will not receive any of her plagues.
Rev 18:4

THE MAJORITY OPINION IS usually the wrong one. That has always been the way of things.

Out of all nations on earth, Israel was to be God's special possession. The majority of the world worshipped idols. That was wrong.

Even within Israel, the majority went astray. When the nation split after Solomon, the larger half turned away from the Lord, and ultimately disappeared altogether. True believers among them were persecuted. At one point, Elijah said, "I am the only one left, and now they are trying to kill me too" (1 Kgs 19:10). The Lord assured him he still had his seven thousand who hadn't bowed the knee to Baal. But it certainly felt like very few.

Of the remaining nation of Judah, only a *remnant* returned from their own exile, and only a tiny proportion followed Jesus when he appeared. Even his closest disciples fled when Jesus suffered most. He was the *only one* who remained faithful, though Peter had sworn, "Even if all fall away, I will not" (Mark 14:29).

Although the church has transformed the world like nothing else, and although Christians like to mention the billions that call themselves Christians, and although there is nothing so significant in all history as the kingdom of God—those who hold to truth as revealed by God are always a significant minority, within both the world and the church. The church fathers observed the distinction between the *visible* and *invisible* church: the majority of those who appear to be Christians are not truly followers of Christ. "Not everyone who says to me, 'Lord, Lord,' will enter the kingdom of heaven" (Matt 7:21).

If you find yourself agreeing with the majority, you ought to feel uneasy.

The Difficulty with Copernicus

You may have heard of the Copernican Revolution of the sixteenth century, when Nicolaus Copernicus proposed that the earth orbited the sun, not the other way round. It was hard for people to accept a new idea, to go against the flow of a received outlook.

> Yet among all discoveries and convictions none may have produced a greater effect on the human spirit than the doctrine of Copernicus. Hardly had the world been acknowledged as spherical and closed in itself when it should abandon the enormous prerogative to be the centre of the universe. Perhaps never a greater challenge has been imposed on mankind; for what did not dissolve by this acknowledgement into vapour and smoke, a second paradise, a world of innocence, poetry and piety, the testimony of the senses, the conviction of a poetic-religious belief; no wonder that they did not want to let go of all this, that they opposed such a doctrine in all manners, which entitled and summoned him, who accepted it, to a hitherto unknown, yea unimagined freedom of thought and greatness of views.[1]

We all know the difficulty of accepting new ideas, ideas that call our assumptions into question. It can be very unsettling. And when you are persuaded by such a thing, it is then hard to go against the flow, to believe

1. Goethe, *Geschichte der Farbenlehre*, quoted in Neuber et al., *Making*.

things when they seem to be outside the box of popular thought. But this book has urged you to think afresh.

Think of the experience of the children in *The Lion, The Witch and The Wardrobe* as each discovered the other world through a rack of fur coats. If your children said such a thing, would you not assume it was nonsense? If they persisted, you might get cross. In C. S. Lewis's story, Lucy was the first to discover Narnia. Her own siblings made life difficult for her when she did, whether unwittingly or out of spite. It's hard to believe things that other people don't believe.

Narnia is a fiction. But it is a picture of the new life in Christ, the eye-opening discovery of the gospel message, the world described by Scripture. And that is not fiction.

Neither is the reaction of people who assume it is.

As a Christian, when you discover new things—or rather, things that are not new at all, that have been believed through history, that have been staring you in the face, that are right there in Scripture—the reaction of those around you can be unpleasant. These are people who think as you used to think, who are friends and family and fellow Christians. When people are challenged, they become frightened. When people are frightened, they will say unkind things, and they might do terrible things.

Such treatment does not prove the majority right. Quite the opposite. The most concerning thing, however, is not that they will shut down ideas outside their own mainstream, by sneering, patronizing, or shouting louder. History shows that truth prevails, whatever stands in the way. What is most concerning is that the majority of the church will be found to be at odds with God.

If you allow your cultural assumptions to cause you to reject Scripture at any point, you have started along a very dangerous path. When the church in a particular culture allows that culture to limit its definition of the gospel, and won't entertain the suggestion that it is doing so, it spiritually stunts its growth and jeopardizes its future. Such a position will include many of our cherished churches, respected gurus, and dear friends.

Squashing the "Flat-Earthers"

The dawn of the Enlightenment, leading up to the great discoveries of the eighteenth century, frightened the church establishment of the day. The church felt so threatened by the new ideas that it had a list of prohibited books, deemed to corrupt the innocent. Back at the time of the Protestant Reformation, that feeling of a threatened establishment led to people doing terrible things to the Reformers. There are whole towns in far-off lands such as South Africa and the United States of America that exist because some European Protestant communities were driven out of their homes to the ends of the earth.

Now much of the church wholly accepts the Enlightenment way of thinking: scientific rationalism is the key to knowledge, things that are *true* are things that can be observed and measured, seen or deduced. Our methods of thinking are Enlightenment-shaped: logical and fixed, consensus-based and peer-reviewed. Much of that is fine and good; we are glad that scientific discovery has replaced medieval superstition. But science is not the sum total of everything. And yet much of the Protestant church in the West is so embedded in the cultural mindset that it is threatened when anyone dares to question assumptions. It scorns anyone who even seems open to truth outside Enlightenment parameters.

There are a growing number of "flat-earthers" of our day; as might be expected, they are often treated as a joke. After chatting to one at a wedding several years ago, one of our kids, on hearing about it, said, "That's stupid. The earth is obviously round. . . . Otherwise, where do globes come from?" That was the final (and only) argument, the end of the discussion. He walked out the door. But more concerningly, how has the rational, Bible-teaching church treated "conspiracy theorists," "anti-vaxxers," "right-wing extremists," or "homophobes" in our own day? Some have been forced to leave churches, some have lost jobs or been evicted from leadership positions in the church, many have lost Christian friends and fellowship. Why? Because the church has the same fear of change that the establishment church had in the early days of the Enlightenment. And it is capable of doing things that are just as terrible as then.

But why should the church be frightened of thinking about new ideas? It doesn't have to embrace them, just by giving them the time of day and a fair hearing. Christianity is different from all other religions in that it is robust enough to have difficult questions asked of it. The truth can cope with challenge and questioning—in fact it is made more secure by being questioned. It is false gospels and false religion that can't cope with being challenged. Those things get exposed and lose their power; but the true faith grows stronger by questioning, because the Scriptures are deep and secure in their integrity.

Instead of dismissing new ideas wholesale because someone important said they are not "Christian," how about having the maturity to listen? Maybe things like yoga, mindfulness, acupuncture, or Reiki healing are not entirely and fundamentally demonic just because they have their origins in other parts of the world or pagan ideologies. Is it so very threatening to just ask what they really mean—even if you conclude they should be avoided in the end? You might even discover glories of God's creation that people have enjoyed for centuries; they grate with the Enlightenment, but perhaps not with the Bible. How will you know without looking? Perhaps "the science" is not right; perhaps disease is in fact more tightly bound up with our emotional health than the drug companies let on; perhaps our material wealth is as much a curse as a blessing because of its insatiable allure. It is good to ask the questions that Christians from outside our culture would ask of us.

What's more, people seeking truth and meaning are not attracted to a church with no imagination. Tradition, maybe: a church standing for the age-old story is exactly what people need. But that is not the same as twentieth-century tradition. Who, seeking *truth*, wants a church that is a religious version of the very Enlightenment-shaped culture that has left them cold in the first place?

It's Ok to Stand Apart

In Revelation, the anti-Christ culture of Babylon is described in ways that seem evermore literally true with every passing year. By chapter 18, her dreadful and deserved end is announced. What horror and surprise awaits the world on judgment day! In the middle of it, one simple command is given to Jesus's followers: "Come out of her, my people" (Rev 18:4).

It is hard to notice how much you are in her, when year by year, small decision by small decision, tiny compromise by tiny compromise, the ways of Babylon are the air you breathe, the water you swim in. How dreadful for the church that blinds itself to God's word because of its *Babylon* assumptions. What courage it takes to believe the bits of the Bible that others don't. Relationships can be broken. But the stakes are too high to do otherwise:

> "Come out of her, my people,"
> so that you will not share in her sins,
> so that you will not receive any of her plagues.

We really can't afford to go with the crowd.

It Feels Good to Discover More of God

Yes, accepting new ideas can be pretty hard, because of the things I have just been describing. But it's good too. The unhinged wildcard who is always reading between the lines for insights hitherto undiscovered, or always seeking to dismiss the normal teaching of the Bible—that person is tiresome, a pain in any church, and a troublemaker. But the member of the Bible study who causes the group to pause on a tricky verse, who even risks derailing the leader from his or her carefully prepared questions with questions of her own—now that is someone who brings Bible study to life. Difficult for the leader, maybe; but good if the aim is to genuinely feed on the word of God.

The Christian life should be one of endless new discovery. Any healthy relationship grows over time. What of our ultimate relationship? To lack hunger for more and more insight into his word is to be bored of God.

Nothing brings joy to life like growing relationships. When you know God, all other relationships grow in meaning too. The whole of life brightens as we know God better. I hope something in this book has given you a taste for fresh discovery, a gap through the walls of our limited cultural outlook. As for me, I also expect to discover more things in the Bible that I have hitherto not believed. I reckon that going five years without changing your mind on something is a problem. Perhaps I will even rethink things I have written here. But we must all keep discovering more of God and his ways. I hope you will enjoy that voyage of wonder.

> All Scripture is God-breathed and is useful for teaching, rebuking, correcting and training in righteousness, so that the man of God may be thoroughly equipped for every good work. (2 Tim 3:16–17 NIV, 1984)

Bibliography

Adams, Richard. *Watership Down*. Harmondsworth: Puffin, 2014.

Adamson, Andrew, dir. *Shrek*. DreamWorks Animation, PDI/DreamWorks, 2001.

AdOYo. "The Wormingford Dragon Window." Atlas Obscura, December 9, 2022. https://www.atlasobscura.com/places/wormingford-dragon-window.

Aelianus, Claudius. *On the Nature of Animals*. Translated by A. F. Schofield. 1958. https://www.attalus.org/info/aelian.html.

Anderson, Neil T. *The Bondage Breaker*. Crowborough, UK: Monarch, 1997.

Andrews, Helen. "The Great Feminization." Compact, October 16, 2025. https://www.compactmag.com/article/the-great-feminization/.

Anglican Church in North America. *The Book of Common Prayer and Administration of the Sacraments with Other Rites and Ceremonies of the Church According to the Use of the Anglican Church in North America Together with the New Coverdale Psalter*. Huntington Beach, CA: Anglican Liturgy, 2019.

———. "Largest Anglican Church in Canada Protects its Faith." October 4, 2011. https://anglicanchurch.net/largest-anglican-congregation-in-canada-protects-its-faith/.

Annaud, Jean-Jacques, dir. *Seven Years in Tibet*. TriStar Pictures, Mandalay Entertainment, 1997.

Archeology World. "Magellan's Strange Encounter with the 10-Foot Giants of Patagonia." June 7, 2022. https://archaeology-world.com/magellans-strange-encounter-with-the-10-foot-giants-of-patagonia/.

———. "The Mystery Behind the 18 Giant Skeletons Found in the USA." March 31, 2020. https://archaeology-world.com/the-mystery-behind-the-18-giant-skeletons-found-in-the-usa/.

Arterburn, Stephen, and Fred Stoeker. *Every Man's Battle*. Colorado Springs: Waterbrook, 2000.

A. R. *True and Wonderfull*. London: Trundle, 1614. https://archive.org/details/truewonderfulldiooarrauoft/.

Augustine. *Expositions on the Book of Psalms*. Vol. 8 of *The Nicene and Post-Nicene Fathers*, series 1, edited and translated by Philip Schaff. New York: Christian Literature Company, 1888.

Austen, Jane. *Sense and Sensibility*. Edited by Ros Ballaster. London: Penguin Classics, 2003.

Baden-Powell, Robert. *Lessons from the Varsity of Life*. London: Pearson, 1934.

———. *Scouting for Boys*. London: Pearson, 1951.

Barclay, William. *The Gospel of Luke*. Philadelphia: Westminster, 1965.

Barrand, Claire. "Did Welsh Giants Once Roam the Valleys?" Spooky Isles, January 3, 2020. https://www.spookyisles.com/welsh-giants/.

Bonhoeffer, Dietrich. *The Cost of Discipleship*. Translated by R. H. Fuller. London: SCM, 1959.

Breckman, Andy, creator. *Monk*. Mandeville Films, Touchstone Television, USA Cable Entertainment, MBC Universal Television Studio, 2002–2009.

Brooks, Phillips. "O Little Town of Bethlehem." Hymnary, 1868. https://hymnary.org/text/o_little_town_of_bethlehem.

Bunyan, John. "He Who Would Valiant Be." Adapted by Percy Dearmer, arranged by Ralph Vaughan Williams. In *Complete Anglican Hymns Old and New*, edited by Susan Sayers and Michael Forster, 281. Suffolk, UK: Mayhew, 2000.

Cameron, James, dir. *The Terminator*. Hemdale, Pacific Western Productions, Euro Film Funding, Cinema '84, 1984.

Cary, James. "Which Dragon Does St. Michael Need to Slay Today?" Seen and Unseen, September 26, 2024. https://www.seenandunseen.com/which-dragon-does-st-michael-need-slay-today.

Charles, R. H., trans. *The Book of Jubilees, or The Little Genesis*. London: Black, 1902.

Cherry, Kendra. "What Is Confirmation Bias? Cherrypicking the Facts to Support an Existing Belief." Verywell Mind, updated November 13, 2025. https://www.verywellmind.com/what-is-a-confirmation-bias-2795024.

Chesterton, G. K. *The Everlasting Man*. London: Hodder and Stoughton, 1947.

Chomsky, Noam. *Understanding Power: The Indispensable Chomsky*. Edited by Peter R. Mitchell and John Schoeffel. London: Vintage, 2003.

Church of England. *The Book of Common Prayer and Administration of the Sacraments and Other Rites and Ceremonies of the Church According to the Use of the Church of England*. 2nd ed. Cambridge: Cambridge University Press, [1953?].

———. Preface to the Marriage Service. https://www.churchofengland.org/prayer-and-worship/worship-texts-and-resources/common-worship/marriage#mm095.

Churchill, Winston. *The Gathering Storm*. Vol. 1 of *The Second World War*. London: Reprint Society, 1951.

Cliff, Norman. "Eric Liddell in Weihsein Camp—1943–1945." Weihsein. https://www.weihsien-paintings.org/NormanCliff/people/individuals/Eric01/txt_personal.htm.

Cohen, Baruch C. "Nazi Medical Experimentation: The Ethics of Using Medical Data from Nazi Experiments." Jewish Virtual Library. https://www.jewishvirtuallibrary.org/the-ethics-of-using-medical-data-from-nazi-experiments.

Coulson, Charles A. *Science and Christian Belief*. London: Fontana, 1958.

Cusumano, Joel. "'Dragon Bones' of Santa Maria e San Donato." Atlas Obscura, January 18, 2019. https://www.atlasobscura.com/places/dragon-bones-of-santa-maria-e-san-donato.

Cutts, Edward L. *Turning Points of English Church History*. London: SPCK, 1908.

Dahl, Terje. "Old Newspaper Articles Are Serious About Giant Skeletons." Sydhav. https://www.sydhav.no/giants/newspapers.htm.

Damick, Andrew Stephen. *The Lord of Spirits: An Orthodox Christian Framework for the Unseen World and Spiritual Warfare*. Chesterton, IN: Ancient Faith, 2023.

Damick, Andrew Stephen, and Stephen De Young. "A Land of Giants." *The Lord of Spirits* (podcast), November 26, 2020.

Darwin, Charles. *On the Origin of Species*. London: Murray, 1859. Project Gutenberg. https://www.gutenberg.org/files/1228/1228-h/1228-h.htm.

Department of Education. "Relationships Education, Relationships and Sex Education (RSE) and Health Education: FAQs." Gov UK, April 5, 2019. Last updated July 9, 2020. https://www.gov.uk/government/news/relationships-education-relationships-and-sex-education-rse-and-health-education-faqs.

Dickins, Rosie. *How Your Body Works*. Illustrated by Océane Meklemberg. Usborne Lift-the-Flap. Tulsa: EDC, 2019.

Dobson, James. *Bringing up Boys*. Carol Stream, IL: Tyndale House, 2001.

Dreher, Rod. *Live Not by Lies: A Manual for Christian Dissidents*. London: Hodder and Stoughton, 2024.

Duncan, David, and Sons, proprietors. "Petrified Giant." *Cardiff Times and South Wales Weekly News*, August 22, 1908. https://newspapers.library.wales/view/3434284/3434296.

Dunning, Robert. Introduction to *Jocelin of Wells: Bishop, Builder, Courtier*. Edited by Robert Dunning, 1–6. Studies in the History of Medieval Religion 36. Cambridge: Boydell & Brewer, 2010.

Edoworld. "Arhuanran of Udo Deity." Edu Culture, August 4, 2023. https://www.edoworld.net/Arhuanran_Of_Udo_Deity.html.

Environmental Working Group. "The Dirty Dozen." EWG. https://www.ewg.org/foodnews/dirty-dozen.php.

Ferguson, N. M., et al. "Estimating the Human Health Risk from Possible BSE Infection of the British Sheep Flock." *Nature* 415 (2002) 420–24. https://www.nature.com/articles/nature709.

Freeman, Richard. *Dragons: More than a Myth?* Devon, UK: CFZ, 2005.

Fulfer, Mac. *Amazing Face Reading*. Self published, 2011.

Fund, John. "'Professor Lockdown' Modeler Resigns in Disgrace." National Review, May 6, 2020. https://www.nationalreview.com/corner/professor-lockdown-modeler-resigns-in-disgrace/.

Garrett, Ben, and Brian Sauvé. "Giants (Part II): Giants in Myth." *Haunted Cosmos* (podcast), season 2, episode 7, November 29, 2023.

———. "On Dragons." *Haunted Cosmos* (podcast), season 3, episode 8, June 26, 2024.

Gawler, Grace. *Women of Silence: The Emotional Healing of Breast Cancer*. Melbourne, Aus.: Hill of Content, 1994.

Gessner, Conrad. *Historia animalium*. 5 vols. Zurich: Tigvri, 1551.

Greenfield, Beth. "Cardiologist and Cohort of RFK Jr. Warns Americans to Avoid Foods with 5 or More Ingredients: Here's Why." Fortune, January 14, 2025. https://fortune.com/well/2025/01/14/rfk-jr-cohort-aseem-malhotra-diet-avoiding-food-5-ingredients/.

Grinnell-Milne, Duncan. *Mafeking: Baden-Powell's Heroic Defence of the Besieged Town During the Boer War*. London: Landsborough, 1960.

Groening, Matt, creator. *The Simpsons*. Gracie Films, 20th Television, 20th Television Animation, 1989–.

Hacker, Jess. "How Many People Were Treated in Nightingale Hospitals?" Full Fact, September 20, 2024. https://fullfact.org/health/how-many-people-treated-nightingale-hospitals/.

Haley, Alex. *Roots: The Saga of an American Family*. New York: Doubleday, 1976.

Harrison, David. “Farmers Rise from the Ashes of Foot and Mouth.” Telegraph, February 19, 2011. https://www.telegraph.co.uk/news/earth/agriculture/8335705/Farmers-rise-from-the-ashes-of-foot-and-mouth.html.

Heiser, Michael S. “Deuteronomy 32:8 and the Sons of God.” *Bibliotheca Sacra* 158 (2001) 52–74.

———. “The Nephilim.” Sitchin Is Wrong. https://sitchiniswrong.com/nephilim/nephilim.htm.

———. *The Unseen Realm: Recovering the Supernatural Worldview of the Bible.* Bellingham, WA: Lexham, 2015.

Henson, Jim, creator. *The Muppet Show.* ATV, Henson Associates, ITC Entertainment, 1976.

Highfield, Roger. “Has the A-Team Defeated the Virus?” Telegraph, April 12, 2001. https://www.telegraph.co.uk/news/science/science-news/4762033/Has-the-A-team-defeated-the-virus.html.

Huxley, Aldous. *Brave New World.* London: Flamingo, 1994.

Huxley, Elspeth. *A New Earth.* London: Chatto & Windus, 1960.

Ibrahim, Raymond. *Defenders of the West: The Christian Heroes Who Stood Against Islam.* New York: Bombadier, 2022.

Ilbonito. “Dinosaur of Ta Prohm: Hoax, Mistake, or Evidence of Dinosaurs in Human Times?” Atlas Obscura, September 4, 2009. https://www.atlasobscura.com/places/dinosaur-angkor-wat.

Inspired Podcast. “Generous Living in Preparing to Die | Richard Garnett.” YouTube, August 28, 2024. https://www.youtube.com/watch?v=mOXgEGVQmfE&t=1148s.

John Muir Trust. “Why We Love Bogs (And You Should Too): 11 Fascinating Features of the Humble Peat Bog.” April 7, 2022. https://www.johnmuirtrust.org/resources/1139-why-we-love-bogs-and-you-should-too

Kennedy, Robert F., Jr. *The Real Anthony Fauci: Bill Gates, Big Pharma, and the Global War on Democracy and Public Health.* New York: Skyhorse, 2021.

Kipling, Rudyard. *The Jungle Book.* London: Macmillan, 1894.

Kircher, Athanasius. *Mundus subterraneus.* Amsterdam: Waesberge & Filios, 1678. https://archive.org/details/mundussubterraneo2kirc/.

Konishi, Shino. “‘Inhabited by a Race of Formidable Giants’: French Explorers, Aborigines, and the Endurance of the Fantastic in the Great South Land, 1803.” *Australian Humanities Review* 44 (2008). https://australianhumanitiesreview.org/2008/03/01/inhabited-by-a-race-of-formidable-giants-french-explorers-aborigines-and-the-endurance-of-the-fantastic-in-the-great-south-land-1803/.

Koonin, Steven E. *Unsettled: What Climate Science Tells Us, What It Doesn’t, and Why It Matters.* Dallas: BenBella, 2021.

Lee, Dulcie, and Jasmine Andersson. “Same-Sex Marriage: ‘MPs Tried to Force Church on Issue,’ Says Archbishop.” BBC, February 13, 2023. https://www.bbc.co.uk/news/uk-64621127.

Lee, Harper. *To Kill a Mockingbird.* London: Arrow, 1989.

Leendertse, Paul. *The Root Cause of Cancer: How to Begin Healing from Within.* Self published, 2025.

Leithart, Peter J. *Delivered from the Elements of the World: Atonement, Justification, Mission.* Downers Grove, IL: IVP Academic, 2016.

Lewis, C. S. *The Chronicles of Narnia.* 7 vols. London: Bles, 1950–1954; Bodley Head, 1955–1956.

———. Introduction to *On the Incarnation*, by St. Athanasius, 9–15. Translated by John Behr. New York: St. Vladamir's, 2011.

———. *The Lion, the Witch and the Wardrobe*. London: Fontana Lions, 1984.

Lipton, Bruce. *The Biology of Belief: Unleashing the Power of Consciousness, Matter & Miracles*. London: Hay House, 2011.

Lyte, Henry Francis. "Jesus, I My Cross Have Taken." Hymnary, 1825. https://hymnary.org/text/jesus_i_my_cross_have_taken_all_to_le.

Macfarlane, Robert. *Landmarks*. London: Hamish Hamilton, 2015.

Macfarlane, Robert, and Jackie Morris. *The Lost Words*. London: Hamish Hamilton, 2017.

Magnusson, Sally. *The Flying Scotsman: A Biography*. New York: Quartet, 1981.

Mansley, L. M., et al. "Destructive Tension: Mathematics Versus Experience—the Progress and Control of the 2001 Foot and Mouth Disease Epidemic in Great Britain." *Revue Scientifique et Technique* 30 (2011) 483–98. https://pubmed.ncbi.nlm.nih.gov/21961220/.

Marshall, Frank, dir. *Alive*. Touchstone Pictures, Paramount Pictures, The Kennedy/Marshall Company, 1993.

Maté, Gabor. *When the Body Says No: The Cost of Hidden Stress*. London: Vermilion, 2019.

Mathetes. *Epistle to Diognetus*. In vol. 1 of *The Ante-Nicene Fathers*, edited by Alexander Roberts and James Donaldson, 25–30. https://logoslibrary.org/mathetes/diognetus/.

McKenna, Kyle Christopher. "Use of Aborted Fetal Tissue in Vaccines and Medical Research Obscures the Value of All Human Life." *Linacre Quarterly* 85 (2018) 13–17. https://journals.sagepub.com/doi/10.1177/0024363918761715.

McNabb, Andy. *Bravo Two Zero*. London: Bantam, 1993.

Mehl-Madrona, Lewis. *Coyote Medicine: Lessons from Native American Healing*. New York: Fireside, 1997.

Mendelsohn, Tom. "Wild Boars Have Joined the War Against ISIS." Shortlist, April 26, 2017. https://www.shortlist.com/news/isis-terrorism-wild-boars-war-iraq.

Metaxas, Eric. *Bonhoeffer: Pastor, Martyr, Prophet, Spy*. Nashville: Thomas Nelson, 2020.

———. *Martin Luther: The Man Who Rediscovered God and Changed the World*. New York: Penguin, 2017.

Moore, Patrick. *Fake Invisible Catastrophes and Threats of Doom*. Self published, 2021.

Morgan, M., publisher. "Giant Skeletons Unearthed." *Abergavenny Chronicle*, April 10, 1914. https://newspapers.library.wales/view/4120759/4120761.

Moritz, Andreas. *Cancer Is Not a Disease: It's a Survival Mechanism*. Brevard, NC: Ener-Chi Wellness, 2016.

Morris, Jackie. "Biography." Jackie Morris Artist. https://www.jackiemorris.co.uk/biography/.

Murray, Douglas. *The Madness of Crowds: Gender, Race and Identity*. London: Bloomsbury, 2019.

Musker, John, and Ron Clements, dirs. *Moana*. Walt Disney Animation Studios, 2016.

Nash, Ogden. *Many Long Years Ago*. Boston: Little, Brown, 1945.

Neuber, Wolfgang, et al. *The Making of Copernicus: Early Modern Transformations of a Scientist and His Science*. Intersections 36. Leiden: Brill, 2015.

Newton, John. "Amazing Grace! (How Sweet the Sound)." Hymnary, 1779. https://hymnary.org/text/amazing_grace_how_sweet_the_sound.

Ober, Clint. "About Clint Ober." Earthing. https://www.earthing.com/pages/about-clint-ober.

Ortiz, Juan Carlos. *Disciple*. Carol Stream, IL: Creation House, 1975.

Orwell, George. *As I Please: 1943–1945*. Vol 3 of *The Collected Essays, Journalism and Letters of George Orwell*, edited by Sonya Orwell and Ian Angus. Harmondsworth: Penguin, 1971.

———. *Nineteen Eighty-Four*. Harmondsworth: Penguin, 1984.

Osterloff, Emily. "Dinosauria: How the 'Terrible Lizards' Got Their Name." Natural History Museum. https://www.nhm.ac.uk/discover/how-dinosaurs-got-their-name.html.

Parker, Matthew. *Monte Cassino: The Story of the Hardest-Fought Battle of World War Two*. London: Headline, 2003.

Patagonia Cascada. "The Truth About Patagonia's Giants." Cascada Expediciones. https://www.cascada.travel/blog/the-truth-about-patagonia-s-giants.

Pigafetta, Antonio. *The First Voyage Around the World 1519–1522: An Account of Magellan's Expedition*. Edited by Theodore J. Cachey Jr. Toronto: University of Toronto Press, 2019. https://archive.org/details/magellans-voyage-pigafetta/.

Piper, John. *Don't Waste Your Cancer*. Wheaton, IL: Crossway, 2011.

Pliny the Elder. *The Natural History of Pliny*. Translated by John Bostock and H. T. Riley. Vol. 6. London: Bohn, 1857. www.gutenberg.org/files/62704/62704-h/62704-h.htm.

Reitherman, Wolfgang, dir. *The Jungle Book*. Walt Disney Productions, 1967.

Rinehart, John. *Gospel Patrons: People Whose Generosity Changed the World*. London: Reclaimed, 2014.

Ryle, J. C. *Expository Thoughts on Luke*. Vol. 1. Edinburgh: Banner of Truth, 1986.

———. *Five English Reformers*. Edinburgh: Banner of Truth, 1981.

Scriven, John, and Tim Dieppe. *Beyond the Odds: Providence in Britain's Wars of the 20th Century*. London: Wilberforce, 2021.

Shakespeare, William. *Hamlet*. Edited by Barbara Mowat et al. Washington, DC: Folger Shakespeare Library. https://www.folger.edu/explore/shakespeares-works/hamlet/read/.

Siegel, Bernie. *Love, Medicine and Miracles*. London: Rider, 1999.

Simonton, O. Carl, et al. *Getting Well Again*. New York: Bantam, 1992.

Smith, W. Ramsay. *Aborigine: Myths and Legends*. London: Senate, 1996.

Solzhenitsyn, Aleksandr. *Cancer Ward*. London: Vintage, 2003.

———. *Warning to the West*. London: Vintage, 2019.

Stark, Rodney. *God's Battalions: The Case for the Crusades*. New York: Harper Collins, 2010.

Stobart, Eddie, et al. *Only the Best Will Do*. Belfast: Ambassador, 1998.

Story, Joanna. "The Viking Raid on Lindisfarne." English Heritage. https://www.english-heritage.org.uk/visit/places/lindisfarne-priory/History/viking-raid/.

Sturcke, James. "Bird Flu Pandemic 'Could Kill 150m.'" Guardian, September 30, 2005. https://www.theguardian.com/world/2005/sep/30/birdflu.jamessturcke.

Taylor, Charles. *A Secular Age*. Cambridge: Belknap, 2018.

Tertullian. *Apology*. Translated by T. R. Glover. In *Tertullian: Apology, De spectaculis; Minucius Felix*, 2–229. Loeb Classical Library. London: Heinemann, 1931.

Tolkien, J. R. R. *The Lord of the Rings*. 3 vols. London: Allen & Unwin, 1954–1955.

Toplady, Augustus. "Rock of Ages." Hymnary, 1776. https://hymnary.org/text/rock_of_ages_cleft_for_me_let_me_hide.

Trapnell, D. H. "Health, Disease, and Healing." In *The New Bible Dictionary*, edited by J. D. Douglas et al., 457–65. Leicester, UK: IVP, 1993.

Tucker, Alfred R. *Eighteen Years in Uganda and East Africa*. 2 vols. London: Arnold, 1908.

Turner, Kelly. *Radical Remission*. New York: HarperOne, 2014.

Tyler, Dominick. *Uncommon Ground: A Word-Lover's Guide to the British Landscape*. London: Guardian, 2015.

United Nations (AP). "A senior U.N. environmental official says [. . .]." AP News, n.d. https://apnews.com/article/bd45c372caf118ec99964ea547880cd0.

Uyiedos. "Aruan of Udo, the Giant of Benin Kingdom." Steemit, December 21, 2017. https://steemit.com/history/@uyiedos/aruan-of-udo-the-giant-of-benin-kingdom.

Van der Kolk, Bessel. *The Body Keeps the Score: Brain, Mind and Body in the Healing of Trauma*. Harmondsworth: Penguin, 2015.

Van der Post, Laurens. *The Dark Eye in Africa*. London: Hogarth, 1956.

———. *The Lost World of the Kalahari*. London: Hogarth, 1958.

Van Dorn, Douglas. *Giants: Sons of the Gods*. Dacano, CO: Waters of Creation, 2023.

Varga, Tamás. "Dinosaur Rock Art: Did Dinosaurs Coexist with Humans?" Earthly Mission. https://earthlymission.com/dinosaur-rock-cave-art-did-dinosaurs-coexist-with-humans/.

Visagie, Jescey. "How Do Namibian Himbas See Colour?" Gondwana Collection Namibia, September 2, 2016. https://gondwana-collection.com/blog/how-do-namibian-himbas-see-colour.

Warburton, Olivia. "King Alfred School Dudley Closes Citing Government VAT Hike." Dudley News, August 20, 2025. https://www.dudleynews.co.uk/news/25404260.king-alfred-school-dudley-closes-citing-government-vat-hike/.

Wark, Chris, and Micah Wark. *Beat Cancer Kitchen: Deliciously Simple Plant-Based Anticancer Recipes*. London: Hay House, 2023.

Watts, Isaac. "When I survey the Wondrous Cross." Hymnary, 1707. https://hymnary.org/text/when_i_survey_the_wondrous_cross_watts.

White, Charles. "Four Lessons on Money from One of the World's Richest Preachers." DCI, 1988. https://www.dci.org.uk/zipped/wesleyonmoney.pdf.

Wikipedia. "You'll Own Nothing and Be Happy." Last updated January 6, 2026. https://en.wikipedia.org/wiki/You%27ll_own_nothing_and_be_happy.

Wilder, Laura Ingalls. *Farmer Boy*. New York: Harper Trophy, 1981.

Wilkinson, Hugo, and Andrew Szudek, eds. *Battles That Changed History*. London: DK, 2018.

www.ingramcontent.com/pod-product-compliance
Lightning Source LLC
LaVergne TN
LVHW050634100826
845148LV00011B/1855

* 9 7 9 8 3 8 5 2 4 9 4 7 3 *